Machine Learning Forensics for Law Enforcement, Security, and Intelligence

Machine Learning Forensics for Law Enforcement, Security, and Intelligence

Jesus Mena

CRC Press
Taylor & Francis Group
Boca Raton   London   New York

CRC Press is an imprint of the
Taylor & Francis Group, an **informa** business
AN AUERBACH BOOK

CRC Press
Taylor & Francis Group
6000 Broken Sound Parkway NW, Suite 300
Boca Raton, FL 33487-2742

© 2011 by Taylor & Francis Group, LLC
CRC Press is an imprint of Taylor & Francis Group, an Informa business

No claim to original U.S. Government works

Printed in the United States of America on acid-free paper
Version Date: 20110510

International Standard Book Number: 978-1-4398-6069-4 (Hardback)

Visit the Taylor & Francis Web site at
http://www.taylorandfrancis.com

and the CRC Press Web site at
http://www.crcpress.com

Contents

Introduction

Many years ago as an Internal Revenue Service Artificial Intelligence Specialist, I discovered exciting new software—first, expert systems, then, neural networks and machine learning programs—for constructing detection models. The IRS used the models for predicting noncompliance, nonpayment, identifying tax shelters, and underreporting.

Several years later after I left the IRS, I worked as a consultant for several federal agencies, such as Sandia Laboratories, the Terrorist Integration Center, and the Department of Homeland Security, Office of Inspector General (DHS-OIG). In one engagement for the DHS-OIG, I was asked to be the technical consultant in the first audit of all the analytical systems at DHS.

During that DHS–OIG audit, we looked at all advanced detection systems by all DHS components, including Secret Service (SS), Customs and Border Protection (CBP), Transportation Security Administration (TSA), etc. That audit showed a lack of knowledge about the use of machine learning technology and software by DHS analysts and management.

The purpose of this book is to remedy this lack of knowledge and integrate an assortment of deductive and inductive tools, techniques, and technologies for chief information officers; federal, state, local, and military law enforcement personnel; legal and IT professionals; fraud and criminal investigators; and competitive intelligence analysts.

Increasingly, crimes and fraud are digital in nature, occurring with real-time velocity and at vast volumes. This book is a guide on how to conduct forensic investigations using software to "interrogate the evidence"; the book also provides a step-by-step guide on how to construct adaptive criminal and fraud detection systems for private and government organizations.

The Author

Jesús Mena is a former Internal Revenue Service Artificial Intelligence specialist and the author of the following data mining, web analytics, law enforcement, homeland security, forensic, and marketing books:

- *Data Mining Your Website* (1998)—the first book on web analytics
- *WebMining for Profitability* (2002)—how to use AI for behavioral targeting
- *Investigative Data Mining for Security and Criminal Detection* (2003)—a forensic university textbook
- *Homeland Security Techniques and Technologies* (2005)—how to use COTS for combating terrorism
- *The California Chingasos* (2006)—a data mining novel about the Juarez cartel
- *Triangular Marketing: Behavioral Analytics for the Anonymous Advertising Anywhere (A3) Bible* (2011)—an interactive e-book

Mena has also written dozens of articles for *Competitive Intelligence Review, New Architect, Intelligent Enterprise, PC AI, DM Review, Marketing Tools, Software Development Magazine, Washington Technology, WEB Techniques*, etc.

Mena has also consulted with NCR, SPSS, SAS, the General Accountability Office, Raytheon Corporation, Boeing Corporation,

Booz Allen Hamilton, the Department of Justice, Grumman Corporation, the National Counterintelligence Center, the Department of Homeland Security (Office of Inspector General), and Sandia National Laboratories.

Mena has over 20 years' experience in expert systems, rule induction, decision trees, neural networks, self-organizing maps, regression, visualization, machine learning, etc., and has worked on data mining projects involving clustering, segmentation, classification, profiling and personalization with government, web, retail, insurance, credit card, financial and healthcare data sets.

Mena has worked, written, and lectured on various behavioral analytics and social networking techniques, personalization mechanisms, web and mobile networks, real-time psychographics, tracking and profiling engines, log analyzing tools, packet sniffers, voice and text recognition software, geolocation and behavioral targeting systems, real-time streaming analytical software, ensemble techniques, and digital fingerprinting.

1

WHAT IS MACHINE LEARNING FORENSICS?

1.1 Definition

Machine learning is at the core of behavioral forensics. Originating from the field of artificial intelligence, machine learning algorithms can be used to analyze vast amounts of data to discover risk and to segment and detect criminal behavior and intent. For criminal detection, machine learning software enables the investigator to interrogate vast and diverse data sets via social and wired networks, the web, and cloud computing. Behavioral analytics is at the core of modeling, profiling, and prediction—in marketing, medicine, manufacturing, advertising, counterterrorism, business intelligence, and now law enforcement.

Machine learning is a branch of artificial intelligence employing pattern recognition software that analyzes vast amounts of data to predict some behavior, which in the case of forensics is criminal intent and activity. The field of machine learning seeks to learn from historical activities in order to predict future criminal behaviors; these can be, for example, burglaries, money laundering, or intrusion attacks.

In addition, machine learning forensics can include remote analyses via networked tools and software. One of the advantages of machine learning investigations is that the data detective can calibrate crime and risk with precision and in an understandable format. The outputs of most machine learning programs are conditional IF/THEN rules that are easy to understand:

```
IF second visit to website
AND IP Address Sector 5
AND transaction price range $46.99 - $76.98
THEN Fraud Risk Score 87%
```

The success of machine learning forensics involves strategic planning and measured improvement of predictive evolving models and clusters. For example, the key strategy for executing and leveraging behavioral analytics for the marketer is to plan and design a framework from which consumers' behaviors can be captured and modeled. Similarly, the forensic strategy should be to create a continuous and systemic method of quantifying behaviors and to continuously measure everything—this can include arrest rates, risk rates, false positives, intrusions detected, incident reports, fraudulent transactions, money recovered, etc.; data is evidence for machine learning forensics.

1.2 Digital Maps and Models: Strategies and Technologies

Behavioral analytics is the underlying process enabling digital marketers such as Google to push targeted products, content, or services via multiple channels to consumers, in a relevant and personal manner. This same behavioral technology, tools, and techniques can be leveraged in the field of forensics. Behavioral analytics is commonly bundled with the term *data mining*. But data mining is actually a marketing term coined by HNC, a San Diego–based company, over a decade ago to pitch their Data Mining Workstation. Over time the company went into the business of detecting credit card fraud for banks via their FALCON service. HNC eventually morphed into Fair Isaac, the generator of the universal FICO risk scores.

So, what is the point? Data mining is a marketing slogan; what we are really talking about is the prediction of human reactions and server actions by quantifying their behaviors: whether online shoppers or fraudulent transactions, network intrusions, criminal modus operandi, etc. As with online marketers, investigators can use the vast amounts of digital data collected with every credit card swipe, every cell call, twitter, chat, e-mail, browser history, keyword used—not to sell but to combat crime.

Machine learning forensics is the capability to recognize patterns of criminal activities in order to predict when and where crimes and intrusions are likely to take place. Machine learning forensics can also be enlisted to detect network intrusions and to discover evidence in litigation, and competitive and corporate investigations. For this type of digital forensics to work, there is a need to create a framework to capture and analyze server, criminal, Internet, wireless, and other types of data for visualization, link association, clustering, segmenting, and predicting criminal activity.

There are two main approaches to machine learning forensics: inductive and deductive. Inductive is self-learning involving clustering analysis, link analysis, and text mining analytics. The second approach is deductive and involves supervised learning. It involves the use of rule generators and decision trees, and also requires "training" a model to predict a behavior, such as a fraud or an intrusion. The investigator needs to have in his toolbox several of these programs in order to progressively advance his investigation from the extractive, inductive, and deductive phases.

1.3 Extractive Forensics: Link Analysis and Text Mining

Two extraction technologies, link analysis and text mining, can be used by machine learning forensics investigators to uncover hidden associations between individuals as well as to extract content from unstructured data formats. Link analysis can be used to discover "who knew whom, where, and when," while text mining can be used to discover hidden content buried in massive amounts of unstructured information sources.

Link analysis generally is the initial type of technology used to direct investigators to suspects and other objects of interest, which may warrant additional surveillance and attention. Link analysis is rooted in the core technology known as graph theory and can be used by the behavioral forensic investigators to discover associations or relationships between individuals via an assortment of communication channels. Link analysis can be used to combine leads and the focus of machine learning forensic investigations by analyzing cell phone calls, e-mails, and text messages between suspects and their associates.

In link analysis, individuals can be represented as circles in a graph; these are known as *nodes*. Links displayed as connecting lines in the graph, known as *edges*, can convey the strengths of the relationships between these entities: the stronger the link, the thicker the line connecting the entities being investigated. Link analysis graphs can be used to investigate relationships between individuals, organizations (cells), and associations among individuals and organizations. Some link analysis tools support counts and directions of connections and relationships. The entities under investigation can also be sequenced in order of the times at which the events took place.

While link analysis is a good technology for discovering what is going on between criminals and their activities and associations, it is limited. Its main limitation is that with a large number of nodes, objects of interest become so numerous that graphical map link analysis becomes worthless. This occurs when a link analysis graph becomes populated with a large number of lines connecting the sources of interest in an investigation (Figure 1.1).

Link analysis is unlike other technologies used in machine learning forensics in that it doesn't discover patterns in large data sets; it instead visually exploits relationships between individuals being investigated on a one-to-one basis. Link analysis assists investigators in discovering relationships—rather than finding large data patterns autonomously—as is the case with decision trees, text mining software, and rule generators. For this reason, link analysis should be the first analysis performed by a digital forensic investigator when warranted; it simplifies and narrows the scope of an investigation.

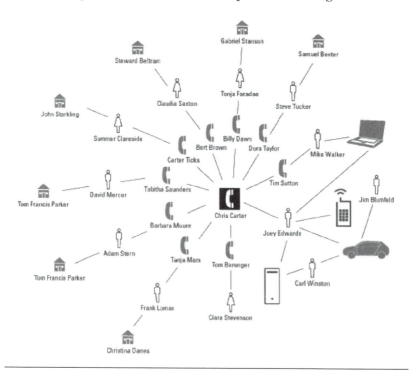

Figure 1.1   A link analysis graph showing associations via a cell phone.

Link analysis is typically used to explore associations between suspects in an ongoing investigation. For example, a common forensic technique is to examine the behaviors of suspects such as their cell phone contacts, e-mails sent and received, and texts they have generated. Investigations using link analysis can also be used to discover financial transactions between different accounts and individuals undertaken during a given time frame. Link analysis can be used to discover ongoing and previous relationships between suspects and their networked contacts as well as financial exchanges and transactions over time, as part of terrorist, financial, or criminal investigations. Care, however, must be taken in the use of link analysis since it could lead to guilt by association.

Another technology known as text mining has become increasingly important for investigators in sorting and organizing the massive amounts of unstructured information that they need to review and investigate. Unstructured text is in the form of documents, notes, e-mails, chat, web forms, voicemail, news stories, texts, regulatory filings, repair records, field representative notes, spreadsheets, presentations, invoices, blogs, etc. Although traditional machine learning forensics can find what is going on, the whys and wherefores remain buried in unstructured content and can represent the hidden story behind the data. Text analytics generally includes such tasks as the categorization of taxonomies, the clustering of concepts, entity and information extraction, sentiment analysis, and summarization.

Why is text analytics important to machine learning forensics? Because investigators need to deal with large numbers of documents, e-mails, and other types of unstructured data formats, which do not reside in structured databases and depositories. In addition, investigators need to leverage the power of machine learning in the extraction and organization of key concepts from these types of unstructured content. Increasingly, companies and individuals are accumulating nearly 80% of their data in unstructured formats; this evidence is too important for the machine learning forensic investigator to ignore.

Machine learning forensics investigators using text mining tools can conduct deep analysis of patents, blogs, reports, e-mails, surveys, orders, and other documents that would take too long to be performed manually. Text analytics provides an automated solution to organizing key concepts from this unstructured content. This involves analyzing large amounts of unstructured data to discover previously unknown patterns and concepts. The information might contain hidden relationships or patterns that are buried in this unstructured content which would otherwise be extremely difficult, if not impossible, to be discovered via traditional manual investigative methods.

Text analytics can use information retrieval (IR) and information extraction (IE) as well as natural language processing (NLP) techniques to organize and prioritize documents about any subject. These text analytics techniques can be used by investigators to gain new insight into unstructured-content data sources within their legacy and operational systems. In addition, text analytical tools can convert unstructured content and parse it over to a structure format that is amenable to forensic behavioral analysis via decision trees and rule generators. For example, all of the e-mails that an organization accumulates on a daily basis can be organized into several piles of groupings, such as customers with low, medium, and high risk. Aside from organizing key concepts, groupings of risky transactions can also be clustered by investigators using a combination of text analytics and other investigative tools.

IR systems identify the text in a large collection of documents or web pages that match a user's query. It is the most basic level of text analytics. The most popular IR systems are today's search engines such as Google and Yahoo, which identify *keywords* within pages and documents on the web that are relevant to a set of given words. IR systems are often used in public and corporate libraries, where the documents are typically not the books themselves but digital records containing information about the books. IR text analytics systems allow digital forensic investigators to narrow down the set of documents that are relevant to a particular type of fraud or crime.

Text analytics involves applying computationally intensive algorithms to large collections of text, and can speed up the analysis considerably by reducing the number of documents for the investigator to focus on. However, the most useful text analytics systems for forensic investigators are the NLP and IE technologies and tools. They provide a method with which a behavioral forensic investigator can analyze a large percentage of information normally archived by organizations.

NLP is one of the oldest fields of artificial intelligence and also one of the most difficult to execute. NLP systems convert unstructured content into readable human language. NLP software can convert human language into a more formal format that makes it easier to apply behavioral analytics. NLP is the analysis of human language so that computers can understand natural languages as humans do. NLP is a subset of computational linguistics. NLP can perform some types of analysis with a high degree of success, such as tagging words into major categories such as nouns, verbs, or adjectives.

NLP can perform disambiguation to identify the meaning of a word, given its usage, from the multiple meanings that the word may have. NLP can also perform parsing of a grammatical analysis of a sentence. Shallow parsers identify only the main grammatical elements in a sentence, such as noun phrases and verb phrases, whereas deep parsers generate a complete representation of the grammatical structure of a sentence. Companies that provide this type of NLP software include Crossminder and Basis Technologies.

Information extraction (IE) is the process of automatically obtaining structured data from unstructured content. Often, this involves the parsing of the unstructured content into one or more structured templates, which are then used to guide the extraction process. IE systems rely heavily on the data generated by NLP systems. Tasks that IE systems can perform include term analysis, entity recognition, and fact extraction. IE software can parse structured tables from documents, e-mails, etc., so that subsequent forensic investigations can be performed. Companies that provide this type of IE software include Attensity and Megaputer.

By using both NLP and IE text tools, investigators can convert the vast amount of data from silos of unstructured content they collect from all channels into a structured format (database or tables) by which multiple analytics can be performed to discover previously unknown knowledge about digital crimes and fraud. Text analytics can be used to convert unstructured content for subsequent modeling to advance an investigation and improve real-time detection systems.

1.4 Inductive Forensics: Clustering Incidents and Crimes

Clustering software is available that can be used to create groupings based on human behaviors and words such as those from text analytics. This is the inductive modeling approach to machine learning forensics, in which the clustering is autonomously performed by the program directly from the data. Inductive forensics is performed when an investigation is randomly exploring the grouping of behaviors by individuals and machines.

It is an exploratory type of analysis performed to isolate anomalies in the data such as avoidance behavior indicating some criminal activity, for instance, a suspicious use of a computer port for a network attack or a questionable financial transaction that may indicate money laundering. The core algorithm used for this type of inductive forensics is known as a Self-Organizing Map neural network, or SOM for short. The clustering of words, for example, can be performed from call site transcripts, e-mails, instant messages, chat, website forms, texts, and phone calls for the creation of matrixes of words by investigators; for instance, the frequency of terms used by an individual in his or her e-mails to associates and superiors can be discovered (Figure 1.2).

This type of clustering is done automatically by the software and is known as "unsupervised learning"; that is, the analysis organizes by itself along key words or human and server behaviors. This is a

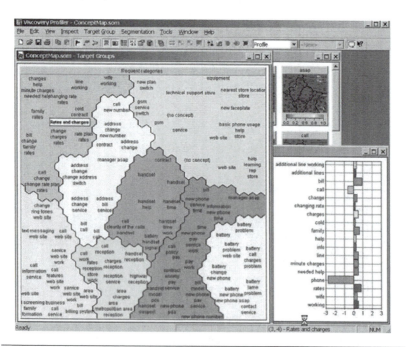

Figure 1.2   The clustering of words as used in a call site of a wireless company.

useful initial step for a machine learning forensics strategy. That is, it lets the behaviors or words of individuals organize themselves into distinct clusters of groupings without bias. The behaviors in the data can be automatically grouped into distinct clusters warranting further attention. The technology and techniques will be covered in detail in Chapter 4.

A Checklist for Conducting Inductive Forensics Investigations

1. Identify the source of words or behaviors you want to cluster. It is useful for the investigator to determine what he or she is looking for, such as suspect names, locations, cell numbers, IT addresses, e-mails, etc.
2. Build and train a cluster of words or behaviors, using SOM software: let the words and behaviors organize themselves into natural groupings.
3. Evaluate the accuracy of the clusters against new words and behaviors. Take unseen words and behaviors from the same source used to build the model and check the accuracy of the predictions.
4. Consider what the clusters have revealed and generate new analyses. This usually involves supervised learning using other types of machine learning algorithms, such as decision trees.

This type of undirected, unsupervised knowledge discovery with SOM software can also be used for exploratory analyses. They can lead to clues an investigator might never come across. However, clustering and text analysis can be used to sort and detect deviant and suspicious criminal behaviors. This type of initial analysis leads to further analyses, which will be covered in detail in subsequent chapters, in which one cluster is compared to another and new knowledge is discovered as to why one cluster is different from others.

Using a set of different algorithms (decision trees), the deductive type of forensics can now be used to answer such questions as why one cluster is different from another in its behavior and what the unique features of each grouping are. For example, the network behaviors can be discovered and examined to determine potential unauthorized transactions, and a decision tree may be generated from multiple clusters to determine the features of normal behaviors versus criminal behaviors. This process involves the use of both inductive forensics (clustering/text analytics) and deductive forensics (decision trees/rule generators). (See Figure 1.3.)

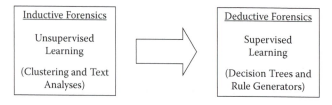

Figure 1.3 Knowledge discoveries (inductive) and the calibration of crimes (deductive).

1.5 Deductive Forensics: Anticipating Attacks and Precrime

Everyday criminals, hackers, terrorists, and other bad guys leave a digital trail behind them. They cannot help it in this digital world; today, a person cannot exist without the web, e-mail, wireless, etc. Digital investigators have come to realize that these behaviors can be captured, modeled, and deployed in order to anticipate potential cyber attacks and other types of crimes. To succeed in this objective, a behavioral forensic investigator's strategy is to recognize and identify where and how to retrieve, organize, and leverage these historical behaviors for modeling to detect and prevent crimes.

Critical to machine learning forensics is getting top management to understand the value and benefits of these types of inductive and deductive analyses. A framework needs to be established to capture behavioral data and conduits set up for their modeling. Machine learning technology cannot only generate conditional rules that segment the good guys from the bad, the software can also create graphical decision trees that can dramatically show the process of drilling down the data using such algorithms as classification and regression trees (CART), chi-squared automatic interaction detection (CHAID), and C4.5, which uses "information gain" to drill down data sets (Figure 1.4).

For example, in the classification and prediction of, say, fruit, the algorithm C4.5 would segment along the lines of information gain using such variables as weight, shape, and color to identify a banana, an apple, and an orange in this manner:

> *Weight*—Little information gain to discriminate between a banana, apple, and orange
>
> *Shape*—Provides more information gain since "round" would eliminate a banana

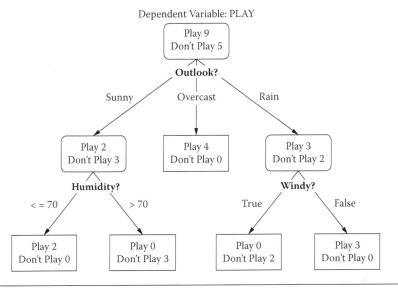

Figure 1.4 A decision tree interrogating data using three variables: outlook, humidity, and wind.

Color—Provides the most information gain: red (apple), yellow (banana), and orange (orange)

In this analysis, the C4.5 algorithm found that color was the most important attribute for classifying fruit types. The point is that the same autonomous process of information gain can be used to differentiate between legal and criminal behaviors. The decision trees and rules extracted from machine learning forensics can be embedded in operational systems, such as those that concentrate on monitoring server activities, surveillance and investigative monitoring systems, websites, call site operations, and other law enforcement and intelligence systems.

Decision trees are a graphical representation of the IF/THEN rules as applied to a given situation, such as, is this transaction fraudulent or not? To develop the rules and risk classifications, two common algorithms are commonly used, usually CART or CHAID. With both, an initial training data set of FRAUD versus LEGAL transactions are used to "train" a model to generate a tree or a set of rules that are statistically significant for discriminating between fraudulent and legal transactions. CHAID, unlike CART, is restricted to categorical variables, and continuous variables must be categorized to be used in the tree.

These machine learning algorithms compute observations of fraudulent and legal observations by repeatedly dividing samples of data into smaller and smaller subgroups. One way to see this process is like the game of "20 Questions" in which one player asks questions to determine the kind of object another player has in mind. Presented with a data set of 283,000 legal and 6 fraudulent transactions, the algorithms in decision trees and rule generator software interrogate the data about the values of each record, with the goal of developing a model to classify future transactions.

These forensic tools will interrogate every field in every record until it sufficiently "learns" the patterns for identifying the key characteristics of FRAUD versus LEGAL. Some of these tools also provide rankings on the statistical importance of every independent variable (inputs) such as time of day, dollar amount, IP address, etc., for predicting the dependent variable (output) of FRAUD. Using this type of rank table, an investigator can eliminate the bulk of the data. Since often only two or three attributes tend to be important for making such predictions, this is important because it is a form of data compression, which can become an important factor once rules are deployed for real-time detection.

Because of their ease of use, decision trees and rule generator software are ideal tools for security and law enforcement personnel and analysts. Their output, whether rules or graphical trees, can easily be presented in court or shared with decision makers. Both types of tools are capable of extracting IF/THEN rules that can serve as filters to issue alerts and targeted communications to elevate risk for multiple applications. These types of IF/THEN rules can be used to oversee operations to detect fraud in real time, as well as the conditions leading to criminal behaviors.

Digital forensics can be employed to model any criminal; however, organizations must carefully plan on how they will capture and create important data streams. The problem for organizations is that these multiple data streams originate and flow from websites, call sites, processing centers, e-mail servers, and an array of other transactional and criminal records legacy systems scattered in different locations, each in unique formats performing diverse operations in a totally disjointed manner.

There are several Internet mechanisms that track users, such as log files, cookies, beacons, forms, and JavaScript; there are also databases, e-mail servers, call sites, and operational and transactional legacy systems that can be enlisted to enhance internal-organization structured and unstructured data streams. There are also real-time demographics products—they offer lifestyle cluster segments and profiles—that can be used to enhance the quality of these internal data sets, in order to gain a more entity-centric view and precise ensemble of segmentation models from machine learning forensics.

In this new machine learning forensics paradigm, data collection, integration, and analysis make up a seamless stream of activity taking place over a "reactive network" and not a static warehouse, allowing an organization or department to customize targeted alerts and assist field investigations based on what it knows about criminal behavior. The core strategy for an organization is regarding how to create, connect, and analyze all of these data streams in a global architecture that can react with precision and value.

Machine learning forensic rules can be strategically positioned to react and take action as criminal events take place with no latency. These forensic rules are created from behavioral analytics gathered from multiple and diverse data sources and networks. The true challenge is gathering support from multiple data owners and keepers about the benefits of machine learning forensics. An organization, department, and agency can enlist both deductive and inductive streaming analytical software products and services that are event driven to link, monitor, and analyze its data streams for behavioral forensics.

Decision tree software can be used to model criminal behaviors in order to develop models for specific types of crimes and criminals. More descriptive names for these decision tree models are classification trees—which can be used to predict who will commit fraud or the magnitude of a fraudulent transaction—that is, the software can predict a discrete outcome, or the amount to be lost. This is an example of a conditional rule extracted from a classification decision tree for deployment by a behavioral forensic investigator:

```
IF Third visit to site
AND Netmask: 255.255.255.0 = 24
```

```
AND Product purchase price range $346.99 - $476.98
THEN Fraud 78%
```

Another type of decision tree is known as the regression tree. These trees are used to predict how much will be stolen. It generates a continuous outcome. This is an example of a fraudulent rule extracted from a regression decision tree:

```
IF Third visit to site
AND Netmask: 255.255.255.0 = 24
AND Product purchase price range $346.99 - $476.98
THEN Fraud Loss $413.78
```

Decision trees represent a very accurate and discrete method of mapping criminal behaviors. However, for these types of forensic models and deployable rules to be developed for generating real-time alerts, it is necessary to have a framework for capturing and leveraging the data. This requires some strategic planning by the investigator. A key question is, what data sets will be used to develop the models and the predictive rules?

The data used to make up the models must be the same data used to derive and deploy these predictive detecting rules. In other words, the data used to train the models is the same data used to make predictions. A series of behavioral forensic rules needs to be set up by an investigative entity across multiple data channels. These rules represent conditions that warrant the issuing of alert rules, and can be used to react to and fire off targeted notifications of potential criminal risks or intrusions and attacks.

These conditional rules take the form of risk signatures representing potential criminal behaviors for organizations. The behavioral models can be strategically placed across transactional touch points in the form of a network of dynamic risk rules. As previously mentioned, a framework needs to be set up to capture and monitor behaviors in order to develop predictive models and alert rules.

The following software can be used to create decision trees for anti-crime models:

AC2: a graphical tool for building decision trees
Alice: a decision tree product for investigators
ANGOSS: decision trees for sales and fraud detection

C5.0: constructs classifiers in the form of decision trees and rule sets

CART: multiple winner of decision tree (modeling) competition

Compumine: rule-based predictive modeling software

Datamite: enables rules to be discovered in relational databases

DMT Nuggets: analytics based on Sift Agent(TM) technology

DTREG: generates classification and regression decision trees

Fair Isaac: tree-building software

Neusciences aXi: discrete and continuous rules from trees

PolyAnalyst: supports decision tree and fuzzy logic rules

Shih Tree Builder: regression and probability trees

SPSS AnswerTree: CHAID and other decision tree algorithms

WizWhy: automatically finds all the IF/THEN rules from data

XpertRule Miner: provides association rule discovery from ODBC data sources

FREE:

C 4.5: the "classic" decision tree tool

CBA: builds classifiers using a subset of association rules

GAtree: genetic induction and visualization of decision trees

IND: provides Gini and C4.5 style decision trees

KINOsuite-PR: extracts rules from trained neural networks

Mangrove: visualization decision tree

OC1: decision tree for continuous feature values

ODBCMINE: analyzes ODBC databases using C4.5 decision tree

PC4.5: a parallel version of C4.5 built with Persistent Linda (PLinda) system

PNC2 Rule Induction System: induces rules using a cluster algorithm

SMILES: decision tree with nongreedy search extraction

Some of these vendors offer services that investigators may want to consider as part of their overall behavioral forensic strategy and project. The investigator or client organization should use a request for proposal (RFP) to evaluate and document expectations and parameters of performance by these solution providers. Test and compare the results of these decision tree and rule generator solution providers, and plan and test what behaviors, demographics, criminal, transactional, contextual, and other types of data will be captured.

Everything can be measured in terms of revenue loss, relevance of results, speed of detection, and rule and tree performance. Every transaction, visit, or activity resides in some digital format that is amenable to behavioral forensic modeling and measurement. The strategic problem for the investigator is mapping it into a viable framework for testing and gradually perfecting it into action and measuring the revenue it saves an organization.

For online fraud and cybersecurity investigations, an organization's website and servers are the primary evidence engines since they generated much of the data used for modeling criminal behaviors. Machine learning forensics involves the tracking and measuring of these criminal and intrusion events, and their sequential patterns of criminal behaviors. Tracking depositories such as log files and other server-level evidence can be used as part of the data gathered by investigators. Cookies, for example, are an important web mechanism for the behavioral forensic investigator insofar as they allow organizations, networks, and ISP providers to track and model criminal behaviors.

Cookies facilitate how an investigator gathers evidence since they allow automatic authentication of a web browser entity to a web server setting the cookie. The fact that this type of tracking technology can identify a user by the web browser's unique identification number is of great value to a behavioral forensic investigator because they can be used to track what web pages have been viewed and what other activities a user has participated in over time.

The advantage to digital investigators is that machine learning forensics supports the quantitative ability to measure detection success and failure in a continuous and flexible manner in near real time. Key indicators such as revenue savings and improved security can be easily tracked, validated, and improved. Not only can behaviors be captured instantly as criminal events take place, but the resulting detection success can also be measured and adjusted for optimization.

The tracking mechanisms such as cookies and JavaScript for the web have expanded to the mobile industry, which means the data they collect can serve as new wireless evidence for the investigator. Several years ago, AT&T filed a patent for a wireless cookie (Figure 1.5) in

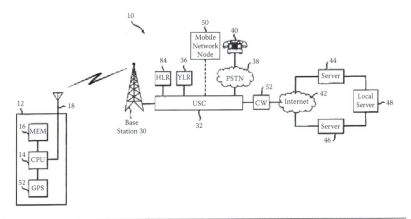

Figure 1.5   AT&T patent for wireless cookie (Pub. No. WO/2002/102025).

anticipation of the value these mechanisms can provide; the following is an abstract of the application:

> Location information for a wireless device is obtained at the wireless device using a positioning unit such as a global positioning system. The location information is stored on the wireless device. The wireless device operates a client engine with a microbrowser or the like to communicate with a web server. The microbrowser and wireless device support the reception of cookies from the web server. The user of the wireless device is presented with an option of adding the location information associated with the wireless device to the cookie. If the user approves, then the location information is added to the cookie information and transmitted to the web server. The web server may then utilize the location information and present content to the wireless device related to its location, such as weather, traffic conditions, or local hotel/restaurant services.

The big issue with cookies in mobile devices such as smart phones has been the stripping of them by the carrier gateway. However, investigators should be aware of solution providers such as Ringleader Digital and their Media Stamp, which can replicate wireless cookies comparable to those online and may prove to be of value to an investigation. Media Stamp compiles profiles of each device by tracking mobile online usage patterns across nearly 100 discriminators that include device type, geography, and mobile carrier information. As with web cookies, these wireless server cookies are anonymous. The "stamping" of mobile devices enables investigators to identify unique users and track their clicks, impressions, and acquisitions across all browsing sessions, mobile sites, and wireless carriers. These types of anonymous investigations are important since they ensure standards of security and privacy.

The wireless digital fingerprints (cookies) can include the ICC-ID (Integrated Circuit Card ID) number, which is a 19- or 20-digit serial number for every subscriber identity module (SIM), which is a removable SIM card from wireless devices. They store the service-subscriber key (IMSI) International Mobile Subscriber Identity, a unique number associated with all GSM (Global System for Mobile Communications) and UMTS (Universal Mobile Telecommunications System) mobile phone users. All of this data is stored in the SIM inside the phone and is sent to the network used to identify a subscribers' mobile devices. This is vital data an investigator needs to know about in a wireless case.

Then there are search engine web cookies for tracking user behaviors over multiple sessions and websites such as those by Yahoo and Google. They set cookies based on what users are searching for, such as a flight, a rental car, or specific content, etc.; they differ in how long they retain this type of evidence. Some of these search engines maintain their cookies for different periods, some look at what a user did a few days earlier to show them ads about the same topic today. Google retains only the most recent searches; others set their cookies to expire in a month, a week, or a day. Google goes only as far back as your current searches: time is money. The investigator needs to know about this type of digital evidence that may impact his or her queries.

There are also more sophisticated and expensive analytical tools that incorporate multiple algorithms which support all of the tasks a forensic investigator needs; they are highly robust and have intuitive interfaces, and include the following software suites:

ADAPA® from Zementis: a framework for deployment, integration, and execution of various predictive algorithms, including neural networks, support vector machines, regression models, and decision trees

Clementine: from SPSS; visual rapid modeling environment for behavioral analytics

KINOsuite PR: extracts rules from trained neural networks

Knowledge Studio: featuring multiple models in a visual, easy-to-use interface

MarketMiner: automatically selects the algorithm: statistical networks, logistic and linear regression, K-nearest neighbors, and decision trees (C4.5)

Mathematica: multimethod system for computational models from data

Oracle 9i Data Miner: embeds into Oracle9i database, for classifications, predictions, and associations

PolyAnalyst: multiple classification algorithms: decision trees, fuzzy logic, and memory-based reasoning

Predictive Dynamix Data Mining Suite: integrates neural network, clustering, and fuzzy models

PredictionWorks: includes decision tree, logistic and linear regression, etc.

Previa Classpad: neural networks, decision trees, and Bayesian networks

prudsys DISCOVERER: decision trees and sparse grid methods for classification

Rank from VADIS: multiple behavioral analytics algorithms software suite

STATISTICA Data Miner: multiple modeling algorithms

Tiberius: neural networks, logistic regression, 3D visualization, etc.

Most of these software suites offer a comprehensive selection of algorithms for automated analysis of text and structured data. Numerous data analysis problems for various applications are readily solved by these toolboxes, enabling investigators to perform numerous knowledge discovery operations, such as categorization, clustering, prediction, link analysis, keyword and entity extraction, text mining, pattern discovery, and anomaly detection. Some are quite expensive, but there are cheaper options and freeware, which we will cover in Chapter 4.

A Deductive Forensic Checklist

1. Ensure that the information technology department and the behaviors they capture are available for analyses and are aligned with the goals of the investigative project.
2. Design the forensic framework and system to capture the right internal and external behaviors.
3. Leverage existing legacy systems with external analytics data and services, such as real-time demographics, government filings, patent searches, wireless billing systems, etc.
4. Incrementally measure the results of the unsupervised (descriptive) and supervised (predictive) models to optimize their performance.
5. Recognize that machine learning forensic techniques, data, and systems need to be flexible and adaptive to change within a rapidly evolving criminal environment: model often and adapt continuously.
6. Every organization is unique—as will be the behaviors a system is designed to detect—so the forensic system needs to be adaptive in its architecture, its components, and its design.

For deductive forensics, the most important issue is the aggregation and use of *the right data*. First, knowing this from the start can lead to improved ROI, high detection rates, and optimum model performance. Second, the investigator should create a framework for measuring everything, with the goal of learning and evolving to new levels of investigative performance and high detection success. The investigator should strategically plan on what and how criminal behaviors will be captured, continuously measuring their significance and detection value.

This, by the way, should be a group effort involving decision makers from the website, call site, operational, security, and production departments and divisions. Every level should have a stake in the forensic project—from the CIO down to the production programmers. Having a stake in the strategy and project can be associated with their performance evaluation and will ensure a commitment to making it succeed by all in the team. Securing the support of stakeholders is critical to the forensic investigator since he or she is dependent on gaining access to their expertise, knowledge, data, and networks.

Recognize that developing, testing, and deploying these predictive models and rules is a learning process conducted in an iterative fashion for purposes of developing a preemptive detection system. The end result will be twofold: knowledge discovery and improved detection for organizations. The insight gained will influence strategic direction and operational design, as well as improved detection of crimes as they happen or even before crimes are committed. Effective behavioral analytical solutions require a set of inductive rules that facilitate the automation of investigative processes and should be flexible and ongoing as conditions change.

1.6 Fraud Detection: On the Web, Wireless, and in Real Time

The single most dominant asset for machine learning forensics investigators is the data organizations generate and store from their daily interaction with clients, taxpayers, website visitors, customers, and other entities. These data repositories capture and allow for the creation of models and rules directly from the behaviors of individuals created from their day-to-day transactions with organizations and websites. Leveraging and modeling these behaviors can be used for fraud detection and allows organizations to identify poorly designed processes, discover hidden relationships within data that can lead to improved efficiency, and reduce the lost revenue resulting from crimes and intrusions.

Fraud detection requires that a strategy be formulated and that a data and technology framework be carefully planned and executed. This strategy and framework, however, must be flexible enough to address the unique objectives of an organization. It must also be adaptive to the increasingly devious and evolving methods of operations that criminals employ. Fraud schemes constantly change, as such fraud detection techniques need continuous vigilance, especially for those transactions that take place on the web, and require that wireless channels be developed and constantly evaluated.

The process and strategy for fraud detection need consistent monitoring and refinement. The models and rules created by machine learning forensics need to react to and detect suspicious behaviors in real time. A wide range of data sources, algorithms, and approaches are required to combat fraud. An effective fraud detection strategy includes several steps that serve as a proven framework and methodology for machine learning forensic investigators in their efforts to eliminate improper payments, fraud, waste, and abuse.

A Fraud Detection Checklist

1. What are the data components related to fraud?
2. Where is the data stored and who owns the data?
3. Can external data sets be used to supplement models created with in-house data?
4. How can the investigator have access to the data for the creation of detection models?
5. Conduct a preliminary inductive analysis using visualization and clustering software tools.
6. Conduct a deductive forensic analysis using rule generators and decision trees.
7. Write a report on the forensic results, and make recommendations for improving security.
8. Deploy reactive rules to detect and prevent future fraudulent transactions in real time.
9. Institute an ongoing process for reviewing the accuracy of the fraud detection models and rules.
10. Keep improving the fraud detection data and algorithms; report continuously on the models' results.

Follow this ten-step checklist to streamline and perfect a comprehensive fraud detection strategy. For example, the investigator needs to interview all the strategic owners of the fraud detection system prior to its construction; they have first-hand knowledge about the crime. The investigator needs to review all of the data sources, their schemas, and formats. If the forensic process discovers a new fraud pattern, new information about it needs to be captured in the data for use in models and rules for real-time deployment. The following is another methodology for the machine learning forensic investigator to consider:

1. Understand the crime scene

   The forensic investigator needs to thoroughly understand how, where, and when fraud is taking place. The investigator must have a clear understanding of the crime being committed, how often it takes place, and the total cost of the crime for an organization. A clear understanding of the objectives of the investigation should also be abundantly clear. An investigator must carefully examine the crime scene to determine what took place and in what sequence the events took place; for example, if the investigation is about online fraud, was the password compromised? For wireless fraud investigations, were the electronic serial number (ESN) and telephone number (MIN) cloned?

2. Understand the evidence

Digital evidence is everywhere; for the forensic investigator, the important issue is to focus on what is important for detecting and preventing future fraudulent transactions. The investigator must understand at this juncture what data exists in order to analyze and model the fraudulent behaviors. At this juncture, consideration must be given to organizing this digital evidence, which may reside in multiple servers located in different locations and in different intervals and formats. These formats may include unstructured content. Consideration of privacy issues and confidentiality must also be defined by the investigator to ensure that no illegal disclosures take place during the course of the investigation and in the deployment of predictive preventive models and rules.

3. Understand the forensics

At this stage, multiple concurrent models need to be explored. This can include link analysis, clustering maps, text mining, decision trees, etc. All of these forensic tools need to be considered during this phase of the investigation. The format of the data and the type of crime scene being investigated can dictate what forensic tool to use. Prior to the development of models, a preparation of the data must be considered; for example, how will the investigator treat missing values in the data? The forensics must include the use of an ensemble of treatments, processes, models, and techniques. Consideration should be given to the accuracy and cost of each to maximize return on investment.

4. Understand the value

The purpose of any investigation is to reduce revenue loss and improve efficiency in detecting and preventing fraud. Calculate carefully the potential revenue savings due to the detection of a particular crime. Document the potential savings due to the deployment of the detection system, and measure the cost savings to an organization. At this juncture, the value of the deployment of the rules or models must be documented. The entire process is iterative, designed to determine and validate the value of the project. Detection rates and revenue saved must be measured continuously in order to determine the accuracy of the models. Lastly, what knowledge was gained from the project? This knowledge can provide insight into how a system is designed and improved in the future.

1.7 Cybersecurity Investigations: Self-Organizing and Evolving Analyses

The velocity and volume of web and wireless crimes require real-time detection developed by machine learning forensic investigators. Each day and night, organized and individual attacks take place against corporate and government organizations. The cybercriminals continuously launch persistent and varied attacks against protected and private networks. Of all crimes, this is the most evil and potentially devastating, threatening citizens, organizations, the economy, and even nations.

Detection systems need to be developed to monitor networks in real time, and proactive measures need to be taken to thwart intrusions and attacks. This can be developed by the digital forensic investigator by aggregating and modeling massive amounts of network, web, and wireless data produced by monitoring devices and processes. Marketing mechanisms such as cookies, server log files, forms databases, beacons, and JavaScript can be enlisted in the development of these anti-cybercrime systems.

Investigations of cybercrimes can provide deep insight into the nature, occurrence, and impact of intrusion attacks on an organization's networks. Once there is an understanding of the crime scene, and the evidence, forensics, and value have been determined and documented, an investigator can move on to perform historical trending and analysis, the final objective being to develop a robust but flexible system to forecast and predict future cyber attacks. The idea is to use machine learning forensic techniques and tools to elevate cyber analysis from passive attack detection to building self-organizing and evolving systems for predicting threats, risk, and attacks, and to ensure real-time countermeasures in response.

Cyber attacks are fast and furious; thus, a detective system needs to be constructed to be flexible, adaptive, and accurate. The core technologies of machine learning forensics are based on artificial and swarming intelligence, which by their very nature seek to replicate the behavior of human knowledge discovery. Swarm intelligence is a branch of AI that is very adaptive to machine learning forensics in that it seeks to develop distributive and adaptive systems to replicate the behavior of animals. In nature, there are schools of fish, flocks of birds, and swarms of insects that behave in a unified and organized manner to survive.

As with ants and bees, the cyber security investigations should include the development of code and rules that operate autonomously and in unison with coded intelligence to monitor, detect, and deter cyber attacks. The concept is to develop thousands of detection rules in the form of digital ants, each looking for evidence of a threat or attack. As these digital ants swarm over a network, they leave digital trails that an ant is trained to follow, calibrating continuously their level of risk. This risk score is shared and mapped with the scent from other ants, so that very quickly the software swarms converge on potential points of attacks. The strategy of the design is to construct a network of distributed rules that coordinate their risk scores. Care must be taken in detecting sleeper attacks, which may be especially difficult to discover since they enter and hide for long periods of time before activating. There obviously will be detailed information on how to go about developing such adaptive and self-organizing systems in a chapter to follow; suffice to say it involves the use of software agents for "patrolling" a network to guard against cyber attacks.

An agent is a program that performs an action on behalf of its creators, such as coordinating a counterattack against criminals attempting to penetrate a network. The concept of patrolling is one in which these autonomous software agents and their internal rules—which may be a combination of domain expertise and machine learning analyses—are used to coordinate their decision-making in order to achieve optimal protection, similar to how bees protect their hive.

Patrolling is required when distributed surveillance is needed over multiple servers and networks. Patrolling can be performed using

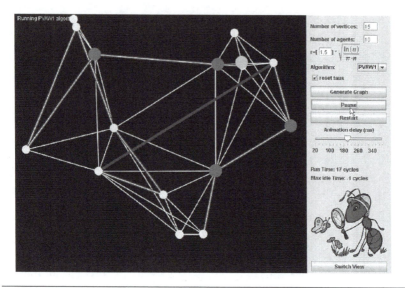

Figure 1.6   Roaming cyber security agents patrolling a network looking for potential intrusions.

multiple detection rules or conditions warranting a coordinated effort to combat criminal behaviors. Anonymous data pointers can be used to access and analyze data located in different locations without jeopardizing security or privacy and will be covered in detailed in the chapters to follow. The point is that patrolling is possible without the need to move any data, and is instead accomplished via a distributed manner over the web and networks in an anonymous and secure manner (Figure 1.6).

As with the web, similar techniques can be used to create self-organizing network detecting systems to prevent wireless intrusions and fraud. Every wireless device contains a SIM (subscriber identity module) that contains its own unique serial number and an internationally mobile subscriber identifier (IMSI). There may also be security authentication and ciphering information related to a local network, which is a list of the services the user has access to along with passwords. The SIM of every wireless device can pinpoint (1) who, (2) when, (3) what, and (4) the location of a cell phone.

The SIM signature can identify the point of time of an individual's communications in digital detail. The SIM can also reveal recently dialed numbers, text messages, and carrier data. Forensic investigators can begin to use off-the-shelf software tools (to be covered in detail in Chapter 4) to extract the SIM's data for machine learning forensic analysis. In a criminal case, this type of digital investigation can lead to identifying affiliations or detecting wireless activity around the time of an event, via link analysis and clustering. There are several wireless scams an investigator needs to be aware of such as cramming, phishing, and evil twin.

Wireless fraud takes many forms. There is cramming, which is when a company or criminal asks a cellular carrier to authorize for voice mail, paging, Internet access, web hosting, and other services that the owner of the wireless device never agreed to purchase. The criminal only needs a subscriber's name and phone number, which the criminal can harvest via phony contest entry forms, offers for product and services coupons, or other promotional gimmicks.

There is also phone phishing, which is initiated via wireless text messages that claimed to be from a bank. Users are asked to dial a phone number regarding problems with their checking or savings accounts. Once the phone number is dialed—which is owned by the phisher and provided by a Voice-over-IP service—it prompts users to enter their account numbers and PIN. Similar scams exist with other payment providers such as PayPal.

Another wireless crime is evil twin, which is a term describing a rogue Wi-Fi access set up by criminals in a hotspot who pose as a legitimate provider but whose true intent is to steal security information from users of wireless devices. Evil twin is the wireless version of a phishing scam. Phishing is, of course, the criminally fraudulent process of acquiring sensitive information such as usernames, passwords, and credit card details by masquerading as a trustworthy entity. These hotspots are an open invitation to criminals, who with the right equipment can locate a hotspot and take its place, substituting their own evil twin.

The forensic investigator can assist an organization, whether a wireless carrier, insurer, government agency, or law enforcement department in detecting and preventing these types of wireless crimes by the use of link analysis, clustering, and the use of decision trees to identify patterns of crimes and criminals' methods of operation and location. Lastly, historical wireless billing information can be used as the core data set for examining these patterns of criminal behaviors. Models and rules can subsequently be developed using wireless patrolling agents to detect and prevent future crimes, thus reducing revenue loss for both carriers, vendors, retailers, and consumers.

1.8 Corporate Counterintelligence: Litigation and Competitive Investigations

Corporate counterintelligence involves combating economic espionage. Both foreign and criminal entities are continuously attempting to break into corporate and government networks in search of classified and unclassified information. Related to this type of corporate initiative is litigation investigations, such as the extraction and analysis of e-mail and documents. Competitive investigations are a form of counterintelligence in that these behavioral analytical tools and techniques can be used to monitor and access the behaviors of competitors. Corporate counterintelligence is in fact the opposite of competitive intelligence and espionage. The former is about protecting corporate intelligence, while the latter is about gaining competitive intelligence.

Machine learning forensics can be leveraged to assist corporations in optimizing their profits, securing their assets, and monetizing counterintelligence via the analysis of digital data patterns. The evidence for accomplishing this exists over private networks and multiple depositories—the role of the investigator is to leverage this content both in structured and unstructured (text) formats. The investigator needs to use a variety of forensic tools and techniques to accomplish this; for example, almost all web and wireless traffic is tracked for marketing and billing purposes and can be one of multiple sources of data analysis for corporate counterintelligence, litigation, and competitive investigations.

Corporate counterintelligence is concerned with the protection of trade secrets, which the Federal Bureau of Investigation defines as "all forms and types of financial, business, scientific, technical, economic, or engineering information, including patterns, plans, compilations, program devices, formulas, designs, prototypes, methods, techniques, processes, procedures, programs, or codes whether tangible or intangible, and whether or how stored, compiled, or memorialized physically, electronically, graphically, photographically or in writing, which the owner has taken reasonable measures and has an independent economic value."

As the FBI defines them, trade secrets are commonly called classified proprietary information, economic policy information, trade information, proprietary technology, or critical technology. The bureau further defines the "theft of trade secrets" as occurring when someone (1) knowingly performs targeting or acquisition of trade secrets or intends to convert a trade secret to (2) knowingly benefit anyone other than the owner. This is commonly referred to as Industrial Espionage (Title 18 U.S.C., Section 1832).

Corporate Counterintelligence Checklist

1. The first task for the behavioral forensic investigative unit is to assemble all of the data owners and conduct a detailed audit of all data depositories and network traffic.
2. Obtain all details about all tracking mechanisms being used by the client organization, such as their use of cookies, registration forms, log files, JavaScript, etc. These mechanisms are commonly used to track the behaviors of users.
3. Use clustering, link analysis, and text mining tools to distinguish abnormal and suspicious behaviors, let the software find the clues, and then concentrate on their findings.
4. Use this type of unsupervised investigation to distinguish what may constitute malicious efforts by criminals, competitors, or foreign entities to steal trade secrets.
5. Use supervised tools such as rule generators or decision trees to map the conditions constituting high-risk behaviors of potential theft or intrusions.

Litigation investigations usually involve conducting in-depth compliance investigations and managing counsel in evaluating and implementing proposed investigative strategies. It may also require conducting multiple analyses to assess risk and determine disclosure strategy within the context of an investigation. A litigation investigation may also require the implementation of preventive compliance programs. The litigation investigator may need to deal with documents, databases, e-mail depositories, and wireless statements. The forensic investigator should strive to be a specialist in dealing with digital evidence involving financial, pharmaceutical, civil, and criminal investigations by employing some basic SQL data extraction skills.

Through the use of various forensic tools, the investigator can take extracts from data sets, in any format, that could turn out to be key evidence for the discovery of potential criminal behavior. For example, in the area of pharmaceutical investigations, this may involve assisting clients with a wide array of enforcement and regulatory proceedings, including the Anti-Kickback Statute, the Medicaid rebate statute, the Prescription Drug Marketing Act, the False Claims Act, the Stark physician referral statute, and multiple state anti-fraud and consumer protection laws.

Litigation Investigation Checklist

1. *Patents*: This involves such tasks as the handling of the Hatch–Waxman legislation (the Drug Price Competition and Patent Term Restoration Act, which established generic drugs) and other patent cases and associated antitrust litigation. For example, the investigator may be required to conduct an investigation into interrelated biotechnology patents and claims of patent infringement, as well as antitrust and other trade secret issues for pharmaceutical clients.
2. *Antitrust*: This may involve dealing with complex civil and criminal antitrust and consumer protection matters, including nationwide class actions, consolidated multidistrict cases, short-fuse preliminary injunction proceedings, and court appeals; clients may include financial, manufacturing, and retailing firms.
3. *Regulatory*: This may involve investigations to challenge federal investigative actions. Another task may also involve handling "reverse" Freedom of Information Act cases, where clients assert their interests in the confidentiality proprietary information sought by competitors, watchdog groups, or other regulators.
4. *Insurance*: This may involve assisting clients in cases in both court trials and in private arbitrations, including both domestic and international proceedings, involving product liability cases against pharmaceuticals and other manufacturers.

Somewhat related to litigation investigations are competitive intelligence strategies, which warrant the monitoring, tracking, and reporting of industry and technology corporate competitors. Two strategies evolve from this endeavor; the first is, of course, keeping an eye on the competition. The second strategy may come as a surprise: it involves an internal audit for competitive intelligence within an organization. A firm may already have an expert on the extraction of oil from water and not know it! Both, however, involve the use of behavioral forensic tools and techniques for extracting, analyzing, and delivering the evidence required for corporate action and potential litigation.

Competitive intelligence is the process of discovering, developing, and delivering relevant information by decision makers in corporate organizations. This type of intelligence may be leveraged for product development, mergers, acquisitions, and alliances, as well as tactical and preemptive initiatives against competitors. Competitive intelligence can be used to support these types of strategic and tactical decisions via the use of machine learning forensics tools, technologies, and techniques. The Central Intelligence Agency (CIA) reduces the process of competitive intelligence to six core phases:

1. *Destination Phase*: Address the preparedness and the capability to perform the task; this is the stage when the processes and systems are put in place to support competitive intelligence activities. For the behavioral forensic investigator and team, it is where the data audit takes place and objectives are established.

2. *Demand Phase*: Identifies what the information needs are and determines the approach to be taken; it identifies the decisions to be supported by the activities of the forensic investigator, such as who owns the data and what software tools and techniques will be used. Funding issues might arise here, but the investigator can always use tools that are free and yet highly accurate and effective.

3. *Discovery Phase*: Involves seeking out and collecting the internal and external information sources. The investigator must identify the sources of intelligence required. For certain industries that are regulated—external data is available from company filings with government regulators—other sources of information include patent searches, chemical abstracts, SEC filings, psychographic, and demographic and corporate profiles.

4. *Development Phase*: Produces a meaningful picture from the pieces of data that have been discovered and analyzed. This is

the phase where the investigator presents the initial results of the analysis and a report is prepared for decision makers.

5. *Delivery Phase*: Communicates the resulting intelligence to the right people at the right time. At this juncture, the investigator needs to determine what intelligence to share and with whom. For example, this may require some changes to network security settings and log-on procedures.

6. *Disengagement Phase*: Involves debriefing clients and thinking of ways to improve the process. For the investigator, this involves closing the feedback loop with the users of the competitive intelligence to ensure their needs are met. This also requires the need to monitor the models and their performance.

One fact about the use of behavioral forensic investigation is that no two organizations will have the same competitive intelligence solution. However, every corporate entity will need machine learning forensics to predict trends and behaviors of competitors and discover previously unknown patterns of opportunities and risk within its own organization. Ironically, machine learning forensics can be used to "machine-learn your business" by conducting analyses of an organization's own employees, in order to get insight into the knowledge residing inside an enterprise. Machine learning forensics can be used to develop competitive intelligence marketing strategies, minimize risk, and reduce losses from fraud and the protection of trade secrets, including the following benefits for an organization:

- Predict and calibrate risk
- Find perpetrators of fraud
- Map competitor's intentions
- Anticipate attacks and crimes
- Be more efficient and competitive

1.9 A Machine Learning Forensic Worksheet

Machine learning forensics generally involves the following tasks:

1. The cleaning or conversion of operational data into a form suitable for forensic analysis.
2. The coding or conversion of the data attributes for analysis.

3. The enrichment of the data used for forensic analysis.
4. The selection of the data sets and certain attributes.
5. The actual analysis via clustering or classification.
6. The reporting of the findings of the investigation.
7. The creation of a real-time detection system.

From the outset, the investigator should be aware of noisy and incomplete data, legal and privacy issues (data cleaning is one of the first tasks), remove duplicate records, and correct errors in data strings and merge with other data sets. Some of the problems a forensic investigator is likely to encounter are the following:

8. Not all departments in an organization will want to share their data.
9. Timing and delay problems in assembling the data sets.
10. Lack of metadata information about databases.
11. Not all data sets are up to date.
12. Legal and privacy restrictions.

Some coding steps commonly performed in preparation of data sets prior to analysis:

13. Convert dates to months, weeks, or days from January.
14. Divide credit scores by 100 to create credit classes.
15. Divide income by 100 to create income classes.
16. Compress addresses into regions.
17. Convert yes to 1 and no to 0.
18. Convert birth dates to age.

Some basic questions an investigator needs to consider:

19. What external new data sets can be used to improve the forensic models?
20. How many data sets are there, how many servers, and how many networks?
21. What processes and transformations are required for the project?
22. What are the criteria for success, and how will they be measured?
23. For what purpose were the data sets created originally?
24. What are the requirements for the forensic project?

The machine learning forensic environment is very much like a production assembly line, a shipyard, or an airport—continuously running, learning, adapting, and improving its detection processes. These are some common steps:

25. Deal with some extremely large data sets.
26. Support data discovery and classification tasks.
27. Deal with historical data sets.
28. Introduce a data-cleaning process.
29. Create a coding framework that is dynamic and flexible.
30. Introduce a flexible architecture that supports heterogeneous data sets.

An inductive forensic checklist:

31. Identify all potential available data sets for the project.
32. Prepare the data sets for analysis, which can answer why, who, and when.
33. Select an inductive forensic approach: clustering and/or text analytics.
34. Identify key attributes discovered by the undirected analysis.
35. Generate a report of the findings.
36. Identify what new processes or steps to take for a real-time detection system.

A deductive forensic checklist:

37. Identify all available data sets for the project.
38. Prepare the data sets for analysis, which can answer why, who, and when.
39. Select a deductive forensic approach: rule generator or decision tree based on the characteristics of the data and forensic goals.
40. Divide the data into training, testing, and evaluating data sets.
41. Use the training data set to generate rules or decision trees.
42. Evaluate the accuracy of the rule and trees by applying them to the testing data set.
43. Gauge the model accuracy by applying it to the evaluating data set.
44. Apply the knowledge and/or code generated from the model to detect fraud and crimes.

45. Measure the success of the detection models and rules.
46. Consider using additional data sets for improving accuracy and performance.
47. Measure and report on all model results.
48. Document all forensic activities.
49. Brief all decision makers on the results of the investigation.

Finally, understand that most forensic investigations are a continuous effort to combat crime, fraud, and destructive network intrusions and attacks. The processes of forensic investigations involve the following:

50. Hypothesis testing.
51. Data aggregation and preparation.
52. The designing of maps, rules, trees, and analyses.
53. The evaluation of maps and models.
54. The development of real-time detection systems.
55. Restarting the entire process all over again.

Crime and fraud are always evolving, and the machine learning investigator must adapt to this fact to ensure success for his or her organization, department, agency, corporation, or network.

2

DIGITAL INVESTIGATIVE MAPS AND MODELS

Strategies and Techniques

2.1 Forensic Strategies

Data aggregation and preparation are tasks an investigator needs to perform before any analysis. When data is properly prepared, the investigator gains an understanding and insight into the criminals' method of operation. This is an important concept: preparing the data means that the map or model is built right. Preparing the investigator means he or she is gaining insight into the crime, ensuring that the right map and model are built. Having a forensic strategy starts with identifying a need and making correct, appropriate, and informed decisions about how to construct the right map, model, and analyses. The investigator needs to start by defining crimes or fraud in a precise way:

1. What crime is being committed?
2. How was the crime detected?
3. When did the crime take place?
4. Where did the crime take place?
5. How often does the crime occur?
6. How much is the crime costing?
7. What criminal clues need to be investigated?

Having a clear picture of the crime is half the battle won for the investigator. He or she should also have an understanding of which direction to take, which method will yield the most returns, and which will be the easiest method to tackle. This generally takes into consideration which crime is the most important, which crime is the most difficult to solve, and which investigation will yield the optimum returns. Somewhat related to this is the question of what kind of solution should the investigation generate: a report, a chart, a map, a graph, a set of rules, code for deployment in real time, a listing of suspects or criminal acts, etc.

As previously stated, it is vital for the investigator to create a framework prior to the investigation. This framework essentially is a data audit that asks the questions: What are the data sets, and do they answer the questions needed to detect the crime? This is a critical question that must be thoroughly answered before investing much time, money, and resources on the construction of the model. The essence of the framework is to build an overall map of the data sets before committing to a detailed investigation. The framework seeks to answer the basic question: What are the factors driving fraudulent or criminal behavior, and how can it be detected?

For fraud detection, it is useful to ask, what are the driving factors? Where is the easiest point in the network or system to detect it? What are the most cost-effective and rapid measures to stop it? What are the patterns of activity leading to fraud? The investigator needs to know what the client organization needs and expects. The solution should be specific enough so that it can be practically implemented. This involves the investigator asking the "six W's": who, how, what, why, when, and where about the fraudulent transactions. Asking these questions in advance will eliminate a dilemma common to data analytics, GIGO: garbage in, garbage out.

It is not uncommon for the preparation of the data for modeling to require various adjustments to be made to the data prior to analysis. Subsequently, the model produced is constructed using adjusted, synthetic, and prepared data. Thus, some processes are needed to ensure that any new data to which the model is applied needs to be adjusted similar to the training data set. If this mechanism is not performed, the model will be unusable as it will not work with raw data, only with data prepared similar to the training data set.

A machine learning strategy and a tracking framework need to be constructed by an investigator. This will ensure that criminal behaviors are captured in continuous data streams so that forensic models can react to crimes in real time. The first task is knowing what incidental data is available for analysis. The second immediate goal is figuring out how these data, which are usually distributed, different, and proprietary, can be used to advance a forensic investigation and a real-time detection system. Some key questions and issues to address in the construction of a forensic framework by an investigator are as follows:

1. Has the crime been defined and will the investigation selected yield tangible results?
2. Has the specified solution (map, rules, models, code) been agreed to?
3. Is there a methodology for refining maps, models, and code?
4. Has the crime driven the investigative strategy and solution?
5. Has the definite solution delivery mode been selected?
6. Is the crime driving the investigation? If not, why not?
7. Have the limitations of the solution been identified?
8. What are the core factors leading to this crime?

In part, an investigation will reveal relationships that work in unison or influence other variables in a crime. To uncover such relationships, an investigator may need to perform multiple analyses involving both inductive and deductive processes and necessitating the construction of clustering maps and predictive models.

Forensic Strategy Checklist

1. Clearly define the crime that when solved yields tangible savings.
2. Specify the required investigative solution.
3. Define how the solution will be deployed.
4. Understand as much as possible about the crime and criminals.
5. Let the investigation drive the tool selection: map or model.
6. Refine the map or model iteratively.
7. Define instability and uncertainty in the map or model.

The key question in formulating a forensic strategy is: Would it be more cost-effective to detect crimes by having human investigators do it manually or by using machine learning code to automate the process? There are two types of investigations: *passive* and *active*. Passive investigations identify relationships and associations, and are explanatory in nature: they are about knowledge discovery. Active investigations generate predictive risk scores, rules, code, etc., and are about reacting to risk, fraud, and crimes as they occur or before they happen. Whether passive or active, the flow of activities in the model creation process is generally as follows:

First Phase

1. Problem Appropriate? => Problem Selection
2. Solution Appropriate? => Solution Selection
3. Data Appropriate? => Data Selection

Second Phase

1. Good Data? => Add Data => Get More Variables => Recode Data
2. Data Problem Fixed? => Identify Data
3. Method Applicable? => Define Modeling Method => Train-Test-Validate => Model Robust?

Third Phase

1. Define Model Parameters? => Model Limitations? => Model Life Expectancy?
2. Model Limits? => Model Accuracy? => Model % Right?
3. Apply Model => Monitor Results => Verify and Adjust

Ideally, a continuous learning system should evaluate incoming data and adapt to behaviors it was trained to monitor and detect—adjusting in real time to a dynamic environment. Forensic rules acting as "sensors" continuously learn to recognize features of criminal behaviors, such as the tendency for fraudulent transactions to take place at specific locations, times, or intervals. In order to execute this forensic strategy, the investigator needs to identify all possible data sets and examine them at the granular level.

The investigator may need to integrate data from different sources, such as different departments or agencies that use different formats, conventions, time periods, degrees of aggregation, and locations. All of this fragmented data evidence can have immense strategic value when brought together by the forensic investigator. This can also include the strategic use of external data from outside an organization; today, such data may include Internet tracking server data and real-time demographics. One possible strategy is to use a clustering analysis to identify subgroups of behaviors and then classify those subgroups into distinct classes of instances or events using a rule generator or a decision tree tool.

However, in the end it is the investigator who is responsible—through an interactive process—for the selection of the right type and level of data aggregation. Domain experts from different departments, agencies, and organizations need to be consulted to explain anomalies, missing values, outliers, and the difference between numeric and categorical values of variables. The investigator is responsible for the strategic selection of the right data inputs and outputs for the forensic system. In the end, the one true measure of success for a forensic system or investigation is the dollars it saves the client organization by detecting fraud or crime.

2.2 Decompose the Data

One of the first tasks an investigator needs to do as he or she gains access to data sets is to obtain counts and summary statistics for each field, as well as counts on the number of different values for all variables. Some machine learning tools incorporate this kind of data profile once a data set is imported into them. Some data sets may consist of free-form text such as postal codes, e-mail addresses, and vehicle identification numbers, which for text analysis do not require any preparation.

On the other hand, there may also be instances when some data conversions will need to be conducted and synthetic classes created; for example, "Juarez, Chihuahua, Puerto Vallarta," can be converted to the country code of Mexico: 52. The important issue for the investigator is that if such a conversion is done for the training data set, then the same conversion needs to be performed when a model is applied to operational data.

Missing values may be another issue the investigator needs to contend with in data sets. There is no clear way of dealing with missing values in data sets; in some instances, it might make sense to use a mean or median value for a numeric variable. For a categorical field, it might make sense to use the most common value in the data set. In fraud and criminal investigations, however, a missing value may be very important and may warrant further analysis. The investigator may want to ask why a contact number or an e-mail address is missing; is it part of an avoidance scheme by the perpetrator?

An investigator should expect to deal with multiple levels of information systems and data sets. Some organizations may have a data warehouse, while others will have middleware tools that provide a single interface to a distributed network of department databases. There are also departmental data warehouses that store summarized data for a single application.

There are also operational databases that have the ability to flag specific information that may need to be retrieved on a continuous basis. Operational databases allow an organization to enter, gather, and retrieve specific enterprise information. Operational databases have the ability to flag specific information that may need to be retrieved on a continuous basis, which is an important capability for the investigator.

The investigator should also be aware of the process of *profile triangulation*, which involves looking at individuals from different perspectives and via a combination of data sources. For example, an organization may have information on an individual internally, but there may be additional information on the same entity in other departments, agencies, or organizations, which when combined expand the knowledge about that individual.

For example, a federal agency may have some master data about an individual; however, a state or local agency may have additional intelligence in their databases that can enhance the overall profile of that individual. There may also be credit and public filing information that can enhance the data an investigator is pursuing. Forensic investigations may also need to integrate additional online and offline information. This includes a mixture of real-time demographics and online clickstream data, as well as wireless access point (WAP) type of information. There are also criminal records, statistics, and multiple criminal national, state, and local databases and networks.

2.3 Criminal Data Sets, Reports, and Networks

In recent years, the federal government has encouraged state and local law enforcement agencies to establish fusion centers to integrate their criminal data and files from different sources to create actionable knowledge. Starting with the lowly 911 call for service (CFS) data set, which is based on observed behavior that is suspicious enough to call 911, the data is organized along the perceived seriousness of the incidents. More importantly, CFS data is public information that can be analyzed without infringing on an individual's privacy and civil rights.

CFS data sets allow for temporal clustering analyses by investigators, so they can focus on concentrations of criminal behaviors over time and space—it also supports the analysis of trends and patterns—enabling countermeasure strategies, deployment of resources, and pre-crime. Clustering of CFS can be performed along crime types and/or keywords to identify incidents that might warrant monitoring and elevated surveillance. These CFS incidents can also be viewed along location, time, and types of activity. The prioritizing of clusters by severity of incidents can also test whether the cluster locations are at risk of being targets for specific crimes, such as burglaries.

The Federal Bureau of Investigation also generates several criminal data reports. The Uniform Crime Report (UCR) contains official data on crime, which it indexes as criminal types, such as homicide and nonnegligent manslaughter, robbery, forcible rape, aggravated assault, burglary, larceny/theft, motor vehicle theft, and arson. UCR is a summary-based reporting system, with data aggregated to the city, county, state, and other geographic levels. The UCR is a reporting file and can only provide some information to the investigator at the aggregate level by states, metropolitan statistical areas, cities, metropolitan and nonmetropolitan counties, and colleges and universities.

There is also the FBI's National Incident Based Reporting System (NIBRS), which is used by law enforcement agencies in the United States for collecting and reporting data on crimes. Data are collected on every incident and arrest in the Group A offense category. The Group A offenses are grouped along 46 specific crimes, which are further grouped into 22 offense categories. Specific facts about these offenses are gathered and reported in the NIBRS system. In addition to the Group A offenses, 11 Group B offenses are also reported with only the arrest information. Again—this type of criminal data set is aggregated and care must be taken on how an investigator uses it—if at all.

Another national criminal data set is the National Crime Victimization Survey (NCVS), which was designed with four primary objectives: (1) to develop detailed information about the victims and consequences of crime, (2) to estimate the number and types of crimes not reported to the police, (3) to provide uniform measures of selected types of crimes, and (4) to permit comparisons over time and types of areas. There is also the National Law Enforcement Telecommunication System (NLETS), an information-sharing system for state and local law enforcement agencies.

Lastly, there is also the National Crime Information Center (NCIC), a central database for tracking crime-related information. NCIC data is received from federal law enforcement agencies, state and local law enforcement agencies, as well as tribal law enforcement agencies, railroad and municipal transit police, and non-law enforcement agencies such as state and federal motor vehicle registration and licensing authorities. The NCIC makes available a variety of records to be used for law enforcement and security purposes. NCIC organizes the data along the following categories:

Personal records:

- Convicted sex offenders
- Criminal conviction records
- Foreign fugitives
- Immigration violators
- Missing persons
- Parolees or people on supervised release
- Persons with active arrest warrants
- Persons with active protection orders
- Secret Service protective alerts
- Terrorist organizations and membership
- Unidentified human remains information
- Violent gang organizations and membership

Property records:

- Firearms records, including lost or missing firearms
- Stolen, embezzled, or counterfeit securities
- Stolen property
- Stolen vehicle and boat parts
- Stolen vehicles and boats

Other criminal data sets and networks that the investigator needs to know about are as follows:

CODIS: The Combined DNA Index System (CODIS) is a database funded by the FBI; it stores DNA profiles created by federal, state, and local crime laboratories in the United States, with the ability to search the database to assist in the identification of suspects in crimes.

NIBIN: The National Integrated Ballistic Identification Network is a specialized computer network in the United States. It contains digital images of recovered pieces of ballistic evidence. NIBIN enables US law enforcers to rapidly determine if a piece of recovered ballistic evidence came from a firearm that has been previously used in a crime.

NICS: The National Instant Criminal Background Check System is a point-of-sale system for determining eligibility to purchase a firearm in the United States of America.

LEO: The Law Enforcement On-Line intranet supports the FBI's ten priorities by providing cost-effective, time-critical national alerts and information sharing to public safety, law enforcement, antiterrorism, and intelligence agencies. With proper clearance, LEO can be accessed from anywhere in the world.

Other systems that focus on specific types of crimes, such as money laundering, include TECS (Treasury Enforcement Communications Systems), JABS (Joint Automated Booking System), NiPC (National Infrastructure Protection Center), and FinCEN (Financial Crimes Enforcement Network).

2.4 Real Estate, Auto, and Credit Data Sets

There are several commercial and government data sets that contain detailed real estate information. Commercial providers include DataQuick, which captures real estate data directly from county assessors and recorder offices nationwide. Other commercial real estate data aggregators are Homesdatabase.com and Accuriz.com, which support searches by address or name of individuals. For vehicle information, no other company matches Polk.com, which maintains detailed data on automobiles, trucks, and both used and new vehicles.

For credit information, there are three nationwide data depositories: Trans Union, Equifax, and Experian. All three provide credit reports that consist of the following main sections:

1. The consumer information section contains information about an individual's name, addresses, and employment.
2. The consumer statement section contains a personal comment that an individual has submitted to the credit bureaus for inclusion in their report.
3. The summary information section contains a list of an individual's payment history, broken down by account type.
4. The account history information section provides detailed information about all credit accounts in an individual's name. Accounts are divided into five categories: Real Estate, Revolving, Installment, Other, and Collection.
5. The public record information section lists publicly available information about legal matters affecting an individual's credit. These public records may include judgments, civil actions, state or federal tax liens, and bankruptcies.
6. The inquiry information section lists details about each inquiry that has been made into a credit history. Details include the name of the creditor or potential creditor who made the inquiry and the date when the inquiry was made.
7. The creditor information section lists the names of all creditors and potential creditors who appear on an individual's credit report. The list includes both creditors that appear in their Account History section and creditors that appear in the Inquiry Section. Each creditor's address is listed to the right of the creditor's name. When available, the creditor's phone number is also listed. Creditors without listed numbers must be contacted via the US Postal Service.

2.5 Psychographic and Demographic Data Sets

There are also several providers of demographic and psychographic information available for profiling individuals or groups. Demographics provide quantitative data based on geography, age, gender, and calendar events. Psychographics provide qualitative data that reflect attitudes, lifestyles, and preferences.

Demographic data providers such as Nielsen, Experian, and Acxiom gather and analyze demographic data from many sources, including local governments, household consumer databases, and postal delivery counts. There are other sources of demographics, including the following websites:

census.gov—The Census Bureau maintains the largest site available on the web and the largest repository of demographic information about Americans.

quickfacts.census.gov—This too is part of the vast US Census Bureau site, but its main value is providing speedy access to basic information for each state and county, such as population, geography, and business.

fedstats.gov—The Federal Interagency Council on Statistical Policy maintains this site to provide easy access to the full range of statistics and information produced by 70 federal agencies for public use.

freedemographics.com—The user can evaluate and compare the market potential of geographic areas down to the zip code level. User-friendly online query forms are available as well as drop-down menus and mapping functions.

zipskinny.com—This site has some basic demographic data for a specific zip code. It shows neighboring zip codes so that the user can easily compare them on some basic demographic variables.

melissadata.com—Provides basic demographic information broken down by zip code with a variety of other information such as media in an area, income tax issues, and types of businesses (SIC codes).

ersys.com—With maps, charts, reports, and relevant links, this site covers over 2,600 US cities with detailed demographics, environmental factors, economic indicators, housing statistics, media, and transportation.

marketingpower.com—The American Marketing Association (AMA) provides several marketing tools that offer free demographics services. Registration is required to access the data, but it is simple and free.

easidemographics.com—Maintained by a research company specializing in demographic analyses. A variety of reports are available for free about almost any place in the country with stats and maps.

markethive.com—Provides a visually rich set of mapping tools that provide free demographics and can help improve targeting of advertising.

esribis.com—ESRI combines demographics, consumer spending pattern intelligence, and lifestyle segmentation with powerful technology.

acxiom.com—Offers streams of real-time demographics and lifestyle information for behavioral analytics to marketers and advertisers, which can also be of value to a forensic investigator. They add a new dimension to the profiling of suspects and criminals, who may not be aware of the personal information and the level of granularity available about them. Firms such as Acxiom are merging their household clusters of millions of US households in the form of networked cookies to target online ads for behavioral analytics, which can potentially also be of value to forensic investigators, since they can track online behaviors with lifestyle information.

These new demographic cookies contain lifestyle information, allowing an organization to profile individuals along specific lifestyle groups and behaviors. This information service can validate a consumer's name and address against their own information and returns relevant data for websites to use, including demographics and diagnostic information; this same intelligence can be served to investigators. For example, the demographics of a 17-year-old visitor will be dramatically different from the median age of, say, an investment firm website, whose typical user's age is 42. Spikes such as these can also be discovered using clustering software, where data outliers stand out for further inspection and analysis for the investigator.

Relevance-X is the result of a blending of Acxiom's EchoTarget ad network, and PersonicX is their proprietary targeting system based on 70 unique household segments. Acxiom is also offering Relevance-X Social, which allows the user to see the social networks of individuals and how many "friends" or contacts they may have within online communities such as Facebook. This real-time demographic product might be of interest to forensic professionals since it readily identifies social intelligence about relationships and communications of individuals under investigation.

2.6 Internet Data Sets

Today, individuals are tracked on the web and wireless networks via cookies, CGI forms, JavaScript, Deep Packet Inspection (DPI), and other proprietary systems and software to cluster them along specific propensities of behaviors and tendencies. Almost all of this tracking is for marketing and advertising purposes, but it can also benefit forensic investigators. For example, a website can generate a unique identification number for each visitor and store their id's on the user's machine using a cookie file—this piece of information is stored as name–value pairs. A cookie is a tracking mechanism created by Netscape over a decade ago to allow for shopping carts to exist for commercial websites. Cookies are sent from Internet servers to visitors' computers in order to track all of their activities at that site, as well as across ad networks and search sites such as Google. A cookie file, for example, could simply be the name of a unique UserID, and a dedicated value assigned to that visitor such as A9A3BECE0563982D:

```
UserID A9A3BECE0563982D
www.jesusmena.com/
```

This is how tracking cookies work. The first time a user visits jesusmena.com, the hosting server assigns them a unique identification number value and stores it on their PC, laptop, or phone. The type of data that cookies can store is flexible; not only can a unique number be stored and used to track the user but it can also record the number of unique sessions and the categories or content of products searched for by that user. For forensic investigators, this can be of value since cookies on suspects' machines can reveal details about their everyday online activities and interests.

For example, Amazon.com stores quite a lot of information about their users. This is what an Amazon cookie captures and how it configures itself on users' machines:

```
session-id-time
 954242000 amazon.com/
session-id 002-4135256-7625846 amazon.com/
x-main eKQIfwnxuF7qtmX52x6VWAXh@Ih6Uo5H amazon.com/
ubid-main 077-9263437-9645324 amazon.com/
```

Amazon stores a main user identification number, a unique identification number for each session, and the time the session started on a user's machine, as well as an x-main value, which could be the type of book a user previously purchased—this is of value since targeted recommendations can be generated every time that user logs on to Amazon. So cookies can be used to make relevant recommendations to users, which are mutually beneficial to both websites and users. However, cookies are also sophisticated tracking evidence that an investigator can benefit from in certain type of cases, such as corporate, litigation, and competitive intelligence investigations.

Cookies make possible the placement of targeted content, products, and services. They can be installed on browsers by either marketers or enterprises; they have also evolved to new levels of sophistication in that they are being placed on consumer browsers by ad networks as well as ISPs. There are also wireless cookies; AT&T has filed for a patent on such a mechanism. It is important that investigators be aware of the potential evidence this tracking data can provide in fraud and cybersecurity cases. This is how cookies get created, installed, and used by websites:

1. The process starts when a user selects the URL of a website into his or her browser or phone; for example, this can be when the user clicks on a site from, say, the search engine results or a bookmark on his or her browser.
2. The browser will check the user's computer hard drive for a cookie associated with that website the user just clicked on. If it finds the appropriate cookie, the browser will send the cookie information along with the URL to the web server that sent the original cookie. If the browser doesn't find a cookie, no data is sent and no tracking occurs.
3. The web server receives the request for a page. It then checks to see if a cookie was sent as well. If so, the web server can use that information to tailor the web page specifically for that

user, such as a book recommendation by Amazon. Tracking takes place; every search term and page visited is recorded continuously, 24/7.

4. If the web server didn't receive a cookie, it knows that the user has never visited the site before. The web server then creates a new ID for that user in the web server's database and sends a cookie in the header for the web page to that machine. The machine then stores that cookie on that user's hard drive. From that point on, that user will be uniquely identified when he or she lands on that particular web server.

As previously mentioned, ad networks can also create cookies that are visible on multiple sites. DoubleClick uses networked cookies to serve banner ads on all of their client sites. This is how most ad networks such as DoubleClick work: they place small (1×1 pixels) GIF files, also known as *beacons*, on a site that allows DoubleClick to load cookies on users' machines. DoubleClick can then track their movements across their network of multiple client sites. Some networks can see the search strings that users type on search engines, thus providing them information about user preferences, needs, products, services, and content they are looking for.

Because ad networks can gather extensive information about users' behaviors from multiple sites, DoubleClick, for example, can form very rich profiles. These are anonymous, but they are still valuable buckets of web and wireless behaviors. DoubleClick and companies like it are in a unique position to do this sort of thing because they serve ads on so many sites, enabling them to perform cross-site profiling, which is not a capability available to individual sites, because cookies are site specific. For an investigator, knowing that this type of evidence exists can sharpen his or her inquiries.

Ad networks also have the ability to collect consumer data from their client's ad servers and e-mail databases, and then merge that information with their client's subscription, contest, and registration form databases. These profiles contain both demographic and behaviors information, which an investigator can merge with other data sources, whether it's their cookie and form databases or with other operational legacy systems.

Cookies are the key to tracking and creating behaviors (while online CGI forms are also an excellent source of individual-provided demographics), and by merging them, an investigator can leverage all that valuable information to provide important profiles of online and wireless behaviors. So, cookies are used to carry out session management, identify users, and store their preferences; however, this tracking information can also be used by investigators. So far, cookies have been limited to the web; however, today many users rely on mobile devices to conduct online searches, send and receive e-mail and text messages, and communicate with others.

The problem with using mobile cookies is that most devices do not implement cookies; for example, Nokia only supports cookies on 60% of its devices, while Motorola only supports cookies on 45% of its phones. In addition, some gateways and networks (Verizon, Alltel, and MetroPCS) strip cookies, while other networks simulate cookies on behalf of their mobile devices. There are also dramatic variations in the wireless markets around the world; for example, in the United Kingdom 94% of the devices support wireless cookies, while in the United States only 47% support them.

The support for cookies is greater in the Far East, where wireless devices are more commonly used to access the web. Mobile cookies is a practice already in place in Japan, so that whether watching a podcast, a video, TV, clicking on a loan calculator or a GPS map—on almost all wireless devices—cookies can be set for tracking and capturing wireless behaviors. Wireless investigations can also capture rich IP-addressable information across wireless devices, which has a greater penetration in Asia followed by Europe, while in the United States, this ability is largely not possible on nearly half of the wireless devices.

Progress is being made in support of wireless cookies, forms, beacons, and even widgets that makes it possible for investigators to analyze wireless behaviors of individuals independent of their location and the digital device they are using. These targeting mechanisms such as web and wireless cookies can be used to anonymously monitor and track the content users read and the sites they visit by a designated unique identification number or even an IP address as that user surfs the Internet, or by their GPS location as they use their mobile devices while traveling.

Finally, these cookies can be set by enterprises, marketers, ad networks, search engines, ISPs, and wireless carriers. These tracking mechanisms and their codes, implemented as cookies, enable investigators to construct detailed user profiles. These behaviors can represent sites visited, content viewed, and searches done via the web or wireless devices, all of which can be stored in central databases and analyzed to predict criminal or fraudulent behavioral patterns.

2.7 Deep Packet Inspection (DPI)

All of these tracking mechanisms can be used to enhance web data streams, but a relatively new technology can make it even better: deep packet inspection (DPI). Strangely, the improvement of this tracking technology was made possible by a US government-ordered Internet wire-tapping directive known as the Communications Assistance for Law Enforcement Act (CALEA), a US wiretapping law passed in 1994. CALEA allows ISPs to block, shape, and prioritize their traffic. However, CALEA was originally intended to preserve the ability of the FBI to conduct electronic surveillance of Internet Protocol (VoIP) services. The core technology allowing for CALEA is DPI, which allows for intrusion detection and network security, but most importantly for investigators, it also allows for the construction of very sophisticated models for detecting and anticipating criminal behaviors.

DPI, which is also known as complete packet inspection and Information eXtraction (IX), is a form of network packet filtering that examines the data rather than just the header of a packet as it passes an inspection point, usually searching for viruses, spam, intrusions, or some other predefined criteria in the form of filtering IF/THEN rules to decide if the packet can pass. These filtering rules might be the result of domain expertise of security personnel and/or rules derived from machine learning investigators.

DPI devices have the ability to inspect Internet traffic beyond the first level (packet header) to up to seven levels so that they can identify the types of applications and the actual content of packets—so that rather than just reading the header of an e-mail, DPI can actually read its content—which can lead to the use of text clustering analyses by investigators. DPI devices have the ability to look at Layer Two through Layer Seven of the Open Systems Interconnection (OSI) model, which is an abstract description for layered communications and computer network protocol design.

DPI hardware and services allows enterprises, ISPs, marketers, service providers, and governments to implement a wide range of applications for the protection of networks. Of course, it also allows a machine learning investigator to analyze web data streams very precisely. Layer Seven is the application layer, so that the actual messages sent across the Internet can be decomposed by DPI, enabling an investigator to find out if a suspect is using a browser such as Firefox, a VoIP provider such as Skype, or a BitTorrent program such as Vuze; these all represent digital evidence for extracting IF/THEN filtering rules.

Because some ISPs using DPI route all of their subscribers' traffic, they are able to monitor web browsing habits in a very detailed way, allowing them to gain information about their users' interests, which can also assist investigators. With DPI, investigators can analyze users by seven layers of detail such as what network they used, which adds a totally new dimension to machine learning forensics. DPI data streams offer a new level of understanding and allow for the discovery of new types of online behaviors that, coupled with other tracking mechanisms such as cookies and beacons, lead to rich digital evidence.

There are several DPI technology solution providers (services), including Feeva Technology, NebuAd, and Phorm, while there are also DPI (hardware) providers, which include Procera, Narus, and Arbor Networks. There are also ISPs that use DPI as part of their services; they include Knology, Charter Communications, Wide Open West, and Embarq, some of which provide bundled cable television, high-speed Internet, and telephone services. The investigator needs to be aware of these DPI firms and the solutions they provide; the following is a brief description of what each of these vendors offers.

The Procera devices can detect more than 300 application protocol signatures. Harbor Network's Ellacoya also claims that its hardware can look deeper than the Internet network protocol, with the ability to identify particular traffic from specific sites such as YouTube or Flickr. Narus offers four suites of hardware mainly aimed at network security, but their boxes, similar to those of Procera and Arbor Networks, also perform DPI from Layer Two to Layer Seven and as such could be used by an investigator of web data packet streams.

DPI hardware providers such as Procera, Arbor Networks, and Narus allow for the construction of models across a grid of applications so that an investigator can create grouping of behaviors based on, say, the type of browser or website used by individuals suspected of online crimes. They add a new dimension to behavioral investigations: they provide very deep content and new attributes for machine learning models with the addition of DPI's seven layers of features via their decomposition of data packets. An added advantage of these DPI boxes is that they operate in real time, with web data streams with throughputs of up to 30 Gb.

Feeva Technology works to identify, target, and deliver relevant and useful information to their users, in collaboration with online media, content, advertising, search services and, of course, forensic investigators. Their software platform provides DPI services on hotspot, hotzone, and municipal WiFi networks. Feeva was recently awarded a US patent; this is the abstract:

> According to some embodiments of the present invention, a system, apparatus and method of network operation and information processing, including data acquisition, data processing, data provision, and/or data interoperability features is presented. In some exemplary embodiments, the method includes registering users logging-on to a computer network and gathering user-related information from users. In one or more embodiments, user-profile and location-centric information for each user may be gathered and/or processed in connection with processing targeting and content information.

Some of these vendors enable an ISP to insert its own messages to be presented to users as they use their browsers, such as customer service notices. Their technology can be used by both wireless and broadband ISPs and can be used to manage their ad campaigns or billing messages. NebuAd is using DPI to build a categorized dossier of interests of consumers, primarily in Asia, but it is expanding quickly into the United States and other countries as behavioral analytics becomes more popular with marketers, enterprises, and investigators.

The two companies that are clearly looking to partnering with ISPs for behavioral analytics using DPI are Phorm and NebuAd. How they go about it, however, is a bit different: one relies on cookies, while the other uses JavaScript. Both, however, also use DPI. Their DPI equipment performs a couple of functions: first, they insert their anonymous cookie that uniquely identifies each ISP subscriber and reads every web page that the subscriber has asked for, and creates a profile of the subscriber's interests based on a predetermined checklist.

Phorm uses cookies and a "307 Temporary Redirect" command to re-route traffic to get users tagged with their cookies. That is, if a user wants to go to www.jesusmena.com, their ISP—if in partnership with Phorm—will intercept the request and route it to www.webwize.net a domain, owned by Phorm, which then issues the user a first-party cookie with a unique identification number. Phorm then sends another 307 temporary redirect telling it to go jesusmena.com; the Phorm server also sends back a webwize cookie, but it's placed in the jesusmena.com domain and becomes another first-party cookie. Once the query arrives at jesusmena.com, it has a group of cookies, including one from jesusmena.com and one from webwize.net. The results of the original query are scanned by Phorm for key information used to create a browsing profile of that unique user.

NebuAd approaches the stamping of cookies via ISPs with a different method. First, it does not intercept the user's query to www.jesusmena.com; instead, it waits until the query is answered. As the last packet reaches the ISP, the NebuAd server injects one packet to the end of the traffic from the jesusmena.com server. The final packet contains JavaScript, which causes the user browser to go and retrieve a bit of scripting code from the NebuAd website, which places a cookie on the user's machine. Both the Phorm and NebuAd cookies track all users' activities in order to create clusters for segmenting users behaviors for investigators to analyze.

2.8 Designing a Forensic Framework

Today, with the advent of the web, cell phone, chat, text, blogs, and e-mail, new real-time behavioral analytics are required for a faster and more responsive investigation as events take place. Data warehouses were built for reflection, not reaction, which is what is required for forensic analytics. To enable investigators to analyze events as they take place, networks of behavior models need to be created and linked.

Websites provide a gold mine of user real-time data, everything from browsing behavior and patterns, to demographics, transactional histories, sources of online traffic, the effectiveness of searches, changes in conversion, keyword drivers, cross-selling propensities, and average order values. Metrics and adjustments to users' behaviors are paramount in an online investigation—the key challenge is deciding on what core data the digital investigators need—and a strategy to capture it in order to drive their inquiries.

Most importantly, investigators need to leverage the information they currently possess as part of their overall strategy and forensic framework. They need to form a strategy for capturing and analyzing the behavior of future users. They need to ask themselves: "Who are my criminals now, and who are likely to be my future ones?" Knowing the core features of criminals is critical and crucial to investigators, and this is knowledge that machine learning forensics can provide.

Every enterprise has streams of transactional and behavioral data flowing into it 24/7, but few of the enterprises are able to analyze the data simultaneously as events take place at the moment consumers interact with organizations, whatever the medium involved: text, phone, e-mail, web, or storefront. Careful and strategic planning by the investigator can leverage criminal behaviors to advance their knowledge of crimes and fraud. Digital investigators must be aware of the valuable intelligence flowing to them from their current and future criminals. They must be proactive and aggressive in formulating a strategic plan for capturing and leveraging all of these data streams. With every criminal event, perpetrators are communicating their methods and scope of their operations. Forensic analytics is leveraging these criminal events, most of which start at websites but cascade across other operational systems within an organization.

Today, digital crimes occur 24/7, and knowing this ahead of time will ensure a successful strategy, framework, and use of web data streams for investigators. Designing and implementing a framework for creating and leveraging streams of criminal behaviors requires advanced planning on how cookies, beacons, DPI, etc., will be defined, designed, and constructed by investigators. Key building blocks to leveraging web data streams include having the following forensic tactics, techniques, and strategy.

A Forensic Investigation Checklist

1. *Investigative Goal*: What the investigation will strive for; more often than not, it is detecting patterns of crimes and fraud.
2. *Goal or Mission*: This can be qualitative in nature, such as "improve detection or reduce fraud losses."
3. *Objective or Milestone*: This must be quantitative; objectives are the metrics by which something must be done (detect crimes early) to accomplish a goal or mission.
4. *Tactics*: These are the executable action items needed to carry out the overall strategy, and are used to achieve the investigation objectives.
5. *Techniques*: These are the systemic procedures by which tasks are accomplished.
6. *Plan*: Lastly, we arrive at the set of tasks that lead to the achievement of all the objectives.

The challenge for an investigator is being able to construct the framework for leveraging behaviors in order to identify criminal activities. The web today is a major revenue and communication channel for almost all organizations of all sizes. It is a major source of criminal intelligence. With every click, users communicate their intent and targets. Investigators need to focus on what criminal behaviors historically have occurred on either websites or networks, in order to concentrate on what perpetrators are attempting to penetrate and targeting to steal. The criminal web data streams can start with an organization's website or network, but the tapestry of forensic analyses can include chat, transcribed phone calls, e-mail, and wireless and other transactional databases.

2.9 Tracking Mechanisms

At the lowest possible level, criminal behaviors can begin to be captured at the web server log file level. These are the most common formats:

- National Center for Supercomputing Applications (Common, Combined, and Separate)
- Custom Log File Format (information captured is defined by the user)
- W3C Extended (used by Microsoft IIS 4.0 and 5.0)
- IBM Tivoli Access Manager WebSEAL
- WebSphere Application Server Logs
- Sun ONE Web Server (iPlanet)

A Server Log File Evidence Checklist

1. Domains and countries of site visitors with GeoIp detection
2. Search engines and keywords used to find the site
3. Authenticated users and last authenticated visits
4. Number of visits and number of unique visitors
5. Page hits for each hour and day of week
6. Most viewed entry and exit pages
7. Unresolved IP addresses list
8. Visits' duration and last visits
9. Operating system used
10. Worm attacks
11. Browser used
12. Robot visits
13. File types

For an investigator, log files can be used to track the movements and the patterns of website activity. Log files can reveal how visitors arrived at a website; they can show which section of a site is most popular and an assortment of other web metrics. Analog was one of the first log file analysis programs back in 1995; it was released soon after several commercial log analytics program came to market. One of the first was WebTrends, which added various graphs, tables, and other business metrics. Soon, other firms followed, such as Accrue, WebSideStory, Coremetrics, and dozens of others. Today, these are the most popular log analyzers:

Google.com/analytics—A free service with advanced segmentation, custom reporting, motion charts, etc.
WebTrends.com—A leading provider of web analytics and consumer-centric marketing.
Yahoo! Web Analytics—The tool provides real-time insight into visitor behavior on websites.
Lyris ClickTracks.com—Integrates web analytics, bid management, and keyword research tools.

Log files have limitations; they report more on browser activity than on criminal behaviors. There are also problems with search bots, which crawl around sites creating nonhuman traffic. Then there is the problem of recognizing unique visitors, who today are typically assigned dynamic IP addresses. One potential solution is assigning unique identification number cookies. Log files can be configured to report on these unique entity cookies: USERID=CustomerA;IMPID=01234. The advantage to this approach is that this value can be linked with other organizational data sets.

As we found out, cookies are simply small text files that are used for tracking clickstream behavior. A cookie typically contains the domain, a lifetime date, and a value, usually a randomly generated unique number for deep link tracking by the issuing website. However, JavaScript tags have become the most popular method of collecting and tracking web data streams. By simply adding a few lines of JavaScript code to a page, all the data from user activities can be collected via a JavaScript cookie:

```
function createCookie(name,value,days) {
 if (days) {
 var date = new Date();
 date.setTime(date.getTime()+(days*24*60*60*1000));
 var expires = "; expires="+date.toGMTString();
 }
 else var expires = "";
 document.cookie = name+"="+value+expires+";
 path=/";
}
function readCookie(name) {
 var nameEQ = name + "=";
 var ca = document.cookie.split(';');
 for(var i=0;i < ca.length;i++) {
 var
 c = ca[i];
 while (c.charAt(0)=='
 ') c = c.substring(1,c.length);
 if
 (c.indexOf(nameEQ) == 0) return c.substring(nameEQ.
length,c.length);
 }
 return null;
}
function eraseCookie(name) {
 createCookie(name,"",-1);
}
```

JavaScript log files are easier to maintain than server log files and with the shift to the web as the main channel for consumers, enterprises have shifted the responsibility for web analytics, such as log maintenance and reporting from internal IT shops, to outside vendors. Typically, these web analytic vendors rely on JavaScript tagging to track and report on visitor activities. Most report on such web metrics as page views, number of visitors, top exit pages, and other measurements that provide little useful information for forensic investigators. However, new vendors such as Lyris and Omniture allow investigators to capture deeper web data, which is required for the segmentation of visitor behaviors and provide much more insight than a count of website hits.

Putting a few lines of JavaScript code in a page can instantly tag the entire website—the reporting can be outsourced to an ASP vendor. Page caching by server farms such as Akamai Technology is not a problem for JavaScript tagging. Special reporting tags can be placed at carts, checkouts, and order confirmation pages to capture and report on the number of products purchased, order value, inventory control and other revenue metrics, including instances of criminal and fraudulent incidents. The one caveat about JavaScript tagging is that it collects user behavior data on the browser side rather than the server side. So, if the investigator's strategy requires storing behavior data on their clients' servers, tagging will not work.

An optional method of collecting web data is via a packet sniffer, which is a special type of hardware from such vendors as Clickstream Technologies and SiteSpec, some of which work with JavaScript. Packet sniffers are an outsource solution to web analytics that sit between the visitor browsers and an organization's website. Hence, packet sniffer boxes can collect absolutely everything, including passwords, name, addresses, and credit card numbers. One caveat about packet sniffers is that they cannot capture and report from Adobe Flash, Ajax, or RIA files. The optimal solution is to combine packet sniffers and JavaScript technologies for capturing and reporting on visitors' behaviors by investigators.

There is an option for making tracking cookies anonymous so that they focus on tracking behaviors rather than unique visitors. This option is important when security and privacy are issues. For most purposes, a website setting a cookie does not need to know the identity of the visitor; it just needs to remember the browser's prior visit. An investigator may choose to search for illegal patterns of behavior that once detected can then convert the anonymous value issued to potential criminal sessions and use that value, such as ID 511946jm33dd8839, and then convert it to the actual name of that suspect. In this manner, anonymous patterns are the focus of the investigation, thus ensuring the privacy of thousands of innocent visitors, with only suspects being identified.

Investigators have the option of using personal information about visitors in a cookie gleaned from registration forms as long as it is stated in the website privacy policy. If personal visitor information is stored in a cookie, it should be encrypted to protect the privacy of those individuals. The use of cookies for behavioral analytics is totally under the control of an investigator, so that a website may create a cookie with unique but anonymous content; or on the server side, they may create a file that logs that anonymous content alongside any personal information that consumers have provided, such as their zip code, or the type of product, service, or content they prefer via the completion of a registration, survey, contest, or order form.

Registration forms can be used for creating dynamic databases and are excellent data engines. They should solicit enough information for segmentation analyses along product lines and demographics, such as a ZIP code. Forms can be built using Perl, PHP, CGI, or commercial software. The information solicited from online forms can be linked to a unique consumer identification number cookie, enabling an investigator to associate the behavior of suspects.

Web and e-mail beacons, also known as *bugs*, and clear or invisible GIFs can also be used in combination with cookies for tracking behaviors in websites and e-mail. A beacon is typically a transparent graphic image of dimensions 1×1 pixel that is placed on a website or in an e-mail. Beacons allow organizations to record the behaviors of visitors. They also can track the consumers' IP addresses, timestamps, and the existence and content of cookies previously set by websites. There are also software and service providers that offer complete turnkey customer analytics and behavioral tracking services. This is how beacons can be used to track and capture web behavior data.

Beacon Evidence Checklist

1. Consumer uses his or her browser to go to a website.
2. The request is received by the web server.

3. The server returns a page along with a request for a 1 × 1 pixel image from a third-party server.
4. As the page loads, so does the beacon, which executes a call for the 1 × 1 pixel back from the third-party server.
5. The third party sends the pixel along with code for reading cookie information, IP address, and any other data predetermined by the website and the third-party service provider.

Beacons are vital mechanisms for behavioral tracking and reporting, and depending how they are created, can tell an investigator how visitors arrived at a website, what purchases were made, and total sales to those individuals. Beacons can also be used to track e-mails, to find out what recipients opened them, and what URL links were clicked on. Beacons can also be linked back to personally identifiable user profiles and accounts. Beacons can be used in conjunction with cookies and registration forms for forensic analytics. It is important for organizations to fully disclose the use of cookies and beacons, and give visitors the option of opting out.

2.10 Assembling Data Streams

By *combining* the tracking online clickstream data created by these Internet mechanisms with offline demographics, investigators can assemble more complete profiles of perpetrators. There are several types of networks an organization can subscribe to for assistance in this endeavor. These include demographic and advertising networks, which pool information from their vast networks of member websites and offline demographics and psychographics information linked to physical addresses such as a zip code. There are also recommendation engine networks that use collaborative filtering technologies for behavioral analytics as a service.

An organization can mix and match from these behavioral and demographic networks. Organizations can also choose to subscribe to some of these service providers in combination with their own streaming analytical software for optimizing their investigations. A key consideration for an organization is the market and industry they are a part of; second, they need to evaluate what products and services optimize their prevention of fraud. These issues will determine the type of behavioral services an organization will subscribe to. There are also tracking and reporting services such as those by ComScore that work similarly to the television Nielsen ratings. There are also surveying vendors such as ForeSee Results and iPerceptions for finding out why users arrived at a website, what they were looking for, and if they found it; this could be certain type of content, products, or services.

Investigators should be prepared to advise client organizations on the optimum combination; first, they can subscribe or partner with demographic, advertising, and recommendation networks to enhance their online investigations. Second, investigators can construct detection systems exclusively within the use of the organization's data; leveraging all the user data aggregated from their transactional databases, e-mail servers, call site, website, and operational systems using new streaming analytical software, which will be covered in detail in Chapter 5. Third, investigators can combine both subscription services with their own analytical software and techniques based on their specific investigative needs. These are some of the on-demand analytic service providers, which can be leveraged along with in-house real-time analytical streaming software products by organizations:

Revenuescience.com—Marketing platform for digital media reaching over 65% of the US online audience.

SageMetrics.com—Uses a combination of web analytics with targeting based on combined user profiles.

DigitalRiver.com—E-commerce platform for software and consumer technology manufacturers.

Analytics-iq.com—Targeting and risk scoring based on proprietary database consisting of 1,500+ demographic, psychographic, attitudinal, and econometric attributes.

Coremetrics.com—Lifetime Individual Visitor Experience (LIVE) Profiles are the core of their client data warehouse for web analytics.

Foviance.com—Multichannel consultancy for websites, telephone, TV, and print.

Both deductive and inductive streaming analytical software are a new breed of products that can be applied to making forensic analytical "filters" a reality for organizations. Software streamers argue that organizations cannot afford to collect criminal events and deal with them later in batches, long after the crimes have taken place. These new streaming analytical software products enable the creation of criminal and fraud detection filters since they are specifically designed to trigger alerts by either matching them to user-provided business rules or by rules created via forensic deductive and inductive data analyses.

2.11 Forensic Techniques

Modern forensic techniques involve diverse areas of investigation technologies, including computer facial reconstruction and recognition, DNA fingerprinting, autopsy science, forensic anthropology, toxicology, and now with this book, machine learning forensics. There are other types of investigative techniques, such as the following (recall how machine learning forensics is also preoccupied with some of the same objectives of extraction, identity, evidence, time, and circumstances, etc.):

1. Digital forensics: Also known as data recovery; used to extract digital or electronic media
2. Forensic anthropology: Used to recover and identify skeletal remains
3. Forensic archeology: Used to provide evidence on the time and circumstances of a homicide
4. Forensic DNA analysis: Used to place a suspect at a crime scene
5. Forensic geology: Deals with the evidence in the forms of soils and minerals
6. Forensic entomology: Used to determine location or time of death; insects that are on or around the remains are studied to determine whether the body had been moved post mortem
7. Forensic interviewing: Interrogation for eliciting information and evidence
8. Forensic odentology: The study of teeth to determine identity
9. Forensic meteorology: The analysis of weather conditions to discover the time of death
10. Forensic pathology: Used to determine cause of death using medicine and pathology
11. Forensic psychology: Used to study the criminal's mind
12. Forensic toxicology: Studies the effect of a poison/drug on the body

What machine learning forensics contributes to law enforcement is the use of machine learning software, and wireless and web networks to search for clues and evidence to detect and prevent digital crimes. Machine learning forensics has many applications, not only in detecting digital crimes and fraud, but also in assisting investigators in competitive intelligence, regulatory compliance, corporate counter-intelligence, and litigation cases. Machine learning tools, techniques, and technologies allow investigators to gather, standardize, and analyze voluminous amount of digital evidence, such as financial records, general ledgers, Internet and network files, and customer, sales, and inventory databases, etc.

Forensic investigators need to use machine learning techniques to assist attorneys, accountants, security specialists, information technology managers, and supervisors. Investigators may also need to collaborate with other government, wireless, Internet, and corporate personnel during their machine learning investigations. They must also be prepared to interact with clients in pursuit of mapping, planning, and conducting their inquiries. The required forensic skill involves much more than conducting investigations of large data sets; investigators must also have the ability to communicate complex technical concepts and their investigation's results and recommendation to nontechnical clients. Lastly, investigators should have a professional demeanor and strong communication skills, both written and oral.

Forensic techniques involve the application of machine learning to the identification, collection, examination, and analysis of data in ways that preserve the integrity of the information and maintain a strict chain of custody for the data. Organizations have the means to collect growing amounts of data from many sources. Data is stored or transferred by standard IT systems, networking equipment, computing peripherals, wireless devices, and various types of media.

When fraud and security incidents occur, organizations rely on forensic investigators to examine and analyze the evidence data that they have collected, and determine if their systems and networks may have sustained any damage and if sensitive data may have been compromised. As previously mentioned, these forensic techniques can be used for many purposes, not just supporting the investigation of crimes and fraud, but also the violations of internal policies, analyses of security incidents, and reviews of current security operational problems.

Because of the diversity and variety of data sources, forensic techniques can be used for investigating crimes and internal policy violations, reconstructing computer security incidents, troubleshooting operational problems, and recovering from accidental system damage. Practically every organization needs to have the capability to perform machine learning forensics, since without such a capability, an organization will have difficulty determining what events have occurred within its systems and networks, such as exposures of protected, proprietary, customer, and corporate sensitive data.

Forensic Technique Checklist

1. *Aggregation and collection*: This phase involves identifying, labeling, recording, and acquiring data from as many possible sources of relevant data, while following procedures that preserve the integrity of the data.
2. *Data extraction*: Forensically processing collected data using a combination of automated and manual methods, and assessing and extracting data of particular interest, while preserving the integrity of the data.
3. *Machine Learning Analysis*: Forensically analyzing the results of the extraction using standardized methods and techniques, to derive the knowledge and intelligence that addresses the purpose of the investigation.
4. *Reporting*: This can include not only reporting the results of the investigation, but also describing the actions used, explaining how tools and procedures were selected, determining what other actions need to be performed, such as examining additional data sources, attributes, and variables; securing identified vulnerabilities; improving existing security controls; and providing recommendations for improvement to policies, procedures, tools, and other aspects of the forensic process.

Before the investigator begins to collect, extract, and analyze any data, a decision should be made by the client organization on the need to collect and preserve evidence in a way that supports its use in future legal or internal disciplinary proceedings. In such situations, a clearly defined chain of custody should be followed to avoid allegations of mishandling or tampering with evidence. Machine learning investigators need to be cognizant of the fact their inquiries and analyses may lead to legal actions by the client organization.

This involves keeping a log of every person who had physical custody of the evidence, documenting the actions that they performed on the evidence and at what time, storing the evidence in a secure location when it is not being used, making a copy of the evidence and performing examination and analysis using only the copied evidence, and verifying the integrity of the original and copied evidence. If it is unclear whether or not evidence needs to be preserved, by default, it generally should be preserved.

When performing a forensic investigation after an incident attack, it is important to contain the evidence residing in the system or network. Isolating the pertinent system or network from external influences may be necessary to prevent further damage to the systems and its data or to preserve forensic digital evidence. The investigator should work with the client to make a containment decision, such as increasing physical security measures and shutting down a host system and network. This decision should be based on existing organization policies and procedures regarding incident containment, as well as an assessment of the risk posed by the incident, so that the chosen containment strategy sufficiently mitigates risk while maintaining the integrity of potential evidence whenever possible.

Once the relevant evidence has been extracted, the investigator should interrogate the data to draw conclusions from it. Machine learning forensics follows a methodical approach to reach appropriate conclusions based on the available data. The investigation should include identifying people, places, items, and events, and determining how these elements are related so that a conclusion can be reached. Often, this effort will include correlating data among multiple sources. It may also involve keeping all data owners informed about the investigation's findings and the risk implications to the systems and networks. For example, a network intrusion detection system (IDS) log may link an event to a host, the host audit logs may link the event to a specific user account, and the host IDS log may indicate what actions that user performed. Network tools such as centralized logging and security event management software can facilitate this process by automatically gathering and correlating the data for the forensic investigator.

2.12 Investigative Maps

The machine learning investigator can generate visual diagrams of criminal activity using several core technologies, including link analysis, semantic maps, social networking tools, and neural network SOMs. Investigative maps are an aid to representing criminal events, such as the discovery of relationships in criminal activities, and provide a visual representation of them for client organizations. Maps and diagrams can show very quickly what is going on in criminal activities; however, the investigator needs to ensure to use the proper tools for advancing the investigation.

One mapping technology used in law enforcement is link analysis, which is a subset of network analysis and is commonly used to explore associations between subjects and objects. For example, link analysis may be used to examine the addresses of criminal suspects and victims. Link analysis networks can also be created to view the relationships between cell phone numbers the suspects and victim have dialed, or financial transactions that they have been involved in during a given time frame.

Link analysis networks can be used to display the relationships between objects, such as IP addresses, wireless devices, individuals, suspects, and subjects as part of forensic investigation. Link analysis provides a graphical network displaying crucial relationships and associations between very many objects of different types that are not apparent from isolated pieces of information. Link analysis is increasingly employed by banks and insurance agencies in fraud detection, by telecommunication operators in telecommunication network analysis, by the medical sector in epidemiology and pharmacology, and of course in law enforcement investigations and everywhere else where relationships between many objects have to be analyzed.

Semantic maps are another type of graphical representation of text found in e-mails, documents, tweets, and other unstructured content. For example, semantic maps can be created showing a network of co-occurring words. Semantic mapping is a technique used to explain concepts behind words, because for any word, there are at least three associations, including class, property, and example. In semantic mapping, the association of class shows the order the concept falls into; in other words, whether it is higher or lower than another concept. The property association shows the defining characteristics of the concept. The association of example shows things that are similar to the concept. For the forensic investigator, semantic mapping software can be used to discover associations and relationships from transcripts and surveillance documentation (Figure 2.1).

Today, there are also social network analysis mapping software tools. A social network is a structural map made up of individuals known as "nodes," which are connected to "ties." Social network mapping tools display these relationships, within, say, a gang of perpetrators selling stolen virtual assets to resellers. Social network analysis (SNA) can be defined as a set of techniques underpinned by statistical analysis that make visible the hidden connections that are important for sharing information, decision-making, and investigations of links and associations between suspects and their devices and networks.

The outcome of an SNA helps diagnose where collaboration and criminal cliques have been cultivated and organized. More importantly for the forensic investigator, SNA can be a software tool for discovering hidden links between criminals and their accomplices. The data from an SNA provides a picture or map resembling a viral structure or antlike pattern of relationships that enables a set of actions for investigators to discover.

Viewed in a number of different ways, analysis of social network diagrams helps determine the extent to which certain people are

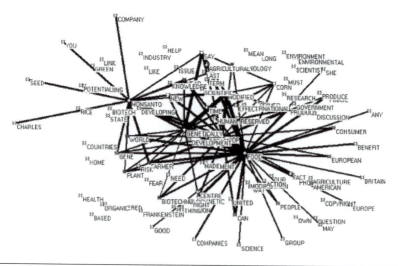

Figure 2.1   A semantic map of concepts from a group of documents.

central to a fraudulent ring or a gang of hackers and criminals. SNA can be defined as a set of techniques and software that make visible the hidden connections that are important for forensic investigations. Viewed in a number of different ways, analysis of social network diagrams helps determine the extent to which certain criminals are collaborating.

Lastly, there is also another type of software used to create investigative maps, self-organizing maps (SOM) neural networks. SOMs are a type of artificial neural network that is trained using unsupervised learning to produce a low-dimensional, typically a two-dimensional map. Self-organizing maps are different from other artificial neural networks in the sense that they self-organized themselves into clusters of, say, legal versus illegal transactions. The SOM neural network was discovered and created by the Finnish professor Teuvo Kohonen, and is sometimes called a Kohonen map. Dr. Kohonen explained his algorithm and approach to the autonomously discovering of clusters in large data sets in the following way:

> The SOM is a new, effective software tool for the visualization of high-dimensional data. It converts complex, nonlinear statistical relationships between high-dimensional data items into simple geometric relationships on a low-dimensional display. As it thereby compresses information while preserving the most important topological and metric relationships of the primary data items on the display, it may also be thought to produce some kind of abstractions. These two aspects, visualization and abstraction, can be utilized in a number of ways in complex tasks such as process analysis, machine perception, control, and communication.

For the forensic investigator, the important part about SOM technology and SOM tools is that they can be used to map in a graphical manner the behaviors of fraudulent and criminal activities from large data sets. They can be used for network intrusion detection, burglary and homicide mapping, fraud detection, and many more forensic applications. Chapter 4 will follow on how to use this inductive analytical technology.

2.13 Investigative Models

Precrime might be a Hollywood term used in science fiction movies, but investigative models based on machine learning can in fact detect crimes before they take place. The forensic models use the supervised path of artificial intelligence known as machine learning: the reason is that machines can process more information in a second than most humans can in a year. Machines can look at entrances to systems and areas; they can create maps and conditional rules about criminal behaviors, which can reveal paths, operations, methods and, eventually, the identity of criminals. The technology is useful for screening millions of transactions in microseconds.

Machine learning is about using the powerful process of observation and reporting on criminal behaviors in our digital environment. The software allows the discovering of patterns from millions of events. Investigative models can be constructed by investigators for building deductive rules for adaptive criminal and fraudulent detection systems. By leveraging this pattern recognition technology, forensic investigators can scrutinize with precise detail fraudulent and criminal behaviors. A major focus of machine learning is to automatically learn to recognize complex patterns and make intelligent decisions based on the data.

Machine learning refers to a system capable of autonomous acquisition and integration of knowledge. This capacity to learn from experience, analytical observation, and other means results in a system that can improve its own speed or performance, that is, its efficiency and effectiveness. Investigative models based on machine learning are thus adaptive, fast, and intelligent; the more crimes they detect, the better they get over time. It is the responsibility of the forensic investigator to ensure that this strategic design and flexible functionality of their detection system comply with this architecture. For example, maintenance of models using rule generators or decision trees will need to be performed on a regular basis.

Investigative models created with machine learning software learn about crimes through millions of observations, calibrating thousands of attributes associated with criminal activities. They mimic how the human investigator goes about gathering evidence and the logic they

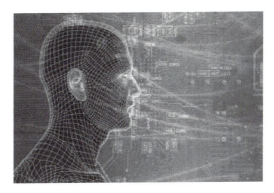

Figure 2.2 The machine learning investigator.

use to detect crimes. The main difference between the human and machine learning investigations is that the machine can examine a huge amount of data from multiple locations, different formats, and at lightning speeds via networks and the web (Figure 2.2).

Two of the first applications of machine learning technology were in the 1990s in the areas of speech recognition and credit card fraud detection. There is a legacy of using investigative models in law enforcement; the early detection systems used neural networks to detect fraud (Figure 2.3).

So, one of the earliest applications of investigative models was employed by credit card issuers, which enlisted machine learning firms such as HNC to monitor and detect potential credit card theft and

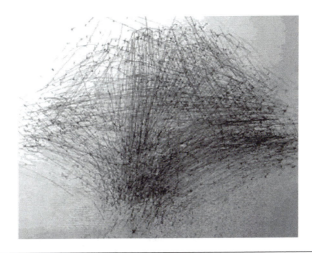

Figure 2.3 The topography of a neural network.

fraud. HNC relied on an early machine learning technology known as neural networks, which were extremely effective at detecting fraud but which suffer from a "black box" dilemma: they could detect patterns very efficiently, but they could not explain them. In addition, new machine learning algorithms such C4.5 and CART were being developed that used the same technique of observing, learning, and evolving; however, they could explain their prediction in the form of IF/THEN rules, which humans could readily understand.

Another aspect of machine learning algorithms, such as SOMs and decision trees, is that they are a form of data compression. For example, a SOM can take a very large data set and segment it into smaller and smaller clusters, allowing the investigator to zero in on a subset of the data, of, say, suspected fraudulent transactions. The same is true with decision trees; again, the machine learning process segments the large data set and subdivides it into smaller fragments of particular interest to the investigation.

One of the main tasks for the forensic investigator is classification via predictive models. For example, a target data set may consist of legal and illegal transactions, a field in that data set indicates this (e.g., L = LEGAL versus I = ILLEGAL), and this then becomes the target categorical variable to be modeled. The investigator thus creates a forensic model, which examines a large set of records, typically known as the training data set, where each record contains information on the target variable; these predictor variables are the inputs for the model.

The investigative predictive model then looks at a new data set, where the value of the target variable is unknown; the model then assigns a classification, LEGAL or ILLEGAL, based on the patterns observed in the training set. Importantly, decision trees can generate different types of code, such as C or Java, in the form of decision rules that can be used by organizations to make real-time decisions about potential criminal transactions. It is important that the model be constantly tested and evaluated for accuracy, as it may need to periodically be refreshed with a new more current training data set. How often this is done is at the discretion of the client and investigator. Be aware that in a dynamic digital business environment, predictive models can become stale.

A proven investigative technique is analyzing a data set using an ensemble technique, which uses multiple algorithms, and then polling their results into a consolidated score or output. For example, an investigator can use a SOM, a neural network, a rule generator, and a decision tree algorithm to converge on the identification of crimes. There are several techniques for creating an analytical ensemble using multiple algorithms, and they will be covered in detail in subsequent chapters; what is important is that the investigator be aware that these options exists and that their investigations center around the data types, sources, formats, and expected results.

The rest of the book will get into the finer details on how an investigator can begin to use these powerful analytical tools to conduct investigations and create strategies and systems for law enforcement purposes. The slant of the following chapters is to instruct investigators on actual forensic techniques and tools for furthering their investigations using machine learning technologies and software.

3

EXTRACTIVE FORENSICS
Link Analysis and Text Mining

3.1 Data Extraction

In this chapter, we will concentrate on techniques and technologies that extract relationships, discover networks of associations, and find key concepts from unstructured content. Data extraction, also known as data scraping, usually involves the process of retrieving data for further processing such as clustering or segmentation analysis. It can also involve the extraction of unstructured data (text) for further processing via a structured type of analytical tool; this may involve some transformation and possibly the addition of metadata. Typical unstructured data sources include web pages, e-mails, documents, PDFs, scanned text, mainframe reports, spool files, etc. A typical application of data scraping is collecting information for litigation investigations, or the scraping of web data for competitive intelligence.

Extracting data from these unstructured sources has grown into a considerable technical challenge. Whereas historically, data extraction has had to deal with changes in physical hardware formats, the majority of current data extraction techniques deal with extracting data from these unstructured data sources and from different software formats. The act of extracting structure from an unstructured data source such as e-mail takes a number of forms. First, extraction from records and their association via the use of their headers and footers; second, the organization into main groupings such as e-mailed resumés by skills, experience, and qualifications; and lastly, the extraction of the data with an attempt to understand its content.

There are a considerable number and types of data extraction tools in the marketplace that a forensic investigator can use. There are tools for extracting different types or classes of data formats, and there are e-mail extraction tools as well as some specializing in extracting relevant content from targeted and multiple websites to databases. Organizations need to analyze massive amounts of data, and one of the first steps is extracting raw data from multiple sources for enforcing cyber security, reducing fraud, and discovering criminal behaviors.

There is also a Data Extraction Language (DEL), which is code for describing data conversion processes from other data formats to XML. A DEL script specifies how to locate and extract fragments from input data and where to insert them in the resulting XML format. The DEL processor executing the DEL script can use the extracted data to either create a new XML document or modify an existing XML document by creating new elements and attributes at locations specified with XPath expressions. DEL is free. The data extraction process generally involves three main steps, which most software tools can perform for the forensic investigator (Figure 3.1):

Step One: Automatic extraction uses pattern recognition to tag and select the data to be collected. Manual extraction allows the use of any criteria the user wishes to define through options or a script; most software extraction products allow the investigator to write these extraction "rules."

Step Two: Transform each input field to each output field. Most tools support automatic mapping, which can be modified by visually connecting and disconnecting input and output fields or through scripting. Scripting can be used for extraction tasks, implementation of business rules, and other logic.

Step Three: Load at run time the data flows from the source, through the transformation process and into the output data table, which can be any database system (SQL Server, ORACLE, MySQL, DB2, MS Access, etc.) as well as in a variety of flat formats including CSV, Excel, FoxPro, DBase, and more.

Data extraction software dramatically simplifies the process of data conversion from computer-generated documents (unstructured content) by identifying the internal document's structure automatically

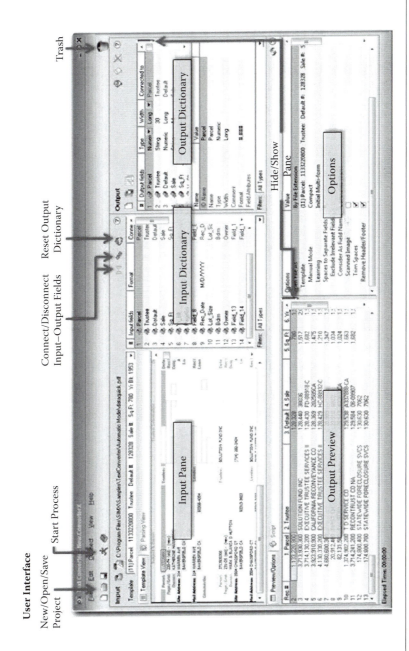

Figure 3.1 A data extraction tool for processing input data streams into analyzable output.

without programming. Some tools employ artificial intelligence (AI) engines that are capable of recognizing recurring patterns of data layout, formatting, and content, thus identifying records and fields to be extracted automatically, which supports script-based data parsing and data transformation so that the investigator can focus on a particular data transformation process without worrying about looping through records or accessing files or databases.

For the investigator, it is important to know about such tools as they can simplify and accelerate projects, which often are delayed by problems of identifying, accessing, and securing the right data for investigations. Most of these data extraction software tools support any-to-any conversion, such as

- Flat file to XML
- XML to CSV
- Any database to XML
- Excel to database
- XML to EDI
- HIPAA to XML
- HL7 to XML
- Date format, string, numerical conversions, etc.
- Any other combination

We next move to two other types of higher levels of knowledge extraction: link analysis and text mining. Keep in mind that this is at the initial, rudimentary level of any forensic investigation, tedious but essential. Scraping the data for analysis is essential, but a detailed map of the processes of extraction and conversion needs to be documented to ensure that whatever models evolve from the investigation can be deployed in real time.

3.2 Link Analysis

Google made a fortune with variations of this technology; it counted the links to sites in order to prioritize their placement in their search engine and their targeted advertising. Link analysis has made billions for those who know how to leverage it. Simple but highly effective, links can disclose relationships and associations that machine learning forensic investigators can use to discover what they could not learn manually. Link analysis for law enforcement is at the lowest level on forensic analysis, and yet it can advance investigations in the right directions. Relationships are everywhere, and these associations often provide a wealth of intelligence that link analysis harvests by combining leads in investigations.

Link analysis software tools, such as i2 Analyst's Notebook, focus on the visualization of links, often assisting the investigator with knowledge discovery rather than discovering criminal patterns. Link analysis is based on a branch of mathematics known as graph theory. A link analysis graph consists of nodes; these are the objects (suspects) that have relationships and edges, which are pairs of nodes connected by that relationship.

Link analysis plays two roles for investigators. First, it enables the visualization of relationships, which could lead to further questions, and second, it can also lead to the discovery of different types of node associations known as a network. A good example of a node network is that of the different devices linked to an organization, such as a mainframe, web servers, workstations, desktops, laptops, and mobile devices. Link analysis has several strengths. First, it capitalizes on relationships; second, it is useful for visualization, and lastly, it creates derived characteristics. Links may suggest important patterns in the data, but the significance of the patterns requires that an investigator manually assemble those relationships and their significance.

The weakness of link analysis is that it requires some human assembly and interpretation. The technology is also limited to the construction of networks that contain thousands of objects; an attempt to construct such a network becomes useless due to the lack of granularity: the human eye is limited to the number of objects it can discern from a highly interconnected and complex graph (Figure 3.2).

Link analysis is not a classification or predictive technology, such as decision trees. It is labor intensive and limited in the scope of data it can process and display. However, link analysis is an excellent tool for the forensic investigator, who can use it to extract relationships for further analysis. Link analysis can be used to view networks of associations that may warrant further investigation. Link analysis, as with text mining, represents the first level of most investigations, where the

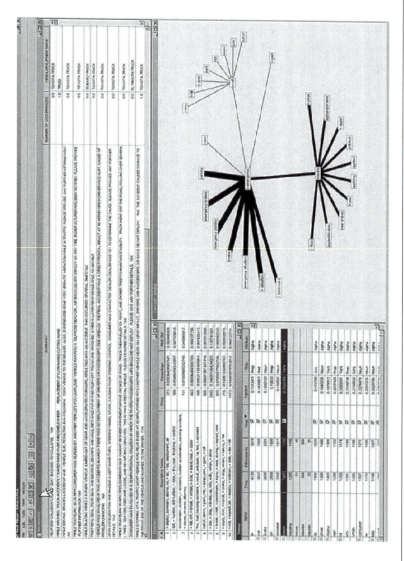

Figure 3.2   A link analysis graph revealing relationships.

extraction of a network of relationships and grouping of unstructured content can lead to new leads and shift the focus of investigations.

Link analysis applications are limited; for example, the Department of Homeland Security (DHS) component the Transportation Security Administration (TSA) uses link analysis to create networks of associations in the screening of travelers. DHS also uses semantic maps in its terrorist investigations. However, link analysis can be used in conjunction with other forensic tools and technologies. For the forensic investigator, it is important to know that most link analysis tools specialize in visualization of relationships in the law enforcement area. The limitations of these tools are they can only provide visualization of a few hundreds or thousands of data elements.

3.3 Link Analysis Tools

The following is a list of some commercial link analysis software:

Analyst's Notebook, from i2 Inc., is software for conducting link analysis, timeline analysis, and data visualization for investigations. The tool provides a comprehensive range of visualization by identifying connections, patterns, and trends in complex data sets; it is the most popular link analysis tool in the world (Figure 3.3).

Centrifuge offers investigators an integrated link analysis suite that can integrate and conduct data explorations on disparate data sources simultaneously. The tool supports a reporting function that can be shared with others in the investigative team—all through a web browser (Figure 3.4).

Maltego is an open source intelligence and forensics application that allows the investigator to identify key relationships and networks; the client license is $650 (Figure 3.5).

marketVisual provides online visual relationship mapping. This website can discover relationships of companies or persons under investigation (Figure 3.6).

NetMap Analytics uses an innovative combination of link analysis and data visualization, with applications for fraud and criminal detection and insurance claims analysis (Figure 3.7).

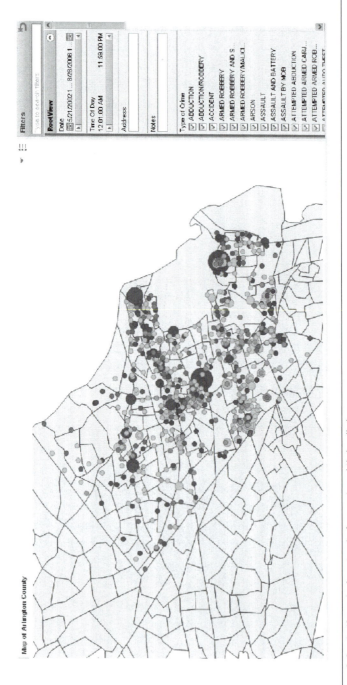

Figure 3.3 An i2 graph of a network of suspects and their cell phones.

Count of Each Crime

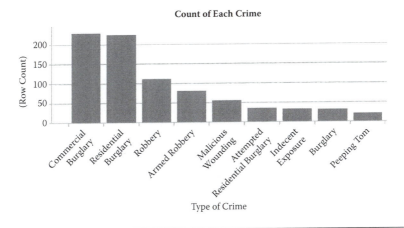

Figure 3.4   A Centrifuge traffic activity graph in a cyber security investigation.

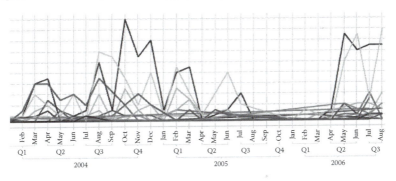

Figure 3.5   A Maltego graph of Internet connections.

NetMap Case Studies

TRACKING A MURDERER

In the early 1990s, seven young backpackers were murdered in what was to become Australia's most notorious serial murder case. The police had developed a profile of the killer. However, to track their suspect down, they faced an enormous volume of data from numerous sources. Investigators therefore applied NetMapping technology to RTA vehicle records, gym memberships, gun licensing, and internal police records.

As a result, the list of suspects was progressively narrowed from an extensive list of individuals to a short list of 230, and then a still shorter list of 32, which included the killer. Thanks to NetMap,

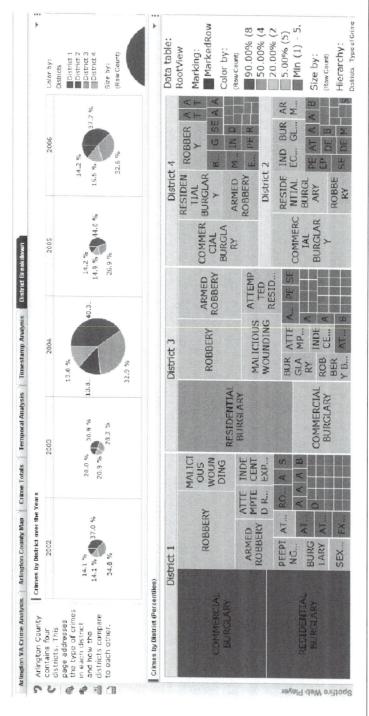

Figure 3.6 MarketVisual can discover the relationships of firms or individuals.

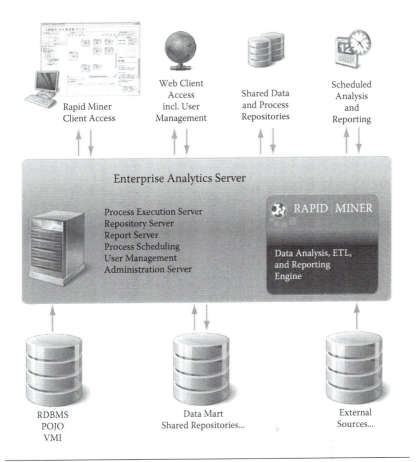

Figure 3.7 A NetMap link visualization graph.

thousands of precious police hours were saved, and police were able to focus their investigations on a more manageable list of potential suspects, leading to the eventual successful conviction of the Backpacker Murderer.

THE CAPTURING OF AN OPTIONS TRADER

The Australian Securities and Investment Commission has the unenviable responsibility of regulating the many millions of transactions that flow across the Australian Stock Exchange. For some years now, ASIC has been a regular user of NetMap technology to successfully detect irregularities. One of the most high-profile examples of this took place in August 1996 when investigators enlisted NetMapping technology to help them track down a mystery TNT options trader who had become a millionaire just two weeks after purchasing options.

The criminal had cleverly hidden behind multiple layers of transactions, false identities, and third-party bank accounts. However, with the help of NetMap, ASIC was able to unravel this complex trail, leading to the discovery and arrest of a Macquarie Bank Director (alias Mr. Booth), who was successfully convicted following his 1999 appeal.

EXPOSING COMPLEX FRAUD

A government fraud agency had six full-time staff working for two years to solve a complex mortgage fraud investigation (i.e., 12 man-years). NetMap Analytics was then given the task of seeing if it could unravel the same case more quickly. A NetMap analyst took ten days to rework the data formats and structures and then entered it into NetMap. NetMap came up with the full solution in less than three hours and discovered additional aspects of the case that had not been previously known.

INSURANCE FIRMS USE NETMAP

Fighting insurance fraud is exceptionally difficult due to the high volume and complexity of the data involved, as well as the increasing sophistication of organized fraud rings. NetMap helps insurance companies fight back. Twenty-seven insurance companies in the United States now routinely employ NetMap solutions.

This includes over half of the 15 largest insurance companies with a total direct written premium of $49 billion. Employing NetMap's state-of-the-art techniques allows forensic investigators to quickly spot irregular patterns of activity within millions of items of data from policies, claims, payments, and medical billing details. These companies are now enjoying a better than nine to one return on their investment.

FORENSICS SAVES CARRIER MILLIONS

Telstra's Forensic and Special Investigations Group handles customer complaints escalated to a "serious" level. These often involve large sums and pending litigation against the corporation for alleged failure of services and lost business. Investigation of the relevant circumstances can be both complex and voluminous, since analysis tasks often involve low-level call records and billing data drawn from disparate warehouses and other sources.

Telstra used NetMap to handle this problem. Telstra conducted formal studies to compare the use of NetMap with previous methods. Telstra's report states "time savings of between 50 and 500 to 1" were achieved and, furthermore, "relevant information was discovered that was not possible to be discovered by any other means." Debt previously classified as "unrecoverable" is now being recovered at the rate of $6,000,000 per annum. ROI is in excess of 20 times the annual outlay.

EXPOSING MONEY LAUNDERING

Following Basel II and other influences in the banking and finance community, compliance with anti-money laundering (AML) standards has become increasingly important. Traditional statistical tools are based on "exception" reporting and the definition of rules that govern those exceptions. Concealment and avoiding detection by known rules are the key weapons of would-be perpetrators, and so the unique "discovery" capabilities of NetMap SuperAudit, which analyzes the data "bottom up," are critical.

In a financial organization that is a client of NetMap, a rule-based system daily processes large volumes of data to flag certain types of transactions. These are passed to NetMap, where the data is further "enriched" with additional information about the parties involved and account information.

The analysts are then able to visualize and detect emergent patterns in the data that are virtually impossible to find any other way. Deemed highly successful, the system provides necessary levels of assurance. It has also led to numerous prosecutions. This organization is now using NetMap via shorter time intervals between data updates and near-real-time viewing.

NetMiner specializes in exploratory analysis and visualization of network data. A free evaluation copy is available, as well as academic copies.

Networked Insights concentrates on the analysis of social networks such as Facebook. Networked Insights discovers and analyzes social network needs as they happen.

Orgnet is an innovative software tool for social network analysis and organizational network link analysis. Mr. Valdis Krebs is the founder of and chief scientist at Orgnet. He contributed the following case study on the detection of a criminal conspiracy.

An Orgnet Case Study

UNCLOAKING A SLUMLORD CONSPIRACY WITH SOCIAL NETWORK ANALYSIS (SNA)

A client of ours—a small, not-for-profit, economic justice organization [EJO]—used *social network analysis* [SNA] to assist their city attorney in convicting a group of "slumlords" of various housing violations that the real estate investors had been side-stepping for years. The housing violations, in multiple buildings, included

1. Raw sewage leaks
2. Multiple tenant children with high lead levels
3. Eviction of complaining tenants
4. Utility liens of six figures

The EJO had been working with local tenants in run-down properties and soon started to notice some patterns. The EJO began to collect public data on the properties with the most violations. As the collected data grew in size, the EJO examined various ways in which they could visualize the data, making it clear and understandable to all concerned. They tried several charting software programs, but to no avail—the complex ties they were discovering made the diagrams hopelessly unreadable. They turned to social network analysis [SNA] to make sense of the complex interconnectivity.

The data I will present below is *not* the actual data from the criminal case. However, it does accurately reflect the social network analysis they performed. The names and genders of the individuals, as well as the names of real estate holdings [LLC] and other businesses, have all been masked. This case will be presented in the sequence the EJO followed: first, they looked at the real estate holdings, then the owners of the holdings, and then their connections, which led to other connections, and more people and entities.

The EJO worked with the tenants and city inspectors to assess the buildings and document the violations. But every time documented problems were delivered to the current LLC owners by city officials, nothing would happen. When the city's deadline approached to fix the violations, the old LLC owner would explain that the property had changed hands and they were no longer involved. The buildings continued to deteriorate as owner after owner avoided addressing the violations.

The following figure shows how a building came under new ownership. The links show the "sold to" flow as building ownership changed from left to right. Every time a property changed hands, it became a new LLC [Limited Liability Corporation] with new owners.

ABC LLC   DEF LLC   GHI LLC   JKL LLC   MNO LLC

The new links in the following figure show ownership/business ties for each LLC. This data was gathered by the EJO from public records. Everything appears normal—a different set of players in each LLC.

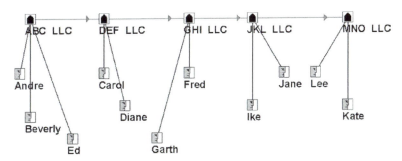

Yet, things were not normal. The EJO discovered that some of the LLC owners were married. As the EJO peeled the onion, more family ties were found within, and between, the LLCs.

The following figure shows us that these LLCs were not as separate as they first appeared. The new links reveal family ties found in public records. The LLCs were *not* independent business entities. The business transactions were happening *within* extended families! A conspiracy was coming into focus.

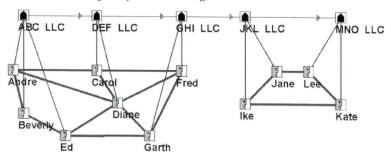

The new links in this figure reveal two family clusters. Yet, there was a curious gap: the transaction between *ghi LLC* and *jkl LLC*. Were these clusters connected? How? These questions soon led to a key discovery: the mastermind behind the conspiracy. Conspiracies often work in this way: masterminds are 2 steps, or farther, from the events they plan. The following figure reveals the family matriarch and patriarch. The matriarch (Heather) was discovered in public records, explaining the gap. Then her current husband (Moe) was a quick deduction. The gap turned out is the dividing line between Heather's first family and her current family. She was the point of overlap between the two groups.

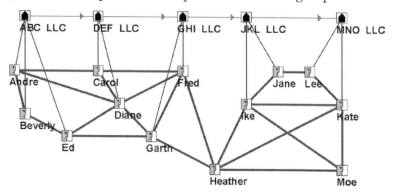

Once Moe was uncloaked, the EJO's chief investigator decided to explore how he was connected—what other business ties did he have? It turned out that Moe had ownership interests in several restaurants throughout the metropolitan area ... and he was on the board of a mortgage company.

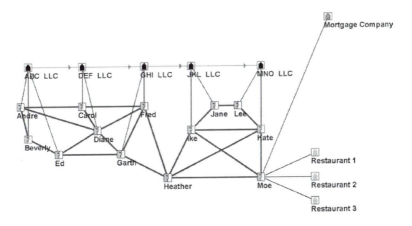

A mortgage company? It was not just any mortgage company; Moe was on the board of the mortgage company that had financed many of the real estate transactions we have been following here. Moe's ties completed the connections of the conspiracy—the "circle of deceit."

The following figure shows the complete conspiracy. It was now obvious that properties exchanged hands not as independent and valid real estate investments but as a conspiracy to avoid fixing the building violations. The darker links represent borrowed money flowing into the buildings through new mortgages.

As time went on, and the buildings appreciated in value during a real estate boom, loans from the mortgage company allowed the owners to "strip mine" the equity from the buildings. This is a common slumlord modus operandi: they suck money out of a building rather than put money back in for maintenance.

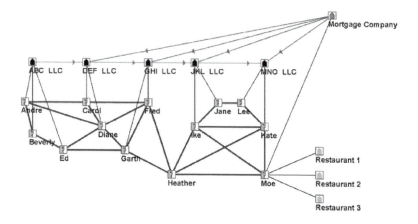

Network analysis is not just about maps. Once a map is drawn, you can measure it. Social network metrics reveal much about the nodes and the clusters they form. Who knows what is going on? Who wields power or influence? Who is a key connector? Who is in the "thick of things" in this conspiracy?

Our metrics reveal that Moe and Heather are the most integrated nodes in the network. The highlighted metrics in the Report window in the following figure, showing the InFlow software, provides mathematical support to what is quite obvious in the diagrams. InFlow allows us to quickly see the relationships between "the maps and the metrics": the pictures and the numbers.

The city attorney combined the network analysis with the city's own extensive investigation and was able to get a conviction of key family members. Later, all of one building's tenants filed a civil suit using much of the same evidence and won a sufficient award to allow all of them to move out into decent housing. Several tenants used a part of their award to start businesses.

The common wisdom is that only big business and government use social network analysis. Yet, there are many individuals and groups that are learning the craft, and solving local problems. Although social network analysis *cannot* be learned by reading a book, it does not require a PhD either. Any intelligent person, with the right guidance and with the proper tools, can apply the methodology to an appropriate problem and gain enormous insight into what was previously hidden.

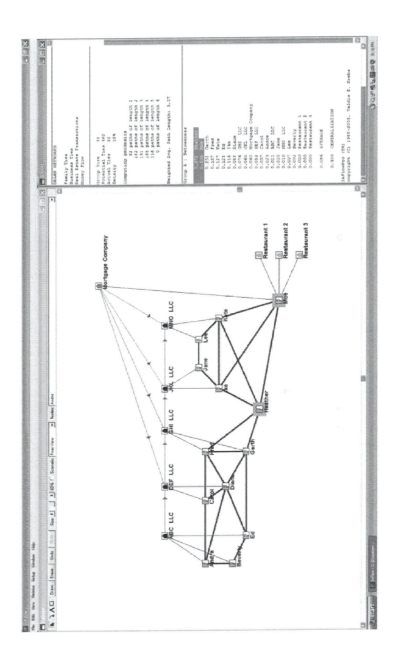

Sentinel Visualizer is an In-Q-Tell portfolio company. They are the venture capitalist firm funded by the Central Intelligence Agency (CIA). Their law enforcement solutions include the graphing of gang activity, money laundering, serial crimes, organized crime, cyber crime, drug investigations, border security, fraud, burglary, and theft rings.

Svivot provides software solutions that analyze data into intelligence used in making critical decisions in law enforcement, and investigative, financial, and commercial organizations. They focus on exposure and analysis of networks, link analysis of high-volume data streams, data fusion of heterogeneous data, and they also provide the visualizing and documenting of complex cases.

VisuaLinks is a provider of data analytics, decision support, and information-sharing solutions for investigating money laundering, financial crimes, narcotics trafficking, terrorism, border security, embezzlement, and fraud in domestic and international commercial and government markets.

3.4 Text Mining

Text mining, also referred to as text data mining or text analytics, refers to the process of deriving content from unstructured free text, such as e-mail or documents. It often involves the extraction of patterns and trends. Text mining can also include the process of structuring the input text, usually via parsing, along with the addition of some derived linguistic features and the removal of others. The point is to extract the valuable content, names, e-mail, and IP addresses. Text mining can also involve the subsequent insertion of unstructured content into a structured format such as a database or table; for example, Attensity software can parse unstructured content and convert it into an analyzable structured format.

Text mining can use a combination of algorithms in its search for relevance, novelty, and interestingness. Typical text mining tasks can also include text categorization, text clustering, the concept or entity extraction, the production of granular taxonomies, sentiment analysis, document summarization, and entity relation modeling such as the discovery of relationships between targeted entities. In the following section, a more detailed explanation will be provided of how some leading text analytic software vendors are doing this. In text mining, the goal is to discover heretofore unknown information or knowledge from unstructured sources.

Text mining is about extracting patterns from natural language text rather than from structured content stored in databases or flat files. Databases are designed for programs to process automatically; text, on the other hand, is written for people to read. A subset of text mining is computational linguistics, also known as natural language processing, which can extract certain phrases from articles, reports, e-mails, and documents, producing a summary of its contents, or extract specific names, addresses, and specific content.

Text mining is also known as text analytics, which more widely describes a set of linguistic, statistical, and machine learning techniques that model and structure the information content of textual sources for a forensic investigation. More broadly, text analytics can also involve information retrieval (IR), which is the science of searching for documents, extracting knowledge within documents, and unearthing metadata about documents. Information retrieval can also involve data retrieval, document retrieval, and text retrieval techniques and technologies.

Text analytics can also involve lexical analysis to study word frequency distributions, which is the process of converting a sequence of characters into a sequence of tokens that programs can analyze. Text analytics can also involve unsupervised pattern recognition, as well as tagging specific terms from documents. It can also involve other techniques, including link and association analysis, visualization, and predictive analytics. The automatic analysis of text can be used to provide an overview of the contents of a large collection of documents, to identify hidden structures between groups of documents, to increase the efficiency and effectiveness of a search process.

Text mining is a multidisciplinary field involving information retrieval, text analysis, information extraction, clustering, categorization, visualization, and machine learning. One group of text mining techniques focuses on document organization, visualization, and navigation, while another group of techniques focuses on text analysis functions, information retrieval, categorization, and summarization.

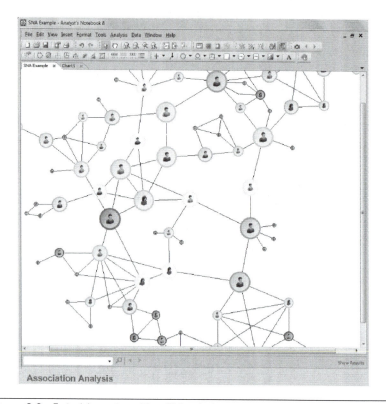

Figure 3.8   Text mining system with multiple outputs.

For example, visualization can organize documents as two- or three-dimensional clusters (Figure 3.8).

The goal of text mining or text analytics is essentially to turn unstructured text into structured data for analysis. The importance of this is that most digital data in organizations—some estimate as much as 80%, although it is likely closer to 50%—is in unstructured format. Text analytics can be used to discover and present knowledge—facts, rules, and relationships for the forensic investigator—that would otherwise remained locked in unstructured formats and be impenetrable for structural analyses, such as segmentation, clustering, classification, and prediction.

3.5 Text Mining Tools

The following are several types of text analytical software solutions that offer various methods of analysis of unstructured content.

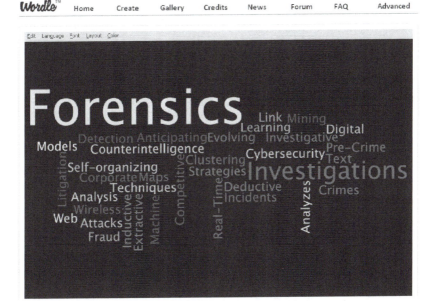

Figure 3.9 A Wordle "word cloud" of this book.

3.5.1 Online Text Mining Analytics Tools

- *Ranks.nl* keyword analysis and webmaster tools
- *Vivisimo/Clusty* web search and text clustering engine
- *Wordle* online tool for generating "word clouds" from text that you provide (Figure 3.9)

3.5.2 Commercial Text Mining Analytics Software

- *ActivePoint* offers natural language processing and smart online catalogs, based on contextual search and ActivePoint's TX5(TM) Discovery Engine.
- *Aiaioo Labs* offers products and services for text analytics and NLP. Labs' areas of expertise include text categorization, sentiment analysis, corpus development, information extraction machine learning, entity recognition, and relation extraction.
- *Alceste* is software for the automatic analysis of textual data (open questions, literature, articles, etc.).
- *Attensity* offers a complete suite of text analytic applications, including the ability to extract "who," "what," "where," "when," and "why" facts and then drill down to understand

people, places, and events and how they are related. A valuable tool for forensic investigations.

- *Basis Technology* provides natural language processing technology for the analysis of unstructured multilingual text. Their Rosette Name Translator (RNT) can convert names written in foreign scripts such as Arabic, Chinese, Korean, and more to English equivalents.
- *Clarabridge* is an extensive text mining end-to-end solution for transforming text to knowledge.
- *ClearForest* offers tools for analysis and visualization of large document collections.
- *Compare Suite* compares texts by keywords, highlighting common and unique keywords.
- *Connexor Machinese* discovers the grammatical and semantic information of natural language. For example, Connexor can locate the time, names, persons, and locations from insurance claims.
- *Copernic Summarizer* can read and summarize document and web page text content in many languages from various applications.
- *Crossminder* does natural language processing and text analytics, including cross-lingual text mining.
- *dtSearch* for indexing, searching, and retrieving free-form text files.

---

dtSearch Case Studies

DeviceLock integrates dtSearch into an endpoint device control and security management platform. DeviceLock endpoint leakage prevention software enables security administrators to centrally control, log, and audit end-user access to peripheral devices and local ports from enterprise systems.

ILook Investigator© Toolsets include dtSearch. The ILook Investigator toolsets are computer forensic tools used to capture and analyze images created from computer systems hard drives and other external storage media. ILook is provided free to qualifying agencies throughout the world. Eligible users must be involved in computer forensics and employed by one of the following: (1) a law enforcement agency whose employees are sworn law enforcement officers; (2) a government intelligence agency; (3) a military agency with authority in criminal and or counterintelligence investigations; and (4) a government, state, or other regulatory agency with a law enforcement mission.

Odyssey Digital Forensics embeds dtSearch with Rosette Linguistics Platform for multilingual investigative data support. Basis Technology's Odyssey Digital Forensics™ enables data capture from hard disks, while documenting the integrity and source of the data. From a captured disk image, the application then analyzes the file system to extract and recover files, and extract text from them. Odyssey next uses the Rosette Linguistics Platform to preprocess multilingual text, including Middle Eastern languages (Arabic, Persian), East Asian languages (Chinese, Korean, and Japanese), as well as a variety of European language content.

Computer Forensic Associates specializes in computer forensics and electronic evidence: "A wide range of scenarios arise where a thorough and detailed assessment of the computer data is required. This can range from looking for hidden assets, uncovering frauds, finding missing persons, performing personnel investigations, and preserving confidential corporate information. I have been using dtSearch for some time now in the majority of cases I handle. I have found it to be an invaluable tool."—Jeffrey Gross, Computer Forensic Associates founder.

SEARCH is a nonprofit membership organization funded by the US Department of Justice and created by and for the states. Dedicated to improving the criminal justice system through the effective application of information and identification technology, SEARCH is now including dtSearch as part of its training.

SYTEX provides training to the intelligence community, local law enforcement organizations, and professionals in the private sector. Initial identification of collection and analysis tools that may enhance and further investigative efforts is a key part of training. dtSearch capabilities make it one of the top tools in analysis efforts. dtSearch is a front-line tool for federal, state, and local law enforcement, and intelligence agencies in forensics and homeland security endeavors. Drives are imaged, hashed, and then indexed with dtSearch on a variety of document types—HTML, PDFs, PSTs, Unicode, and many others.

Forensic Toolkit from AccessData offers a complete suite of technologies for forensic examinations of computer systems. "dtSearch was the perfect choice for what we wanted to accomplish ... fast efficient searching that is easily accessed by any investigator."

SRA's OrionMagic law enforcement customers, who include the Federal Bureau of Investigations (FBI) and other branches of the Department of Justice (DOJ), the New York Police Department (NYPD), and various police departments in California, Florida, and Maryland, use dtSearch for different search options, such as adjustable fuzzy, stemming for root word derivations, numeric range, proximity, complex Boolean logic, and relevancy.

- *Eaagle* text mining software enables the user to rapidly analyze large volumes of unstructured text, create reports, and easily communicate their findings.
- *Enkata* provides a range of enterprise-level solutions for text analysis.
- *Expert System* uses its proprietary COGITO platform for the semantic comprehension of language for knowledge management of unstructured information.
- *Files Search Assistant* enables quick and efficient search within text documents.
- *IBM Intelligent Miner Data Mining Suite* is now fully integrated into the IBM InfoSphere Warehouse software; includes a text mining component.
- *ISYS* searches over 100 file formats across multiple sources; on-the-fly HTML conversion.

ISYS Case Studies

BEDFORDSHIRE POLICE FORCE

As with any police force, Bedfordshire deals with a large volume of information that resides across various systems and formats.

The police department must deal with over 4 million documents and several databases with hundreds of thousands of records dating back to 1990 in support of its 2,100 police personnel. With data that stretches back nearly two decades, Bedfordshire must also account for the constant stream of new information that enters its systems on a daily basis. Accessing key pieces of information contained in these systems isn't a matter of convenience—it's an absolute requirement. To address Bedfordshire's information management needs, its IT staff introduced BORIS— the Bedfordshire Open Research Information System. BORIS brings together information from 4 million documents and multiple databases, offering Bedfordshire a single point of access for investigative research.

The lynchpin to the BORIS portal is the ability to conduct a single search across a broad base of data. To deliver the greatest benefit, this search capability would need to offer speed, efficiency, ease of use, and 100% accuracy. One of the primary challenges for any search technology is the ability to cater to simultaneous searches across multiple information sources, be they unstructured Word, Excel, and PDF documents or the records of structured databases.

ISYS Enterprise Server provided Bedfordshire's IT personnel with tools for customizing the search implementation according to its requirements. Most search systems offer either a basic product with no flexibility or a highly complex technology that requires significant resources and money to configure. ISYS instead offers out-of-the-box capabilities that deliver immediate benefit along with a flexible architecture for customizing the solution to an organization's own unique needs. This approach has been enthusiastically welcomed by criminal intelligence analysts, police forces, and investigative units, where ease of use and a deep understanding of their end-user needs are paramount.

MIAMI DADE POLICE DEPARTMENT

Police Sergeant Gary Smith and the Homicide Bureau at the Miami Dade Police use several tools to refine their investigation process, including DNA, fingerprints, and ISYS software. Sergeant Smith describes how ISYS helped the department crack an unsolved murder.

A company that customized corporate jets won a major contract that involved working with new equipment, which required extra training. Four people were selected for the training, who would car-pool twice a week to Fort Lauderdale. One day, the four were returning from training when gunshots were fired through the roof and sides of the car. Three in the car were injured and one died on the scene. Sergeant Smith and his team began investigations.

A search returned a shotgun with a ground-off serial number. Eventually the serial number was raised and the registered owner traced: Gerardo Manso. Manso was an employee of the same company as the victims, but he had not been selected for extra training. He had positioned himself on the roof with a shotgun, and when the four returned from training he opened fire on the car.

After hours of interrogation, Manso confessed to the homicide. Coincidentally, ISYS had come online at the Bureau for the first time. The first name Sergeant Smith entered into ISYS, Gerardo Manso, appeared in another report.

This case involved a drive-by shooting. The victim worked in a grocery store and was rumored to be having an affair with another employee: Manso's wife. When interviewed, Manso's wife denied the affair and mentioned her husband's name. This was recorded in the report, but because the affair was denied, the investigators were unable to find a motive or a suspect.

When confronted with this murder, Manso also confessed to the previous crime and was booked. "Without ISYS, this information would never have been accessed. Manso's name would never have been entered in the restricted fields of the database we were using, and the case would never have been solved," says Sergeant Smith.

VENTURA COUNTY SHERIFF'S DEPARTMENT

The mission of the Ventura County Sheriff's Department is to protect and serve the people of the county. Steve Sullivan, Crime Analyst II for the East County Jurisdiction, utilizes ISYS in fulfilling this mission. Sullivan supervises a team of computer "detectives" that use databases, information systems, and ISYS to help solve crimes. Other counties share large volumes of information with Ventura County, and bulletins are received from different sources. "Crime Analysts are in the information business. It is imperative that we have access to the information we need, when we need it," says Sullivan.

Several law enforcement databases are often transferred from one agency to another. "The databases are extensive and time consuming to go through when searching for something specific," says Sullivan. The need for immediate access to information prompted Sullivan's decision to invest in ISYS. "The speed at which ISYS retrieves information is remarkable," adds Sullivan.

In one case, a suspect was arrested during a burglary, and the investigating detective believed the perpetrator was responsible for 39 other burglaries in the area. The detective remembered that in one of the burglaries, blood samples were taken from the scene. The detective complained to Sullivan that he'd have to read through hundreds of pages of reports to find the relevant case. Sullivan searched two databases simultaneously with ISYS and found the case within seconds.

When Sullivan transferred from Los Angles to Ventura, he took over a unit that had 15 years' worth of documents, reports, and other information stored on computer. "Imagine trying to wade through 15 years of data and trying to guess where everything was stored. There were files on the system in formats that were no longer installed on our machines. With ISYS, I could access the information I needed regardless of location and format," says Sullivan.

One reason Sullivan invested in ISYS was the Intelligent Agent feature, which allows users to identify their areas of interest and reports back as relevant new information enters the system. "Often an investigator will ask us to provide more information on a particular case. Information might enter our information bank 10 minutes, an hour, or 3 months from now, and ISYS helps us respond to the investigators as soon as the information is available," says Sullivan.

- *IxReveal*, offering uReveal "plug-in" advanced analytic platform and uReka! desktop "search and analyze" consumer product, based on patented text analytics methods.

An IxReveal Case Study

Police officers from Jacksonville Florida's Sheriff's Office were aware of a crime series involving the use of a box cutter in raping transients and prostitutes, but the total extent and characteristics of the perpetrator were unknown. By using the analytic capabilities of uReveal, the crime analyst on the case was able to learn from known cases and discover previously unknown cases.

Based on this information, a suspect was identified and arrested. The analysis was able to relate both crime and information reports that in previous investigations were not possible. Crime Analysis Unit Manager Matthew White recalls initially testing the solution to see if it would help solve a difficult vehicle burglary pattern. Scores of cars are broken into every day in this major city, but in this case the pattern was difficult to detect because the crimes were geographically dispersed and traditional MO information did not have the level of detail needed.

When analysts used uReveal, they were able to see a level of detail in the data that they previously would not have; thus, it was obvious that the string of crimes took place during funerals throughout the city. To detect these patterns, analysts had to know that officers were increasingly using terms such as *funeral*, *graveyard*, *wake*, and *gravesite* to provide context for the crime.

The 18 members of White's Crime Analysis unit are in place to help police become more efficient by supporting ongoing patrols, investigations, and homeland security. From proactive scanning to generating suspect lists and spotting trends and patterns, all these are the unit's responsibility. Traditionally, analyst units have spent an inordinate amount of time reading reports each day, leaving little time to analyze the bank of information they have just barely sifted through.

Covering a large area like Duval County, with so many reports generated through the office, it was impossible for officers to read every single report. For those they were able to read, relying on an officer's memory to identify details and make connections to other events was inefficient and unreliable.

Receiving over 1 million calls each year, police officers create various reports ranging from Incident Field Interview, Truancy and Arrest Reports to phone calls that come into the station. With well over 100,000 criminal incidents each year, and a relative number of arrests, officers tend to write a great deal of narrative detail—all of it in unstructured text format—that information can span from 1 page to over 50 pages of incident descriptions.

This information is dynamic; more information is added through narrative detail or text as cases evolve. "We have a large volume of unstructured data and a lot of the very good information we need is in it," explains White. "Spending all day reading reports is inefficient and kills the time to do analysis. We recognized the need to have a more robust sense of our data. When we learned about uReveal from IxReveal, we knew we had found a solution that would help us better analyze our data."

The ability to learn from the data will enable crime analysts to find connections between events for both those they may be seeking, as well as those unexpected discoveries, such as the funeral vehicle burglaries. In addition to learning from the data, the solution integrates Excel spreadsheets, and enables faster sharing among analysts.

- *KXEN Text Coder (KTC)* text analytics solution for automatically preparing and transforming unstructured text attributes into a structured representation for use in KXEN Analytic Framework.
- *Lexalytics* provides enterprise and hosted text analytics software to transform unstructured text into structured data.
- *Leximancer* makes automatic concept maps of text data collections.
- *Linguamatics* offers natural language processing (NLP), search engine approach, intuitive reporting, and domain knowledge plug-in.
- *Megaputer Text Analyst* offers semantic analysis of free-form texts, summarization, clustering, navigation, and natural language retrieval with search dynamic refocusing.
- *Monarch* is a data access and analysis tool that lets the user transform any report into a live database.

- *NewsFeed Researcher* presents a live multidocument summarization tool, with automatically generated RSS news feeds.
- *Recommind MindServer* uses PLSA (Probabilistic Latent Semantic Analysis) for accurate retrieval and categorization of texts.
- *SAS Text Miner* provides a rich suite of text processing and analysis tools (Figure 3.10).
- *TEMIS* offers an information discovery solution serving the Information Intelligence needs of business corporations and government agencies.
- *Textalyser* is an online text analysis tool, providing detailed text statistics for free.
- *TextPipe* is a text conversion, extraction, and manipulation workbench.
- *TextQuest* is text analysis software; it offers a variety of analyses, from a simple word list up to a content analysis or readability analysis.
- *TIBCO* combines text analytics with graphical clustering and link analysis for the summarization of crime data.

A TIBCO Case Study

ARLINGTON VIRGINIA COUNTY CRIME ANALYSIS

TIBCO combines text analysis with graphical clustering and link analysis to generate views of the Arlington crimes by the day of the week and hour of the day at which a crime took place. The software can also look for keywords in investigator's reports, such as the words "The crime reports by the Arlington County Police Department have been documented and are displayed for analysis in this file." Our initial insight into the crime event data shows information about how often each type of crime has occurred and where the crime occurred.

The Map Chart (Figure 3.11) shows us the location of the crime events through the use of a shapefile of Virginia and the geospatial information in the data. The size of the markers on the Map Chart

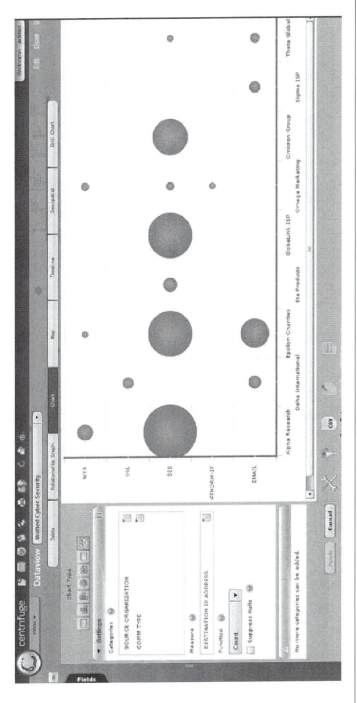

Figure 3.10 SAS text mining concept linking window displays terms grouped by clusters.

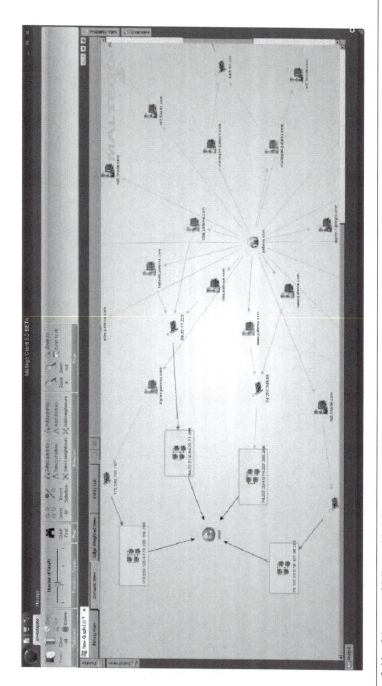

Figure 3.11   Crime map of Arlington, Virginia.

is relative to the number of times a particular type of crime has occurred at a location.

Each type of crime appears in the bar chart (Figure 3.12), sorted by number of occurrences. Marking one or more bars will display details in the cross table. The details in the cross table display the count of the marked crimes for each day of the week.

Several visualizations can be used to analyze data across other data. For this case study, we are considering amount and type of crime over dates. On the following graph (Figure 3.13), a line chart is used to display the rate of each type of crime over date. The chart has the "Date Hierarchy" set as its X-Axis property, in order to give the user the option to slide from one date measurement to another.

And finally, a graph along the lines of Arlington districts (Figure 3.14) can be generated.

- *Xanalys* provides investigative software that automatically extracts entities and cross references from free text documents and builds a database for subsequent analysis.

Xanalys Case Studies

These following are some success stories that Xanalys is permitted to disclose.

NORFOLK CONSTABULARY

The Norfolk Constabulary polices an area of approximately 3,500 square miles and a population of 750,000, with an establishment of 1,500 police officers and 1,200 support staff. As part of the National Intelligence Model guidelines, the Constabulary scans its own policing environment to identify trends and potential crime "hot spots." Information is gathered, analyzed, and shared at regular meetings, at which strategic decisions are made and priorities established for future policing activities.

In this modern model of law enforcement, the Constabulary's analysts are increasingly relied upon for investigations and for following National Intelligence Model guidelines. Norfolk Constabulary analysts have been using XANALYS® Link Explorer (formerly

New Search

marketVisual

Visualize Business Relationships

Search Company or Person   Jesus Mena

Submit

Jesus Mena   Number of relationships: 25   Most relationships with: InferX
Strongest relationships: University of Texas at El Paso   InferX   Sandia National Laboratories   Artificial Intelligence   University of Texas El Paso   Nippon Telephone & Telegraph   Lockheed
Corp   Safeway Inc   Office of Inspector General   WebMiner Inc   Department of Homeland Security

Figure 3.12   A TIBCO table of crimes in Arlington.

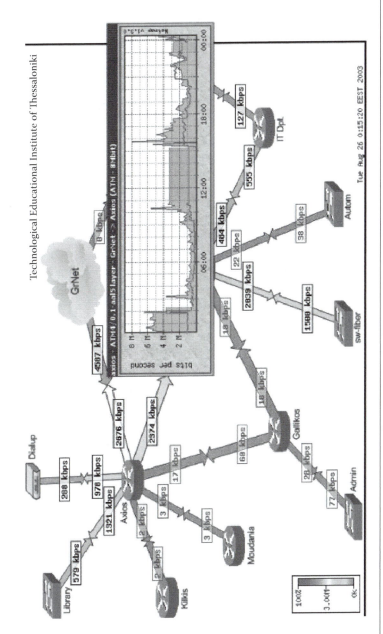

Figure 3.13 A TIBCO graph of crimes across time.

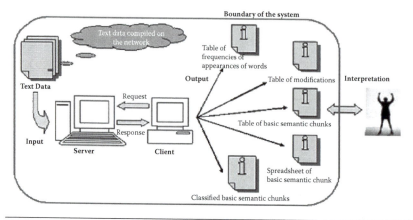

Figure 3.14   A TIBCO map on crimes by districts in Arlington.

Watson®) to aid their investigation analysis since early 2000, and they find it one of the most powerful new weapons to help keep Norfolk safe.

When crime rates began to rise, senior managers and staff within the Norfolk Constabulary had reason for concern. Intelligence relating to crime in the coastal resort town of Great Yarmouth, in the county of Norfolk, United Kingdom, confirmed the expansion of a well-organized drug gang into the community. At the same time, vehicle-related crimes were dramatically increasing in the area.

Drug dealers from other parts of the country were systematically infiltrating the town of Great Yarmouth, Norfolk. The gang eventually grew so bold as to conduct "business" in clear view on street corners. Information collected from varied intelligence sources helped ascertain where and when drug deals were taking place. Simultaneously, intelligence about vehicle-related crimes was being compiled.

"We intuitively knew that tackling the drug gang problem would have a major impact on the auto theft problem," said Detective Chief Inspector Barry Lister, who led the investigation team. "So we combined the vehicle crime data with gang-related intelligence to tighten the noose around our drug-dealing gang."

Crime intelligence analysts working as part of the investigation team used XANALYS Link Explorer software to analyze the structured and unstructured information gathered for both investigations. Using the software, analysts collected and linked relevant information from multiple databases such as mobile phone, driving, and residency records. That structured information was compared with wide-ranging, unstructured information from witness statements, surveillance, and test purchase officer reports.

Using its own analysis techniques and XANALYS Link Explorer to aggregate all information, the police team identified a crime pattern. From the pattern, they outlined a complete crime timeline for local investigators, highlighting a series of actions that began with a drug purchase request on a mobile phone and ended with delivery by a drug runner. To validate the identified crime pattern, mobile phone calls were put through a time series analysis that conclusively proved a correlation between outgoing calls—"orders"—and the timing of street delivery.

With a clear understanding of the drug-dealing pattern on the street, the investigation team ran a similar analysis of auto-related crime activity. Their work showed an obvious pattern of theft and vandalism in the immediate vicinity of the drug-dealing locations.

To make the final arrests, all officers involved with the investigation collaboratively created an enforcement strategy based on suspect profiles and relationships they knew existed between dealers. Ultimately, the Norfolk Constabulary arrested 26 suspects on drug trafficking, most of them high-level dealers and suppliers.

As in any investigation, an arrest is only half of the battle. To prepare the evidence for court presentation, the officers used XANALYS Link Explorer to graphically explain the mapped links between people, places, and events. This clear representation of the identified links, which depicted the activities that took place on more than one instance of crime, was then presented in court.

Through a combination of superb collaborative police work and powerful technology, the Norfolk Constabulary not only stopped Great Yarmouth drug trafficking in its tracks, but it also presented such clear evidence in court that all 26 suspects, upon seeing the evidence against them, pleaded guilty and were convicted. No one walked away. The defendants were sentenced to a total of more than 100 years in prison by the court.

For its dedication, hard work, and the irrefutable evidence it presented in the courtroom, and for conducting a well-run, well-documented investigation, the Norfolk Constabulary was lauded by the judge. In addition, several officers were commended for their management of the investigation.

"This is a clear example where technology enabled our officers to act definitively with a crystal-clear path for our enforcement strategy," said Detective Chief Inspector Lister. "Furthermore, it is very gratifying that when presented with the evidence compiled with the use of XANALYS Link Explorer, all of the defendants knew defense was futile."

ONTARIO PROVINCIAL POLICE

Paul Kenneth Bernardo was suspected of more than a dozen brutal sexual assaults in Scarborough, Canada, within the jurisdiction of the Ontario Provincial Police. As his attacks grew in frequency they also grew in brutality, to the point of several murders. Then just as police were closing in, the attacks suddenly stopped. That is when the Ontario police knew they had a problem. Because their suspect was not in jail, they knew he had either died or fled to a location outside their jurisdiction to commit his crimes.

The events following Bernardo's disappearance in Toronto and his eventual capture in St. Catharines would ultimately lead to an intense investigation into police practices throughout the Province of Ontario, Canada. The investigation results would show glaring weaknesses in investigation management and information sharing between police districts.

Bill Van Allen's belief in a better way of conducting police business pushed him into the leadership role of an elite group of investigators, called the Campbell Commission Implementation Project, which sought to bring Ontario Provincial Police investigation methods to the forefront of law enforcement.

Under the direction of Van Allen, the Campbell Implementation group's charter was to meet 11 objectives relating to investigation management.

In their worldwide hunt to find cutting-edge investigative methods and technologies, officers found shockingly few effective solutions. Then investigators came across XANALYS

PowerCase, an investigation management system based on the best practices of law enforcement organizations around the world. Today, every stage of major investigations is managed by Ontario police, who use the software to collect, organize, link, and present investigation evidence.

Using PowerCase, investigators now capture disparate information concerning a case and then rapidly see connections with evidence already collected and associated with related cases, information that could otherwise go unnoticed. For example, when information is put into PowerCase, connections between statements from witness #1 and witness #103 are presented to investigators, even if the investigators who collected the information never speak with one another. Moreover, should information not be an exact match, such as Bernardo versus Benano, or 805 Main Street versus 508 Main Street, the software will connect the information and present it to investigators.

Another aspect of automating part of the investigative process is linking evidence from seemingly unrelated cases. As part of all investigations taking place in Ontario today, PowerCase alerts are sent to investigators who may not know that they are seeking the same suspect in different cities, or are investigating crimes with similar profiles. In this manner, investigators share information with unprecedented levels of effectiveness and efficiency.

Furthermore, police are liberated from many of the tedious aspects of law enforcement. Leaving phone record analysis to the software, for example, gives an opportunity for officers to question more people, or perform other aspects of police work that lead to faster case resolution.

Among the many additional benefits Ontario's groundbreaking PowerCase investigation capabilities provide is consistently high investigative standards that are able to stand up to increasingly rigorous courtroom scrutiny.

While PowerCase underwent adoption in the Province of Ontario, opposition to investigation management software was encountered on many levels. After all, police work has been done in much the same manner for the past 100 years, and software doesn't solve crimes; police officers do. Nevertheless, crimes, clues, and convictions are all recorded on paper today in many law enforcement organizations. But after dramatic successes mounted in Ontario, including convictions in cold cases, Van Allen and his team steadily changed mindsets throughout the force. Crimes are now solved faster, easily passing courtroom muster as judges and prosecutors recognize that cases investigated using PowerCase consistently stand up to legal challenges.

Today, most of the Ontario Police force uses PowerCase software and methods as they would any other investigative tool. While a minority views its effectiveness with disbelief, others see it as one more weapon in their arsenal against crime.

With the continued commitment of Van Allen's team, the Ontario Provincial Police are leading their profession in investigation management techniques and practices.

As Campbell Commission Inspector Gary Parmenter put it, "the ability to collect, analyze, and share information is far more powerful against criminal activity than any gun we can carry. It's just like when telephones, two-way radios, and cell phones were adopted back in the day. Our ability to collect, analyze, and share information puts us one more step ahead of the bad guys."

Today, all objectives of the Campbell Commission task force have been met, and have put the Ontario Provincial Police in the vanguard of law enforcement. Police organizations from the United Kingdom, Australia, Singapore, etc., now study the case management and information-sharing systems pioneered in Ontario. In these countries, as in the Province of Ontario, cases such as that of Paul Kenneth Bernardo are becoming more rare.

Paradoxically, Bill Van Allen now says one of his most pressing concerns is the fact that law enforcement is often judged by how quickly it solves major cases such as that of Paul Kenneth Bernardo. When cases are solved more rapidly, the instances of high-profile investigations become far fewer. Crimes can now be avoided with greater frequency and that kind of crime fighting success does not make headlines. "It's a problem I'm happy to work with," says Van Allen.

GALVESTON TEXAS TASK FORCE

Law enforcement officials know too well that a criminal can't be brought to justice unless a jury understands the crime. The Galveston County Auto Crimes Task Force recently encountered a criminal scheme so complex that explaining it clearly to a grand jury would ordinarily have been a difficult, day-long challenge. But with the help of a sophisticated software called Watson® by Xanalys, the task force made a clear and convincing argument in just 15 minutes, securing an indictment.

The multijurisdictional Auto Crimes Task Force is dedicated to fighting commercial auto theft, as well as other vehicle-related crimes. Among the many things that are big in Texas, the recent reduction in auto theft is certainly a source of pride. Statewide auto theft dropped 36% over a 5-year period, according to the Texas Automobile Theft Prevention Authority (TATPA), which was established in 1991 by the state legislature. TATPA funds the Auto Crimes Task Force, in concert with the citizens of Galveston County.

When the task force presented its findings to the grand jury in this complex theft and fraud case, it was aided by the intelligence analysis capability of Watson. Watson automates the intelligence analysis process and represents findings in chart form. These capabilities saved the task force time and money in analyzing the data and creating a compelling presentation.

By modeling the offender's illicit activities in Watson, the task force was able to generate charts automatically that clearly showed how different parts of this scheme worked in relationship to one another, explained Sergeant Mike Creech, who directed the task force effort. The software has more than paid for itself by bringing clarity to the task force's grand jury presentation and saving weeks of work in its development, he said.

Watson helped officials on the case sort out what Sergeant Creech described as "a major paperwork nightmare." The case involved the manager of a body shop at an auto dealership who was stealing auto parts, filing bogus insurance claims, making kickbacks to an independent adjuster, and pocketing insurance deductibles paid in cash. He would apply other customers' insurance deductible checks to cover his trail.

The task force reviewed a year's worth of financial records from the body shop, which filled two large file boxes. Investigators meticulously chronicled inventory, insurance claims, and cash deductibles. They were able to trace, for example, when one person's insurance deductible paid by check was fraudulently applied to another customer's deductible paid in cash.

As if the sheer complexity of the data was not frustrating enough for investigators, additional paperwork that would have supported the investigation was destroyed by the defendant's internal auditor, allegedly by accident. The task force had to piece together the sequence of transactions in this multilayered scam using partial information.

Watson was not yet on board when the year-long investigation began, so investigators analyzed data and charted relationships among transactions manually. But the static nature of manual charting was at odds with the constant changes inherent to an ongoing investigation.

"If you're in the middle of the investigation and you draw a chart, then every time you get new information you have to redraw the chart," said Sergeant Creech. "It's time consuming." When Watson arrived; investigators were able to automatically generate updated charts as new discoveries unfolded. Analysis time was dramatically reduced.

The task force chose to present to the grand jury a two-month snapshot of the case that was representative of the year-long scam. The investigative team spent five days selecting a period of activity to model. Then the investigators entered the chosen two months of data into Watson, which they used to analyze the data and automatically chart relationships among events.

Watson charts showed events and transactions in sequence, making it easy for the grand jury to understand how each related to the next, and to see how the overall scheme operated. Not only was the suspect indicted after a 15-minute presentation, but the case never went to trial. Within a week, the offender pleaded guilty to misapplication of funds by a fiduciary. He was sentenced to 10 years in prison, plus restitution.

So clear was the Watson-based presentation that "the scam was right here in front of my face," Sergeant Creech said. "Watson saved me a great deal of time trying to draw and redraw charts." he said. "It saved my investigator time in presentation to the grand jury. And it has saved our taxpayers and our grand jurors a whole lot of headaches."

The task force continues to analyze data for a wide variety of cases using Watson. Cases have ranged from using automobile license data to crack a pyramid scheme, to tracing a missing person.

The task force also uses Watson to do postmortem evaluations of cases. In one case that the prosecution lost, investigators had analyzed and charted the case data manually, before Watson was available. The charts done by hand had been misleading, Sergeant Creech said. Postmortem analysis with Watson shifted the focal point of the case.

- *VantagePoint* provides a variety of interactive graphical views and analysis tools with powerful capabilities to discover knowledge from text databases.
- *VisualText*™ by TextAI is a comprehensive GUI development environment for quickly building accurate text analyzers.
- *Wordstat* is an analysis module for textual information such as responses to open-ended questions, interviews, etc.

Many packages above offer free or limited trial versions.

FREE OPEN-SOURCE TEXT MINING ANALYTICS SOFTWARE

- *GATE* is a leading open-source toolkit for text mining, with a free open source framework (or SDK) and graphical development environment.
- *LingPipe* is a suite of Java libraries for the linguistic analysis of human language.
- *Open Calais* is an open-source toolkit for including semantic functionality within blogs, content management systems, websites, or applications.
- *RapidMiner* (Text Mining Component) is a free software that is extremely powerful and contains dozens of text and data mining algorithms (Figure 3.15).
- *The Semantic Indexing Project* offers open source tools, including Semantic Engine, a standalone indexer/ search application.

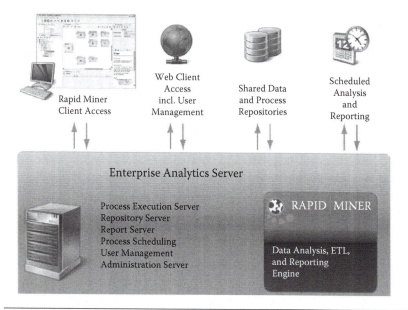

Figure 3.15   RapidMiner incorporates all the functionality of expensive analytical suites.

The following is a checklist of terms and algorithms involved in text analysis. No extensive discussion on these techniques will be given here, as this book is geared toward real-world applications such as law enforcement. However, the investigator should be aware of these underlying text analytic technologies.

A Text Analytics Checklist

1. *Bayesian Models*—They consider all possible parameter values, includes a penalty for including too much model structure. Thus, these models guard against overfitting (creating memories, rather than models).
2. *Concept Decomposition*—A procedure for text retrieval based on a sparsified matrix, which can enhance the accuracy compared with the technique based on latent semantic indexing with singular value decomposition.
3. *Orthogonal Decomposition*—A technique used in exploratory data analysis and for making predictive models; it involves the calculation of a data matrix by centering the data for each attribute.
4. *Probabilistic Models*—Embraces the object-relational nature of structured data by capturing probabilistic interactions between attributes of related entities that can be used to predict link structure.
5. *Vector Space Models*—An algebraic model for representing text documents as vectors of identifiers, such as, for example index terms;

they are used in information filtering, information retrieval, indexing, and relevancy rankings.

6. *Latent Semantic Indexing*—A technique in natural language processing, in particular, in vectorial semantics, of analyzing relationships between a set of documents and the terms they contain by producing a set of concepts related to the documents and terms.

7. *Graph-Based Models*—Are usually described by means of nodes and edges, roughly corresponding to places and their spatial relations.

8. *Text Streaming Models*—An automated unsupervised learning of latent topics from text documents for document organization, retrieval, and filtering of information.

9. *Clustering*—Technique for unsupervised document organization, automatic topic extraction, and fast information retrieval or filtering.

10. *Factor Analysis*—A data reduction method.

11. *Visualization*—Graphical depictions of relationships between sets of concepts, permitting the end user to identify previously unrecognized or unknown relationships.

12. *Metadata Generation*—The use of a self-organizing map (SOM) algorithm to cluster training web pages to discover some semantic descriptions about web pages.

13. *Information Extraction*—Technique for locating specific pieces of data in natural language documents.

14. *Text Classification*—There are two types: supervised document classification, where human feedback provides information on the correct classification for documents; and unsupervised document classification, where the classification is without reference to external information.

15. *Text Segmentation*—The process of dividing written text into meaningful units, such as sentences or topics.

16. *Text Summarization*—Technique based on statistical, linguistic, and heuristic methods of calculating how often certain key words appear in a document by frequency and which sentences they are present in, and where these sentences are in the text.

3.6 From Extraction to Clustering

As we saw in this chapter, there are several tools that the forensic investigator can use to advance his or her inquiries. First, link analysis technology can be used to guide investigations by discovering associations between entities and devices. Second, text analytics can also be used to expedite investigations by discovering hidden patterns in unstructured content, such as crime reports, 911 calls, e-mails, and other types of documents.

These extractive technologies can guide the investigator toward more distinct and productive leads for detecting fraudulent and criminal activities. In Chapter 4, we will discuss how clustering technology can be leveraged by the forensic investigator to discover, group, and view the behaviors of criminals.

However, as some of the case studies in this chapter showed, all of these technologies can be used to supplement each other, such as link analysis, text analysis, and now clustering algorithms and tools, to be followed by decision trees and rule generators. Forensic investigators can begin to develop their machine learning toolbox by downloading open source software such as RapidMiner, which is totally free.

4

INDUCTIVE FORENSICS

Clustering Incidents and Crimes

4.1 Autonomous Forensics

Cluster analysis is the forensic process of decomposing a set of observations into several subsets of observations that have some digital similarity, which can be viewed in a graphical format. Creating visual maps of these findings and creating predictive models for anticipating crimes is one of the missions of forensic investigators. Observations within the same cluster are similar in some sense, which for forensic investigators may point to certain computer ports, locations in a city, intrusions into networks, or fraudulent attempts. Clustering is a method of unsupervised learning that is important for the forensic investigator to understand.

Unsupervised learning is a term used in machine learning and is a class of problems in which one seeks to determine how the data are organized. Many methods employed here are based on behavioral analytic methods used to preprocess data. It is distinguished from supervised learning in that the learner is given only unlabeled examples. However, unsupervised learning also encompasses many other techniques that seek to summarize and explain key features of the data.

For the forensic investigator, unsupervised learning and clustering is a method of discovery of clues. The most powerful and accurate clustering technology is that of a neural network known as a self-organizing map (SOM). The SOM is a topographic organization in which nearby locations in the map represent inputs with similar properties. A SOM is trained to produce a low-dimensional (typically two-dimensional), discretized representation of the input space of the training samples. However, a SOM is different from other artificial neural networks in the sense that it uses a neighborhood function to preserve the topological properties of the input space.

This makes SOMs useful for visualizing low-dimensional views of high-dimensional data, akin to multidimensional scaling. The model was first described as an artificial neural network by the Finnish professor Teuvo Kohonen, and is sometimes called a Kohonen map. Similar to most artificial neural networks, SOMs operate in two modes: training and mapping. Training builds the map using input examples. It is a competitive process, also called *vector quantization*. Mapping automatically classifies a new input vector.

A self-organizing map consists of components called *nodes* or *neurons*. Associated with each node is a weight vector of the same dimension as the input data vectors and a position in the map space. The usual arrangement of nodes is a regular spacing in a hexagonal or rectangular grid. The self-organizing map describes a mapping from a higher-dimensional input space to a lower-dimensional map space. The procedure for placing a vector from data space onto the map is to find the node with the closest weight vector to the vector taken from the data space and to assign the map coordinates of this node to that vector.

SOMs can be used for the creation of models in the clustering of behaviors, as well as words. For the forensic investigator, clustering is an important tool for knowledge discovery. Since a SOM adheres to the unsupervised mode of modeling, the clusters organize themselves; this means there is no bias in the models. This totally autonomous method of inductive data analysis allows the findings to emerge from the raw data, without the restraints imposed by other more structured methodologies such as decision trees and rule generators. Clustering is exploratory data analysis driven by the raw data itself and is an excellent technique for uncovering features of criminals and crimes by isolating their activities and behaviors (Figure 4.1).

Unlike traditional graphing technologies that display the location of crimes over a city, SOM clustering is about using self-organizing graphs to *detect* criminal activities. Rather than just using graphs to represent criminal "hot spots," this type of inductive analysis actually focuses on the mapping of criminal activities, such as network intrusions, fraud, money laundering, etc. The forensic investigator is not

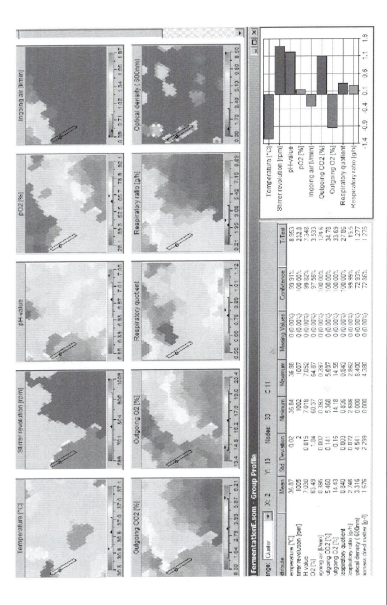

Figure 4.1   A SOM can discover clusters of behaviors automatically.

concerned with reporting about criminal patterns, as much as discovering patterns that identify crimes.

What self-organizing maps achieve for the forensic investigator is to "compress" the data into more manageable chunks of leads, behaviors, patterns, and evidence. A network of SOMs can reduce the complexity of criminal behaviors into simple spatial maps, with descriptive statistics and detailed charts. Most importantly, SOMs provide the power of true machine learning in which the criminal behaviors are discovered by a combination of powerful servers, artificial intelligence software, and seasoned field human investigators.

Thus, clustering refers to the grouping of records, observations, words, behaviors, or cases into classes of similar features or objects. A cluster is a collection of records that are similar in features to one another and dissimilar to records or behaviors in other clusters. For the forensic investigator, this might involve the use of a SOM to cluster the behaviors of legal transactions and the clustering of fraudulent transactions. Clustering differs from classification in that there is no target variable for clustering.

Clustering is about induction or statistical inference, whereas classification is about deduction or logic and deductive inference. The clustering task does not try to classify, estimate, or predict the value of a target variable like a decision tree or rule generator. Instead, clustering algorithms, neural networks such as SOMs, seek to segment the entire data set into relatively homogeneous subgroups or clusters in which the similarity of the records within the cluster is maximized and the similarity to records outside the clusters is minimized (Figure 4.2).

For example, of the six clusters, the large ones might represent legal behaviors, whereas the smaller outliers might represent criminal behaviors. Clustering is often performed as a preliminary step in the investigative forensic process, with the resulting clusters being used as further inputs to a different technique downstream, such as decision tree and rule generator classifiers. For example, those outlier records can be processed via classification algorithms to discover their unique features.

Due to the massive sizes of present-day data sets and databases, it is often necessary to apply clustering analysis first to reduce the search space for the downstream processing via decision trees and rule generators. Also, as with link analysis and text mining, and now clustering

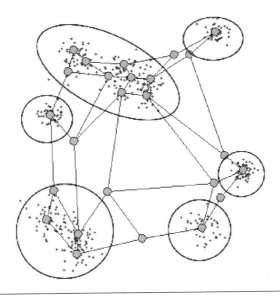

Figure 4.2 A SOM generates six clusters of behaviors.

via SOM, it is a process of data compression and refinement. These processes can be used in different combinations and configurations, all concluding with powerful machine learning classifiers such as decision trees. To a large extent, what tools are used is based on the expectations and results required by the forensic investigation.

4.2 Self-Organizing Maps

The idea behind SOMs is very simple: objects repel and attract each other. Self-organizing maps essentially display these different objects in the form of discrete clusters of information. Depending on the data set, the SOM graphics can be dramatic, displaying the distributions of linkage among the objects; the SOM will break apart and form discrete clusters. The value of these neural networks tools is that they can discover and recognize unknown patterns in the data.

The basic SOM consists of an input layer and an output layer. The input layer is connected to the inputs. The output layer is laid out like a grid. Each unit is connected to all the input units, but not to each other. The output units "compete" with each other for the output of the network. The end result is intense competition between the outputs until eventual "winners" rise from the raw data, much like putting a sheet of cellophane over a map of hills and valleys (Figure 4.3).

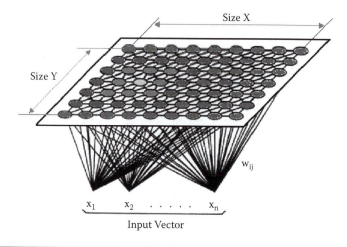

Input Vector

Figure 4.3　A SOM architecture organizing clusters from the input data.

So, how does a SOM recognize patterns and discover clusters? The output layer consists of many units, each connected to all of the units in the input layer. The output layer is arranged in a grid, as if the units were in the squares of a checkerboard. When a member of the training set is presented to the network, the value flows forward through the network to the units in the output layer and presented as distinct cluster groupings. The units in the output layer compete with each other, and the one with the highest value "wins." The reward is to adjust the weights leading up to the winning unit to strengthen the response to the input pattern.

Initially, the map a SOM creates is quite large; however, as with most neural networks, internal units adjust as they recycle the data in their effort to learn the patterns and create smaller clusters that are similar to each other and dissimilar to other clusters. Automatic cluster detection using SOMs can be performed to uncover a hidden structure that can be used to improve the performance of more directed techniques, such as decision trees. Once the final SOM network has been "trained" with the output layer restricted only to the units that identify clusters, it can be applied to new instances in a "test" data set. This is a typical methodology when working with neural networks: data sets are split into a train and test subsets in order to calibrate their accuracy and to view how well they have learned from the raw data.

SOMs have been successfully applied by criminal investigators to cluster burglaries, rapes, and murders; they also have been deployed to detect network intrusion behaviors. Most modern clustering tools provide dashboards for measuring their accuracy; for example, error rates can be generated on the misclassification of clusters. Although SOMs can identify clusters, they sometimes cannot identify what is unique about them; however, powerful tools such as SOMine, which will be covered in depth in the following section, can provide detailed statistics about the clusters it discovers, such as the average mean of each cluster.

Neural networks such as SOMs are highly sensitive to how they learn from data; for this reason, it is important that as many attributes as possible be used in the creation of their maps and models. The results can be dramatically different when important predictive variables are identified; however, to do so, divergent data sets should be used as their inputs. For this reason, multiple maps and models need to be developed and tested when using SOMs, which eventually will lead to the development of predictive rules from decision trees. It is a two-step process, clustering for discovering key features about the targets of investigations—and classification for the quantification of those investigations—precrime and the creation of real-time detection systems.

There are different types of clustering techniques and algorithms, such as K-means, fuzzy c-means, and QT clustering; however, for the forensic investigator, SOMs provide several advantages, including ease of use, quick deployment, and high accuracy, but most importantly, they can deal with massive data sets, which some statistical clustering algorithms cannot. The field of machine learning was specifically developed for the analysis of massive data sets, which SOMs and decision trees have no problem dissecting. SOMs are also known as topology-preserving maps, which assume a topological structure among the cluster units. This property is observed in the human brain, which neural networks are designed to mimic.

Neural networks such as SOMs are unique programs in that they were created to replicate the human process of learning; how they operate imitates the way humans learn, by example. The formation of a SOM occurs in two phases: the initial formation of the correct clusters and the final conversion. The second phase takes much longer, which for certain applications may require many iterations through the training phase. One of the first applications of SOMs was the recognition of faces and sounds. What distinguishes them is the ability to process and learn from millions of interactions and records, something the forensic investigator cannot possibly accomplish. As such, they are excellent tools for the investigator when dealing with large data sets, where there is a need to develop leads from the raw data.

Neural networks such as SOMs are made up of artificial biological neurons that are connected or functionally related in the way the human nervous systems are organized. For example, in the field of neuroscience, they are often identified as groups of neurons that perform a specific physiological function, which for SOMs is to replicate the human process of discovering patterns and creating clusters. SOMs have been used to cluster and match unsolved crimes and criminals' modi operandi (MOs) or methods of operation.

Local, state, and federal law enforcement agencies have mountains of criminal data, which essentially is used for reporting purposes, yet they fail to leverage this valuable information by the strategic use of advanced machine learning forensics. The following section identifies some of the best of these clustering tools that an investigator needs to know about and use; most provide free evaluations, and some have academic free licenses. The investigator needs to know the strengths and weakness of each algorithm; for example, Bayesian networks are different in their performance and accuracy from SOMs and decision trees.

4.3 Clustering Software

4.3.1 Commercial Clustering Software

- *BayesiaLab* includes both Bayesian classification algorithms for data segmentation via supervised learning and Bayesian networks to automatically cluster variables via unsupervised learning.

4.3.1.1 What Are Bayesian Networks? A Bayesian network, belief network, or directed acyclic graphical (DAG) model is a probabilistic graphical network that represents a set of random variables and their conditional dependences with other variables in that data set. For example, a Bayesian network could represent the probabilistic relationships between crimes and criminals. Given information on criminal methods of operations, a Bayesian network can be used to compute the probabilities of the presence of various crimes.

Most importantly, Bayesian networks can be used to model risk; for example, by definition, risk is intrinsically linked to the notion of the unforeseeable. They are particularly adapted to the modeling of knowledge and the cognitive processes in areas containing uncertainties, such as network intrusions, fraud detection, and physical risks. Bayesian networks are recognized to be powerful technology for structuring and the management of risk control.

Bayesian networks can also be used to perform unsupervised learning in order to discover a set of significant probabilistic relations present in the raw data; they can be used to identify the links between multiple risk factors. Using unsupervised learning, they can be used to discover "influencers" and relationships hidden in data sets related to crimes and criminal activities.

They can assist the forensic investigator in discovering relationships between behaviors and targeted crimes. A Bayesian network is also known as a graphic probabilistic model through which the user can acquire, capitalize on, and exploit knowledge. These networks can discover and display factors related to crimes under investigation. Software tools such as BayesiaLab support this kind of clustering ability; in addition, they can also be used to perform unsupervised *and* supervised learning.

Risk is by nature closely related to hazard and, therefore, uncertainty. Bayesian networks are commonly known to be well suited for risk assessment due to their abilities to represent uncertain knowledge and to make rigorous probabilistic calculations. They can identify and prioritize factors influencing risks and crimes a forensic investigator is attempting to discover (Figure 4.4).

- *IBM Intelligent Miner* includes two clustering algorithms.
- *perSimplex* is clustering software based on fuzzy logic. A free download is available (Figure 4.5).
- *PolyAnalyst* offers clustering based on the Location of Anomalies (LS) algorithm (Figure 4.6).

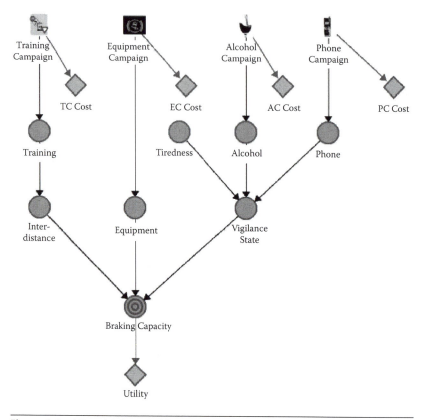

Figure 4.4   A BayesiaLab graph of factors influencing road risk.

- *StarProbe* is cross-platform, very fast on big data, has star schema support, special tools, and features for data with rich categorical dimensional information.
- *Viscovery* is one of the most powerful clustering software tools in the marketplace based on the SOM algorithm, with visual cluster analysis, segmentation, and assignment of operational measures to defined segments. It supports supervised and unsupervised analyses (Figure 4.7).
- *Visipoint* Self-Organizing Map for clustering and visualization; free downloads are available.

4.3.2 Free and Open-Source Clustering Software

- *CLUTO* provides a set of partition clustering algorithms that treat the clustering problem as an optimization process.

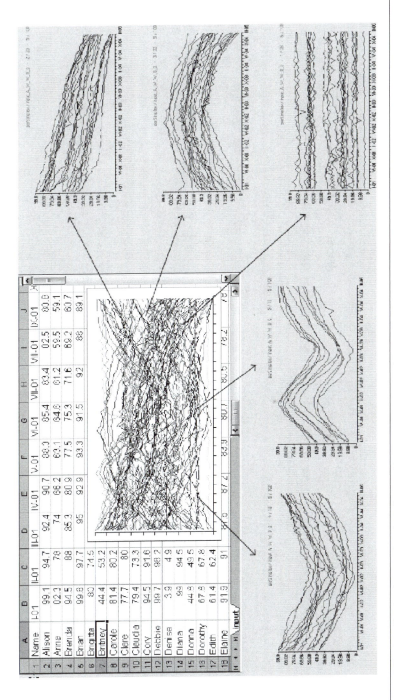

Figure 4.5 A perSimplex decomposing clustering graphic.

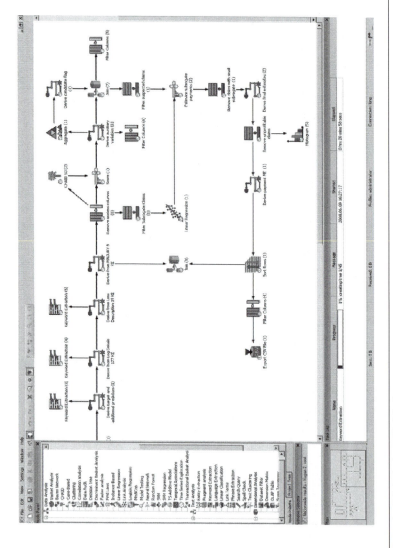

Figure 4.6   The Megaputer PolyAnalyst graphic interface.

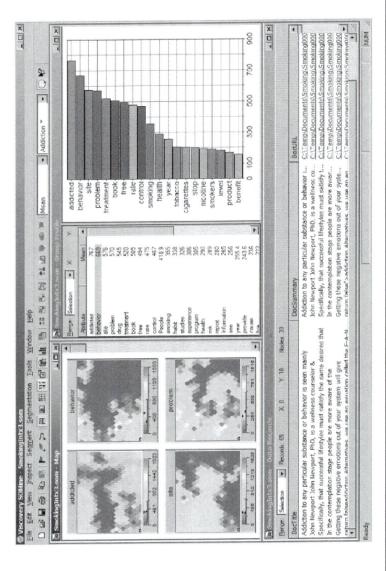

Figure 4.7 Viscovery SOMine can cluster data and text.

- *Databionic ESOM Tools* is a suite of programs for clustering, visualization, and classification with Emergent Self-Organizing Maps (ESOM).
- *PermutMatrix* is graphical software for clustering analysis, with several types of hierarchical cluster analysis and several methods to find an optimal reorganization of rows and columns.
- *Snob* is an MML (Minimum Message Length)-based program for clustering.

4.4 Mapping Incidents

One of the objectives of the forensic investigator is to assist in the creation of a dynamic and adaptive clustering detection system to monitor network traffic, for taking fast and effective countermeasures against high-volume attacks of networks and organizations. This may involve a hybrid solution involving network security information systems and networks coupled with forensic techniques such as clustering of patterns.

Intrusion Detection (ID) plays a vital role in the process of securing network-based computer systems by analyzing communications and reporting on malicious or abnormal activity. On the one hand, the process of ID has to deal with large computational cost due to the volume of data produced by high-speed networks, with the constant evolution and development of new intrusion methods and modern tools making intrusions more stealthy and effective. Most ID systems are brain dead: they capture the data, but they do not have the smarts to act on it; this is where the forensic investigator can come in and offer a solution that combines the brute force of machine learning with the expertise and knowledge of the forensic investigator.

The simplest method of criminal behavior is to observe it evolve, and be aware it can change at any time. For the investigator, it is important to know how and when network intrusions occurred, and are likely to be at risk in the future via specific behaviors of intruders. The methods of defense against intrusions are getting increasingly more time sensitive and sophisticated. Nature-inspired "swarming intelligence" agent-based mechanisms constructed via Bayesian networks, SOM algorithms, and decision trees offer the robustness, speed, and adaptability required for constructing "smart" intrusion detection systems (IDSs). Swarming intelligence architectures, strategies, and software can replicate the avoidance and counterattacks behaviors of insects and all biological species via schools, swarms, flocks, herds, packs, and other forms of organized communication and reaction systems of animals as they struggle to survive.

Denial of Service (DoS) attacks are special crimes in the process of intrusion detection, in which the goal of the attacker is to make some, or all, network services of the target unavailable. The most general classification of DoS attacks categorizes them into vulnerability and flooding attacks. The former type of attack focuses on exploiting certain flaws of networking mechanisms—to disable them requires some carefully crafted strategies and use of pattern recognition tools—to profile their DoS behaviors.

The second class of DoS attack is executed by attacking the target victim with large amounts of "dead packets" that are impossible to process. The packets in the flood usually are not crafted—the volume of the unwanted traffic alone forces the target to deplete its resources while processing the dummy packets and makes network services unavailable to legitimate users—it also renders the targets open to direct kill attacks. This kind of DoS attack is a back-door maneuver, and detection systems must be hard-wired with machine learning rules to recognize these evolving attacking patterns. With the growth of the bandwidth and interconnectivity of Internet and wireless networks, these flooding DoS attacks have become one of the greatest threats in cybercrime, capable of infiltrating and disabling hundreds of thousands of server networks. The following case study is presented courtesy of Dr. Lionel Jouffe from Bayesia.

Cyber-Crimes Detection Case Study*

The growing dependence of modern society on telecommunication and information networks is irreversible. The increase in the number of interconnected networks to the Internet and wireless networks has led to an increase in security threats and cyber-crimes

* Submitted by Nasser S. Abouzakhar, Gordon Manson from the Centre for Mobile Communications Research, University of Sheffield.

such as Distributed Denial of Service (DDoS) attacks. Any Internet-based attack typically is prefaced by a reconnaissance probe process, which might take just a few minutes, hours, days, or even months before the attack takes place (Figure 4.8).

The work presented here describes the use of *BayesiaLab* for learning Bayesian networks in order to detect distributed network attacks as early as possible. This work indicates how a Bayesian network probabilistically detects communication network attacks, allowing for generalization of Network Intrusion Detection Systems (NIDSs). It describes the major results achieved from experiments based on real-time data set as well as the observations that explain the achieved results. Learning Agents that deploy the Bayesian network approach are considered to be a promising

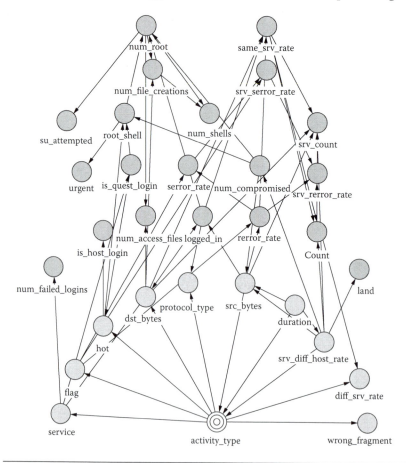

Figure 4.8 A Bayesian network mapping intrusions.

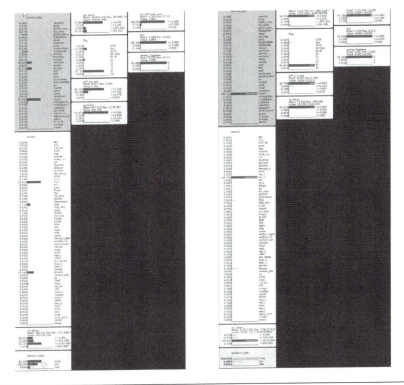

Figure 4.9 A breakdown of the ports and server activities the network discovered.

and useful tool in determining suspicious early events of Internet threats and consequently relating them to millions of port and server activities (Figure 4.9).

The Bayesian network has been automatically constructed thanks to the learning algorithms of BayesiaLab. The target variable, activity _ type, is directly connected to the variables that heavily contribute to its knowledge such as service and protocol _ type.

4.5 Clustering Crimes

Traditionally, solving crimes has been the mission of the law enforcement specialists, such as field detectives; however, computer data analysts in the guise of machine learning forensic investigators can assist traditional law enforcement officers and detectives to speed up the process of solving crimes. More specifically, this may involve the use of clustering-based models to help in identification of criminal patterns.

Criminal clusters have a specific meaning and refer to a geographical or time spatial grouping of different types of crimes (Figure 4.10).

Such clusters can be visually represented using a simple geospatial plot of different types of crimes overlaid on the map of a police jurisdiction or an entire city and are typically used to map "hot spots" of crimes. However, in the context of machine learning forensics, the objective of clustering is to identify criminal patterns or a crime spree. Crime rates differ between different types of urban districts, and these disparities are best explained by the variation of descriptive urban criminal clusters.

However, for the creation of predictive models, tools such as SOMs can be used to create clusters from the criminal data and used to develop these descriptive hot spots in a way that should allow common features to be extracted for mapping predictive criminal data patterns before they take place. The clustering algorithms a forensic investigator uses are for the purpose of identifying groups of criminal records that are similar among themselves but different from the rest of the data. These clusters can be useful in identifying a crime spree committed by one or the same group of suspects. Given this fact, the challenge to the forensic investigator is to find the best variables providing the best insight and prediction about clustering criminal patterns.

Almost all modern law enforcement agencies and police departments use electronic systems and relational databases for crime reporting, to their citizens, city managers, and local government officials, but most importantly, these reports are used to feed criminal statistics to the Department of Justice and other state and federal agencies that oversee their funding resources.

These criminal reports typically contain categorical information such as the type of crime, date/time, location, etc. Then there is information about the suspect, the victim, and the witness. Additionally, there is also some unstructured content in the form of a narrative or description of the crime and Modus Operandi (MO) that is usually in the format of free text. The police officers or field detectives use free text to record most of their observations that cannot be included in checkbox kind of predetermined questions. While the first two categories of information about crimes and criminals are usually stored in structured formats—amenable to forensic analysis via decision trees and rule generators—there is also important unstructured content

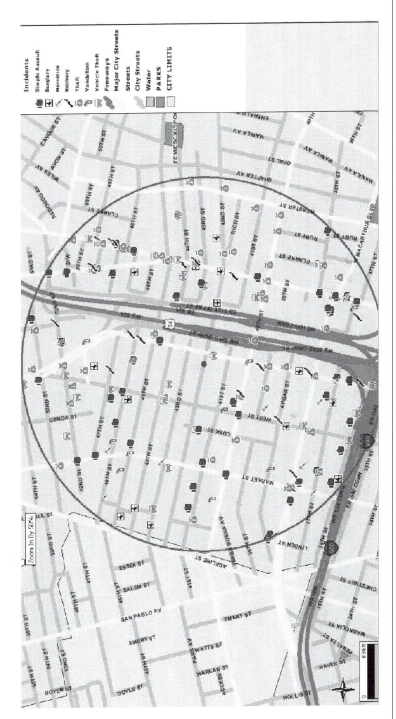

Figure 4.10 A descriptive clustering graph of crimes in Oakland, California.

stored in the free text format of investigator field reports that required the use of text-extracting and clustering software tools.

To illustrate the diversity of standard crime data sets and the challenges a forensic investigator is likely to experience, we provide a case study offered by Megaputer using their PolyAnalyst multialgorithm software suite, which supports both structured and unstructured analyses. As this case study demonstrates, there are strategies and tools for supporting these multiple types of analyses by machine learning forensic investigators.

Crime Pattern Analysis Case Study

Vijay Kollepara and Sergei Ananyan, Megaputer

INDUSTRY SITUATION

Building on the success of employing the analysis of structured data to help solve and prevent crimes, law enforcement and government organizations are seeking to expand the scope of their analysis to include unstructured text data. While typically over 80% of all information available to an organization resides in text form, the analysis has to date been primarily confined to only the structured portion of available data. Missing four out of every five bits of useful knowledge is a very high price to pay for the lack of efficient means for text analysis. An ability to perform in-depth analysis of text data could provide both corporate and government organizations with many new insights. Yet until recently, such analysis required significant manual labor of reading and coding text narratives; the process is too slow and prone to errors.

Today, new data and text mining technologies provide a next generation of tools for the analysis and visualization of both structured data and text. Such tools help increase the quality and productivity of the analysis and reduce the latency period between recording raw data and obtaining key knowledge necessary for making informed decisions.

CASE OVERVIEW

A police department had a large collection of police information reports (PIRs) that were filled out by officers at the time of recording incidents over a period of several years. The main portion of each PIR holds a text description of the incident. The department was seeking a capability to identify historical crime patterns from a large volume of unstructured data.

There are many questions investigators needed to get answered quickly:

- Are there correlations between the crime type and the location of the incident?
- What are the distributions of crime types involving suspects of different ethnic origin?
- How can I quickly extract reports characterized by certain parameters of interest? For example, robberies performed by white teenagers involving the knife threat.
- Are there correlations between the type of crime, weapon employed, and the location of the incident?
- What is the most typical weapon in cases when high school students are charged with weapon possession?

Traditionally, the process of finding answers to these questions involved the analysis confined only to the structured portion of the data, somewhat enhanced by an officer's ability to recollect relevant past cases and repetitive keyword-based searches of the text portions of reports. Manual analysis of all PIRs was a cumbersome, time-consuming process prone to errors and biases. New automated text analysis could help the agency quickly and consistently discover important patterns in crime occurrences and empower police officers and analysts to

- Learn from historical crime patterns, and enhance the crime resolution rate.
- Preempt future incidents by putting in place preventive mechanisms based on observed patterns.
- Reduce the training time for officers assigned to a new location and having no prior knowledge of site-specific crime patterns.

- Increase operational efficiency by optimally redeploying limited resources (such as personnel, equipment, etc.) to the right place at the right time.

METHODOLOGY

Megaputer Intelligence carried out an incident reports analysis project to demonstrate a complete analytical solution for processing a mix of structured data and text in incident reports. This case study discusses a methodology and sample results of discovering knowledge hidden in unstructured data. The project was carried out with the help of the data and text mining system PolyAnalyst™.

An overall objective was to create an analytical solution that investigators can routinely use to identify new patterns and associations between types of incidents, locations, time, and descriptive details of the incident. The developed approach consists of a series of steps (Figure 4.11):

- Preprocess data to a format suitable for further analysis.
- Extract important concepts and terms through text mining.
- Analyze patterns and co-occurrences of identified concepts.
- Develop an automated solution for crime pattern analysis.

DATA PREPROCESSING

The first step in creating an analytical solution involves understanding data and transforming it to a convenient format. The original PIR data was in the form of text documents and contained information entered by the investigating officer at the time of the incident. All this information was stored as unstructured text reports, singling out only the date the report was filed, the corresponding police station, and the classification of an event by a field officer filing the report. These text documents were parsed into a database format separating structured and unstructured portions of PIRs. Data was normalized.

CONCEPT EXTRACTION

The first type of text analysis starts with capturing key concepts and terms in text descriptions present in PIRs with the help of a text mining engine. This engine can run in an unsupervised mode,

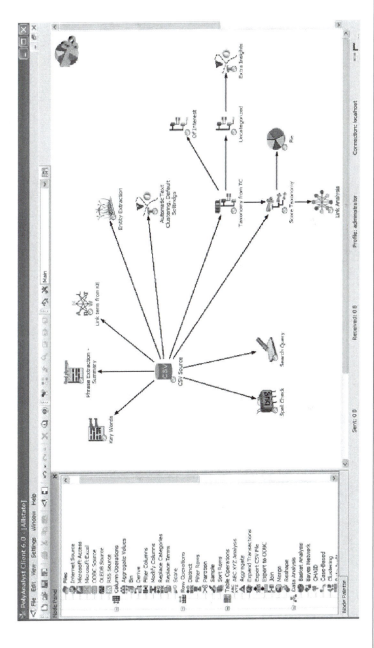

Figure 4.11 The Megaputer interface for launching multiple types of analyses.

when clusters of unusually frequently occurring terms are automatically discovered by the system, or a supervised mode, when the user focuses the analysis performed by a text mining engine to only primary topics of interest to the user.

A police investigator exploring historical reports might want to capture all terms related to weapons, narcotics, and schools and then check if there exist correlations between the discovered items and other crime characteristics (such as event type and location). This was achieved by focusing the PolyAnalyst Text Analysis engine to look for all particular instances of these broad category terms. The user does not have to manually specify all possible particular instances of weapons. Based on a comprehensive dictionary of English terms and semantic relations between them, the PolyAnalyst text mining engine automatically expands the search and finds all possible weapon-related terms in the collection of investigated police reports (Figure 4.12).

It proves quite useful that the system supports interactive drill-down from the discovered weapon-related terms to original records in the data with the corresponding terms highlighted. For example, one can quickly learn that while the term *pike* can potentially represent a medieval weapon, in all cases recorded by police officers the term *pike* represents a certain type of a highway (Leesburg Pike, Columbia Pike, etc.).

Correspondingly, the term *pike* can be excluded from the list of weapons discovered by the system in the investigated police reports. Similarly, the investigator can run the text mining engine to extract all particular instances of drugs or narcotics, as well as particular instances of *school*.

PATTERN ANALYSIS

In the next step of the analysis, all extracted terms were used for tagging individual reports, allowing further usage of these terms as new structured attributes of individual PIRs together with the original structured data: event type and location. Then, the PolyAnalyst Link Analysis engine was applied to reveal associations between the extracted terms and individual values of structured attributes and display a visual map of correlations between individual crime types, locations, weapons or narcotics involved, and school type mentioned.

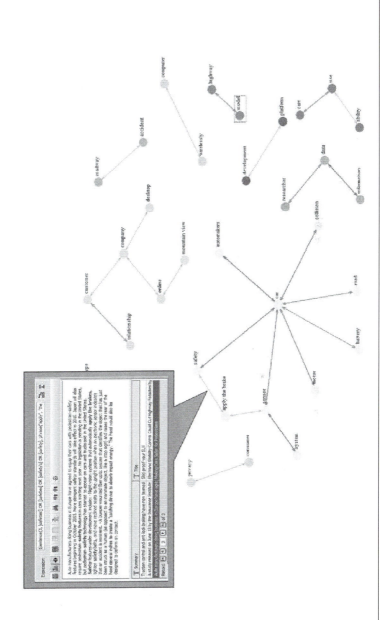

Figure 4.12 The clustering of concepts from free-form text.

TEXT OLAP

Law enforcement officers are often interested in seeing distributions of criminal events by location, type, weapon used, and other characteristics. This task is somewhat similar to OLAP analysis, which is widely used in the corporate world for the analysis of structured data. However, in the case of analysis of police reports, most of the information of interest is buried in unstructured text, and this causes failure of standard OLAP in addressing this task.

PolyAnalyst provides a unique Text OLAP engine capable of organizing a mix of text and structured data in interactively manipulated multidimensional cubes. The text OLAP engine allows the user to define a number of dimensions of interest that include information extracted from natural language text, in addition to regular structured attributes. This makes all information hidden in the text portion of reports available for quick and efficient manipulation, analysis, and reporting: a capability many investigators had dreamed of for a long time.

A matrix defining attributes and values will be used by the PolyAnalyst Text OLAP engine for analyzing PIR data. There is one dimension defined by values of a structured attribute—event type—and four more dimensions defined by values extracted from the main text portion of police reports: ethnicity and age of suspects, location of the incident and weapon used, the suspect ethnicity (which were defined as white, Asian, Hispanic, and black), possible age groups (such as suspects in their teens, twenties, thirties, forties, and fifties), and most frequent incident locations. It is interesting to note that the system was again instructed to search for all particular types of weapons, and returned back all specific types of weapons mentioned in the investigated collection of police reports automatically.

Upon applying the developed Dimension Matrix to data, the system generated an interactive Text OLAP report allowing the user to see distributions of data records across different dimensions, drill-down to subsets of records matching all selected criteria, browse through the corresponding original text records with the terms of interest highlighted, and shift around the order of dimensions of interest.

The user can derive a wealth of information from each view of the Text OLAP report. For example, from this report, one can first observe that out of 540 investigated reports, in 73 cases suspects were described as black, in 47 as white, in 31 as Hispanic, and in 11 as Asian. Drilling down to see the distribution of Event Types involving black suspects, one immediately sees that the most frequent crime type for this group of suspects is Robbery: 52 out of 73 events. All other event types lag robbery by a wide margin. Continuing the drill-down process on robbery events and selecting further branches of interest, one sees that the majority of these robberies involve suspects in their twenties who confront victims when they approach their cars, and display guns before demanding money (Figure 4.13).

The analyst can save all records supporting an investigated drill-down node to an HTML report maintaining the highlighting of terms found by the Text OLAP engine. Such reports listing all records of interest help quickly substantiate recommendations made for decision makers.

Being an interactive decision support tool, PolyAnalyst Text OLAP report allows the analyst to quickly change the focus of the analysis and drill down on other branches of the report or change the order of the defined dimensions to obtain different views of the data.

For example, while robbery is still a number one crime performed by white suspects in the considered county (15 cases out of 47), a relative share of this crime type compared to others is quite low compared to cases involving black suspects. On the other hand, for white suspects there appears a second widespread Event type—Exposure, which occurs almost as frequently as Robbery: 9 cases out of 47. It is interesting to note that in the majority of these cases the age of the suspects is not being reported.

Then, by simply changing the order of defined dimensions in the report, one can read other valuable information directly from the same Text OLAP report. For example, the analysis found that, overall, the most frequent crimes in the investigated PIRs are Robbery (117 out of 540 cases) followed by malicious wounding (30 cases). An investigator interested in the distribution of weapon possession events can immediately learn that a vast majority of

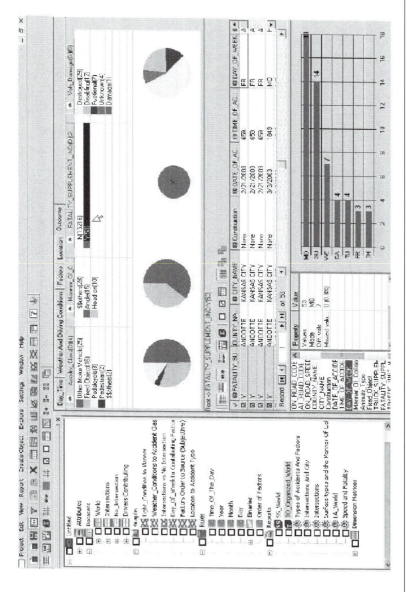

Figure 4.13   PolyAnalyst provides an assortment of reports, views, and charts.

them occur at school (16 out of 18 cases) and most frequently involve either a knife (6 cases) or bb gun (6 cases).

Previously, these types of observations were based only on the experience of local investigators. Now, such conclusions cannot only be made based on new observed patterns but can also be easily substantiated with immediate drill-down to the highlighted text of the relevant reports.

To sum up, we have seen how pattern analysis can be easily performed on large volumes of data containing a mix of structured data and text collected by a law enforcement agency. The ability to quickly draw meaningful conclusions from the analysis of text data becomes an invaluable tool for educating newly inducted officers about historical trends at particular locations, generating aggregate views of data for better decision making, and helping in the allocation of critical resources to appropriate areas.

AUTOMATION

The entire process of pattern extraction and visualization can be automated to a large degree, so that the results of the analysis are easily derived and shared by many users across the organization. It is also possible to interface the discussed analytical techniques with existing IT systems. An access to an easy-to-manipulate front-end implementing the collection of related interactive visual reports with powerful data and text mining engines embedded in the background empowers investigators with a new capability to quickly arrive at reliable conclusions based on objective analysis of large volumes of unstructured data.

CONCLUSION

The considered case illustrates an overall process for implementing a text mining solution and proves the feasibility and value of performing simultaneous analyses of both text and structured data within the same software system.

The discovered results help investigators identify hidden patterns through the automated analysis of historical police reports. To date, this knowledge was largely dependent on local expertise (so called "local veterans"). Moreover, the new approach to the analysis delivers a much more comprehensive and objective overall picture of the incidents as it involves evaluating both structured and textual portions of the database.

Law enforcement agencies and government organizations can benefit from this combination of text mining and pattern analysis technologies by achieving:

- Improved crime resolution rate
- Optimal resource allocation based on dynamically changing patterns
- Faster and more up-to-date results from raw data
- Reduced officer training time and costs
- Better crime prediction and prevention of offenses

Both government and corporate organizations are now redefining the boundaries of traditional analytical solutions that were to date centered on analyzing only structured data. Decisions made are now based on the analysis of all available data, including the most information-rich text portion of the data, rather than on subjective analysis relying primarily on analysts' experience. As compared to the previously employed manual knowledge discovery process, modern analytical tools help accomplish superior analytical projects a hundred times faster, while consuming less than 10% of previously required resources. Text mining is becoming the cornerstone technology in the formation of a new intelligent organization.

4.6 From Induction to Deduction

Deductive forensics is a technique that models historical data with a different objective than inductive forensics, where unsupervised learning is the mode of discovery. Deductive forensics is most interested in predicting criminal outcomes or fraudulent events. This type of predictive analysis is a valuable ability for identifying when and where criminal activity will take place, and in what format. This capability is absolutely needed because most digital crimes occur in microseconds: detection systems using predictive rules from these types of analyses are a requirement for machine learning forensics.

Deductive forensics is the activity of determining what is going to happen in the future by closely scrutinizing historical data and identifying trends, making correlations, and discovering predilections. Activities that can be performed prior to deductive analyses are link analysis, text mining, and inductive clustering. These tools and technologies are a form of data compression allowing forensic investigators to focus their attention on specific criminal behaviors.

Deductive forensics involves a proactive approach rather than the reactive approach of traditional law enforcement activities. Deductive forensics via decision trees uncovers problems before they occur so that enforcement organizations can proactively prevent instead of reactively fixing criminal behaviors and activities. For example, these technologies and tools can be used for fraud detection: to identify anomalies in credit card activity or insurance claims activity so that fraud and abuse are detected early and losses are minimized.

In the end, the use of all of these techniques allows the forensic investigator to do forecasting: identify trends by analyzing historical crime data and predict similar future behaviors and events. This propensity analysis is possible by leveraging techniques such as decision trees, clustering, Bayesian networks, and other advanced analytical algorithms to calculate predilection or predisposition. For law enforcement personnel, the only thing better than catching the bad guys who commit crimes is catching them *before* they actually commit the crime, which the machine learning forensic investigator can discover, enabling them to tell law enforcement personnel when and where a particular crime is going to occur.

Deductive forensics can provide an agency, department, or organization the "when and where" of criminal activities, but there are two fundamental elements that must exist before any analysis can take place: relevant historical criminal data must be electronically stored in a data structure that enables analytical processing; typically, this is not a problem. Next, all data related to crime and criminal activity must be integrated in a common data structure.

At a minimum, the forensic investigator needs various attributes from the city's law enforcement, jail, courts, juvenile records, and geographic information system (GIS) data in the same place. The most common data structure for intense analytical processing that covers these two fundamental needs is called a *dimensional data warehouse*. A dimensional data warehouse combines the data from all of the various sources and then organizes the data into facts (statistics, amounts, etc.) and dimensions (time, place, grouping, etc.). With criminal data, the most common fact is simply a count of the occurrence of a crime. However, there are many important dimensions, such as date/time of crime, location of crime, offender name, and many criminal-related codes used to classify crime types.

Dimensions tell you the "when and the where" as well as the "who and what," and much more. Thus, the forensic investigation can feed the stored years of historical criminal data into a dimensional data model, which quite simply identifies trends. For example, it may discover that most car thefts occur between midnight and 2 am on weeknights in hotel parking lots. Armed with that information, an investigator can instruct on-duty law enforcement officers to frequent hotel parking lots more often between midnight and 2 am on weeknights. The same forensic analysis may discover that 90% of all city burglaries occur at midday in certain city blocks, or the discovery that most network intrusions using DoS techniques take place between 3 and 5 am.

These forensic models, however, become much more sensitive and revealing when external data sets are merged with this purely criminal data. For example, what are the income and education levels of burglars on the midday criminal sprees? What are the educational paths most homegrown terrorists take? All of these factors can assist the forensic investigator in developing robust analyses and clusters. The same dimensional data structure can be used to learn which criminal profiles will be more likely to commit certain crimes or which prevention programs are most effective with would-be criminals. Machine learning forensics can be used to discern criminal patterns and identify possible suspects. In addition, forensics can be used to match suspects to crimes by examining career criminal files, suspect vehicle files, probation and parole reports, and field interrogation files. In addition, behavioral forensics can be leveraged for target profiling by analyzing victim and premises data.

Lastly, some forensic investigators have used SOMs to cluster unsolved crimes and then match them to criminals' method of operations; discovering patterns that can match time of day, time of week, points of entry, and guilt by method of criminal behavior. What makes this interesting for the machine learning forensic investigator is leveraging all of these knowledge discovery models with real-time networks. Agent technologies, for example, are distributed software components that can realign processes to meet goals without intervention: so, if the agent's goal is to detect crime, it will do so in a totally autonomous manner. The goal of the forensic investigator is to assemble such systems for autonomous, silent, swift, and precise detection of criminal behaviors and attacks. For the clustering of crimes and incidents, it is simply knowing when things do not look right and focusing attention on the anomaly or outliers.

5

Deductive Forensics

Anticipating Attacks and Precrime

5.1 Artificial Intelligence and Machine Learning

As early as the 1950s, the quest for computer systems that can learn has been a vision of those involved in the field of artificial intelligence and machine learning. However, it was not until the advent in the 1980s of new algorithms coupled with increased computing power that the vision of machine learning was realized via symbolic classifiers such as decision trees, neural networks, and genetic algorithms. A new generation of researchers began to develop machine learning algorithms such as C4.5 and CART for the classification of arbitrary classes of objects on real-world problems such as segmentation and prediction.

Machine learning forensics is not so much a single technique as much as a "hybrid" approach, which uses multiple algorithms and tools such as link analysis, text analytics, clustering, and decision trees to discover hidden knowledge from multiple data sources. It is important that the forensic investigator be aware that no single algorithm can solve the problem of knowledge discovery; some algorithms will perform well on some part of the data set, whereas others are useless. The important fact is that these algorithms, such as decision trees, scale up very well for large data sets, which increasingly are the norm in most organizations.

It is vital to counsel with domain experts during the course of organizing a strategy as to the data sources and algorithm to be used in forensic investigations. Human guidance and experience are a major component of a digital forensic investigation; at every juncture, consulting with the client is essential to ensure that the machine learning tools are being used properly and with the maximum chance of success. Behavioral forensics will always rely on human expertise coupled with the brute analysis of machine learning algorithms.

Another advantage of decision trees, or rule generators, is that they lend themselves to easy interpretation so that decision makers can readily grasp the graphs and rules they generate, which is not the case with other machine learning algorithms such as back-propagation neural networks, which generate "black box" formulas that contain no information on how they arrived at their solution. The single exception is the SOM neural network, which by design allows for free-form unsupervised learning via autonomous clustering and the generation of easy-to-comprehend clusters and graphs.

In addition, symbolic classifiers such as C4.5, CHAID, and CART and other proprietary decision trees tools outperform neural networks or statistical regression when it comes to analyzing corporate data sets, which typically contain numeric and categorical attributes such as gender, married status, etc. This, coupled with their transparency in explaining their finding in a simple set of conditional rules, make them ideal for the presentation of the finding to decision makers. A major multinational, multi-industry, multi-data sets project known as StatLog during the 1990s concluded after comparing several classification algorithms that symbolic classifiers were superior in the classification of corporate data sets to regression and neural networks. It is important that the forensic investigator be flexible and be prepared to develop hybrid solutions, detection systems, and investigations using various techniques and algorithms.

5.2 Decision Trees

Decision trees are powerful machine learning algorithms that use a treelike graph of decisions and their possible consequences, and are a descriptive means for calculating conditional probabilities. A decision tree takes as input an object or situation described by a set of properties; the outputs can be a yes/no binary decision, or it can be a continuous value. Some decision trees can also have multiple branches. When a businessperson, marketer, or a forensic investigator needs to make a decision based on several factors, a decision tree can help identify which factors to consider and how each factor has historically been associated with different outcomes of the decision, such as a legal transaction versus a fraudulent transaction. Modern decision tree tools are highly robust and intuitive; their interfaces are easy to navigate and use, and their segmentation results can readily be inspected for quick insight into the partitioning of the target variable (Figure 5.1).

Machine learning forensics involves using these types of software tools, which produce decision trees that create graphical models and text rules which can both predict behavior and explain patterns. The key benefit to all is the generated graphs and rules, which end users can easily understand and apply. For example, given one attribute (e.g., fraud), a decision tree can be used to try to predict the value of new customers, visitors, or shoppers who may be criminals by examining some of the other available attributes, such as the number of website visits, types of payment, types of products being purchased, the visitors' GPS location, etc.

This can be accomplished by examining all other attributes via machine learning iterations in which these independent attributes are measured in terms of their "information gain." In machine learning, this concept can be used to define a preferred sequence of attributes to investigate—that is, which of these variables contribute to predicting the dependent variable of fraud the investigator is trying to predict, via a decision tree tool. Almost always, a few attributes can be discovered to provide high information gain and should be preferred to other attributes—this type of analysis is a form of information compression.

One common technique for machine learning investigators is to use decision trees to eliminate a high number of attributes from, say, a fraud investigation. To accomplish this, the investigator can start with hundreds of attributes and, through the use of decision trees, eliminate many of them in order to focus just on those with the highest information gain, as they pertain to predicting fraud in future transactions from new unseen data purchases. Decision trees are the single most popular machine learning tools because they are easy to understand, easy to implement, easy to use, and computationally cheap. The elimination of nonpredictive variables is an important technique for the forensic investigator because being able to use only a limited number of predictive variables is important when trying to construct compact reactive real-time detection systems.

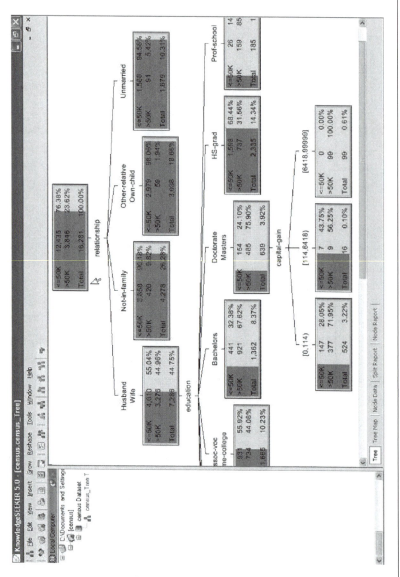

Figure 5.1   Decision tree segmentation of income according to the most important predictors.

A particularly efficient method for producing classifiers from historical data is to generate a set of multiple decision trees to explore all possible search spaces. They are a supervised learning method for uncovering what drives crimes and criminal behaviors from a set of inputs samples. Greedy search methods of decision trees typically involve growing and pruning different decision tree structures to explore the exponential space for possible detection models. Some early decision trees worked only with categorical attributes, while others used only numeric variables; today, however, most tools work with both. Since this is a supervised method of modeling, a training data set must first be used to develop a tree structure—next, a test data set unseen earlier is exposed to the tree structure—and error rates are computed that most modern decision tree software tools support via their internal instrumentation.

The algorithms used to subdivide the data in decision tree models seek to find those variables or fields in the data set that provide maximum segregation of the data records. Any field in the data set may theoretically be chosen as the important "clue" in a forensic investigation, but the field is only useful if it successfully divides the records. In the vernacular of information theory, the objective is to let the algorithms select those variables that provide the most information and that reduce the most uncertainty.

Information theory provides a mathematical means of formalizing the transmission of information that reduces uncertainty. Information theory defines the possibilities and their probabilities within a problem space; it allows the forensic investigator to calculate the amount of relevant information transmitted for any illegal event or criminal transaction. For the investigators, decision tree tools enable them to calibrate the information that is transmitted whenever the numbers of possible alternatives are reduced. When an investigator discovers that some alternatives are more likely than others, then less uncertainty about the outcome of events exists, and less reduction of uncertainty is possible.

5.3 Decision Tree Techniques

Decision trees are designed to be classifiers. In classification, there is always a target variable (e.g., fraud, intrusion, theft, risk, etc.) that is partitioned into predetermined classes or categories variables and grouped into classes such as high, medium, and low. So, for the machine learning forensic investigator, the first step in using decision tree is to randomly split a data set being used to create a model into both training and testing data subsets. Once the decision tree is in place, the investigator will want to evaluate its performance. This is commonly accomplished by testing the tree model with a new data set not used for training; at this juncture the investigator uses the unseen test data set to evaluate the accuracy of the decision tree predictions.

For each extracted rule, the investigator can measure how often the submitted test data records are properly classified. The investigator at this point can begin to compute the error rate of the entire tree as a weighted sum of the error rates for all the individual leaves of the model. The investigator can now observe the error rates and computational efficiency so that he or she can incrementally improve the model by pruning the tree to get rid of less useful rules. Thus, the investigator may want to prioritize the most important attributes and rules represented by the decision tree. Some rules and attributes will be very important for predicting criminal behaviors.

On the other hand, the investigator will gain further insight by discovering that certain attributes and rules may be nonsensical in the context of the investigation, and so will be of little use. In these cases, some attributes and rules can be eliminated from the tree and the forensic investigation. The dearth of data in these trees may be quite informative for the investigator, since that in itself may be a clue as to the failure of certain attributes to be predictive and fail to find a pattern in that investigation. The investigator can now narrow the focus of the query on only those rules or attributes that are of value in predicting criminal behaviors. Failure is just as important as success; it may force the investigators to ask whether they are posing the right question from the data. Depending on the failure to find good results, the investigation may change the direction of the analysis and question what additional data sources need to be included for the creation of a more predictive tree.

The decision tree tools can work directly with standard spreadsheet forms or related databases; some tools can process coded categorical features without explicitly preparing them as multiple true-or-false binary features. Modern tools can also handle missing values through automatically generated surrogates. As mentioned earlier, decision tree algorithms rely on recursive partitioning of the data by picking the predictive best features to separate the data and repeating the process on a subdivision of a data set. Lastly, many variations are possible, including binary and multiple trees, which can be pruned by the investigator to reduce a tree's size and complexity.

Tree induction is well suited for high-dimensional applications such as fraud detection and the mapping of other criminal behaviors. Decision trees are the fastest nonlinear prediction method for dynamic feature extraction and selection. Trees can take advantage of various types of data reduction and incremental forensic case analysis. The size of the completed tree, expressed as a number of terminal nodes, is a measure of the complexity of a forensic solution.

Less complex solutions are found by pruning cases in the training data; this is accomplished by removing nonpredictive attributes and measuring error rates on progressively smaller trees. There are many ways of pruning a tree, for example, by significance testing at varying levels. Most decision tree methods provide for automatic complexity adjustment either by testing many trees of different sizes or by pruning to a fixed significance level. The main point to remember is that tree induction is by far the fastest prediction method (Figure 5.2).

The main advantage of decision trees is that they are logic-based solutions with strong explanatory capabilities. Small compact trees are highly interpretable and intuitive for humans to instantly discover how attributes are interrelated in large data sets under investigation. Decision trees are fast and usually produce high-quality solutions for forensic investigators and their clients. Decision trees and rules are related logical representations. Rules, however, are equally expressive and may be preferred because their solutions are often simpler and more intuitive. Any decision tree can be represented as a set of decision rules that may not overlap. Of all the prediction methods, decision rules have the greatest potential for managing missing values because of the overlapping, disjunctive rules. Missing values in data sets are quite valuable in fraud detection investigations.

Decision trees are useful for the forensic investigator who must deal with incoming data records and future transactions of uncertain quality; spurious results are obvious in the explicit rules. The rules

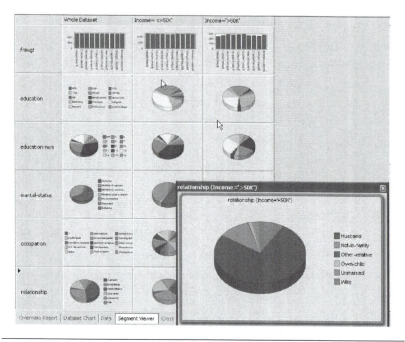

Figure 5.2 The results of decision trees can be graphically viewed in many dimensions.

themselves can be expressed easily as logic statements, in multiple language codes, such as SQL, C+, Java, etc., so they can be applied directly to new records and transactions. Because of the nature of forensic investigations, it is vital that rules can be used as evidence to demonstrate to the satisfaction of, say, a court of law, regarding the processing of an empirical field investigation and the method of detection from multiple attributes and rules.

Forensic investigators need to ensure that they take the time to know the data they are working with: the data detective needs to understand the definition of each field attribute, and how it is used by the client organization. If a working data dictionary does not exist, this intelligence must be obtained through interviews with those who created and use the data. The investigator must have access to domain experts and their working expertise. If the investigator is not a practitioner in the field of analysis from where the data originated, he or she may not be able to appreciate which rules are important and which relationships within or between attributes should be made explicit. Predicting the future is one of the most important applications of machine learning forensics.

5.4 Rule Generators

Rule induction and decision trees are related approaches to discovering logical patterns within data sets. Although rules and decision trees may seem similar at first, they are in fact quite different both in terms of the information they discover from databases and in terms of their behavior with new data items. In essence, decision trees may be viewed as a simplistic approach to rule discovery. Rule induction is yet another field from the area of machine learning in which formal rules are extracted from a set of observations. The rules extracted may represent a full scientific model of the data, or merely represent local patterns in the data.

In decision theory, a decision rule is a function that maps an observation to an appropriate action. Decision rules play an important role in the theory of statistics and economics, and are closely related to the concept of a strategy in game theory. However, decision rules can also be used for fraud detection and intrusion detection for the forensic investigator. In order to evaluate the usefulness of a decision rule, it is necessary to have a loss function detailing the outcome of each action under different states.

There are also other algorithms for generating rules that include association rule learning, which is a popular and well-researched method for discovering interesting relations between variables in large databases. Association rules are most commonly used in "market basket" analysis by retailers. They are used for analyzing and describing strong rules discovered in databases using different measures of interestingness. Association rules are used for discovering regularities between products in large-scale transaction data recorded by point-of-sale (POS) systems in supermarkets; for example, they are used to examine what shoppers buy in combination, such as

```
IF sale of ONIONS
AND sale of POTATOTES
THEN sale of BEEF 76% Probability
```

This information can be used by retailers to organize their product lines in their shelves and stores. Association rules can also be applied to the field of forensic investigations such as intrusion detection and other types of criminal behavior where the discovery of one rule or feature is associated with another in tandem. The following case study is presented by XpertRule software and demonstrates the application of predictive rules in a real-world scenario:

An XpertRule Case Study Breaking the Rules

Martin Baldock

Operations Director, Kroll OnTrack Legal Technologies

For many auditors, testing of controls forms a major part of the audit year. Controls are designed and put in place to, perhaps, segregate duties; rules are agreed between businesses and audit not only to limit risk but also to permit commercial transactions to take place. A typical rule might be that for purchases above £2000 a director's signature is required. One might, therefore, assume that data mining techniques, such as rule induction, would form an important part of the internal auditor's computer-assisted auditing techniques (CAATs) toolkit. If you can think of the question, then you do not need data analytics, so you may well not need this type of technique. However, I think advanced data analytics is vital if you want to do much wider testing of controls across large data sets, rather than just taking a sample.

RULE INDUCTION

Rule induction software comes in many guises, often as part of a suite of tools. Although not a recommendation, a product I have used in the past is XpertMiner from XpertRule software, and I will be using this for my examples.

At the most basic level, rule induction software, when run against a data set with default settings, simply sorts and filters a database on criteria set by the user. Most systems attempt to divide the data into branches with yes or no tests on certain attributes contained in the data. These branches or divisions of the data result in a treelike structure; software that uses decision trees attempts to classify or group the transactions together into sets.

Also, as I have said before, just having a great tool is not enough. Around 60% to 70% of your time and effort will be spent getting the data you want to examine imported and in the correct form. Most tools in this space have great data import screens; XpertMiner is no exception. It has a number of filters and routines that you can apply to the data almost as simply as representing a diagram as a process flow. The user can, with a simple drag-and-drop mechanism, build a sophisticated import mechanism, including bespoke filters and operations. The import into these tools is also very fast—this product took only seconds to load a million records onto my standard laptop.

Having got the data into the tool, there are many things you can do with it. For me, the most useful in an audit sense is the tree profiling technique. The "Tree Miner" in XpertMiner has automatic induction, making it very easy to discover rules and patterns in data. Conversely, there are many instances where the auditor will have great knowledge of the data set, perhaps from a previous audit. In these cases, tools similar to this often allow the user to interact with the rule induction process to force knowledge extraction based on statistical information.

It has to be remembered that we often do not have the time or resource to investigate every minor anomaly, and it is therefore necessary to focus on the high-risk areas. Using the interactive capability, the auditor can add splits on each node of the tree to get a better understanding of the rule discovery process, or use a process of guided queries to explore how the frequencies divide into each path.

What I really like about this sort of product is the graphical display. The information in the screenshot is simple loan application data and shows, based on historical information, whether a loan application should be accepted or not. The same technique could be used on purchase ledger data, stock control, or even call centre data. If this technique was applied, without any preconceived ideas or expected rules imposed, the data itself would show whether controls were being bypassed. For me, this type of technique makes computer audit an exciting field to work in and really helps remove the drudgery of tick and bash audit techniques of the past. The way I like to look at testing is that if you can think of the tests, then so can the bad guys: use these types of understandable data mining techniques, and you may well be ahead of the game.

As auditors you may have to check areas of the business where you have little knowledge of the underlying technical decision-making process. For example, using rule induction techniques you could look at maintenance and repair schedules, allowing the software and data content to show what rules are in place. These actual rules—that is, what really happens—could then be audited against procedures. Payments of any kind will have some form of process surrounding them, whether it is a sign-off level or a segregation of duties; these types of scenario are ideal for rule-based techniques and quickly and graphically show any anomalies.

If the same analysis is run every year and the rules have not changed, then it may be possible to compare the resulting tree diagrams, which would highlight any issues quickly. Likewise, branch comparison may be possible simply by comparing the pattern produced by the tree mining process.

5.5 Decision Tree Tools

- *Alice d'Isoft,* a streamlined version of ISoft's decision-tree-based AC2 data mining product, is designed for mainstream business users. This decision tree software is both powerful and has an intuitive easy-to-use interface that allows the creation of segmentation models by forensic investigators. The software makes it possible for the user to explore data online interactively and directly. As simple to use as a table, Alice d'ISoft is an ideal tool for the forensic investigator; it does not require any previous statistical skills. It allows, in complete autonomy, for rapid development of decision tree analyses, and then, the improvement of their pertinence (Figure 5.3).

  ISOFT also provides what it calls a *FraudManager* module; these are some of its features and capabilities:

  Electronic fraud is a growing risk for a great number of enterprises. A well-known example is the falsification of credit cards. Unfortunately, banks are not the only companies affected by this problem. Commercial cell phone sites, medical declarations,

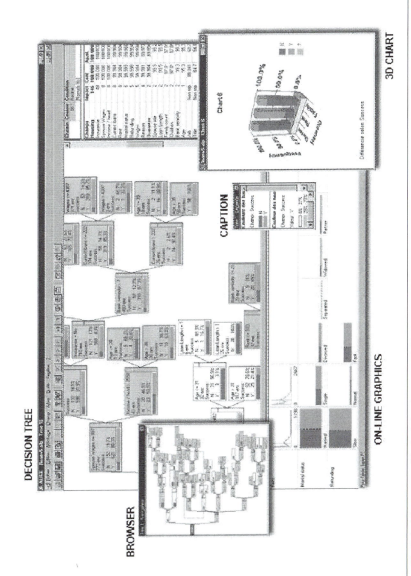

Figure 5.3 Alice d'Isoft decision tree graphics include a browser and 3D chart.

insurance payment and network intrusion: electronic fraud is affecting more and more sectors of activity.

The advent of these new cyber criminals is to a great extent linked to the development of information systems by companies and the progressive replacement of paper transactions by electronic transactions (check, credit card). Computer systems are not sheltered from breaches, and the fraudsters have the time and imagination to keep up.

Recent cases of fraud allow two observations:

1. The swindlers are becoming professional. This is no longer just about isolated individuals, but more and more it is about structured groups with significant means at their disposal.

2. The scams are no longer just large occasional attacks, but there are also numerous transactions of small amounts lost in the shuffle and more difficult to get back.

Tools proposed to fight against this new fraud must therefore be more and more sophisticated and offer a high level of dynamism. Electronic fraud is difficult to detect and requires adequate tools. Fraud is a generally diluted phenomenon. Detecting fraudulent transactions is like looking for a needle in a haystack.

A tool to fight against fraud must have the capacity to process large quantities of data rapidly and easily. Then, it must identify fraudulent transactions with a weak ratio of error (false positives). Indeed, imagine what a disaster it would be to label a good customer as a swindler.

Finally, criminals have a recognized capacity to rapidly modify their questionable behavior. The fraud control solution must ensure dynamism by offering sufficient flexibility of use. The efficiency of a solution to fight fraud depends on the methodology proposed to put it to work. For every establishment fighting against fraud, the stakes are high. It comes down to effectively diminishing risk without limiting the market, its level of service, or penalizing its good customers.

- *Angoss KnowledgeSEEKER* provides risk analysts with data processing, analysis, and knowledge discovery capabilities to better segment and understand behaviors. KnowledgeSEEKER is one of the most powerful, robust, and accurate decision tree tools in the marketplace.

Angoss also offers *ClaimGUARD*, an application for predictive claims fraud and an abuse detection solution: it provides a suite of analytics capabilities and domain expertise to reduce and prevent the costs of fraudulent or abusive transactions for health care and benefits insurance.

Another module from Angoss, its *Credit Lifecycle* solutions, extends industry-standard credit evaluation tools with analytics scores resulting from a more strategic use of your own customer and transactional data. Through the mining of existing data and the creation of proprietary scores and scorecards to target new opportunities for growth, lending organizations and credit departments are able to improve their ability to proactively manage and optimize the risk/reward choices for individual lending decisions, and across their portfolios (Figure 5.4).

- *C5.0/See5* constructs classifiers in the form of decision trees and rule sets. It includes the latest innovations such as boosting.
- *CART 5.0 decision-tree software* provides advanced facilities for data analytics, data preprocessing, and predictive modeling including bagging and arcing. Salford Systems' flagship software, CART, is a robust, easy-to-use decision tree that automatically sifts large, complex databases, searching for an isolating significant patterns and relationships. This discovered knowledge is then used to generate reliable, easy-to-grasp

Key Features of KnowledgeSEEKER

Data Discovery   Advanced Visualization   Decision Trees

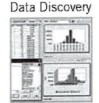 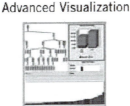 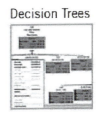

Figure 5.4 Angoss decision tree tool KnowledgeSEEKER.

predictive models for applications such as detecting credit card fraud and managing credit risk.

Designed for both nontechnical and technical business users, CART can quickly reveal important data relationships that could remain hidden using other analytical tools. The most recent release includes modeling automation technology that dramatically accelerates the process of generating accurate and robust models; CART is currently in use in major web applications.

Technically, classification and regression trees (CART) is based on landmark mathematical theory introduced in 1984 by four world-renowned statisticians at Stanford University and the University of California at Berkeley. Salford Systems' implementation of CART is the only decision tree software embodying the proprietary code written by CART co-author Professor Jerome H. Friedman.

The CART creators continue to collaborate with Salford Systems to enhance CART with proprietary advances. With CART 6.0 ProEX, Salford has introduced patented extensions to CART specifically designed to enhance results for market research and web analytics. CART supports high-speed deployment, allowing its models to predict and score in real time on a massive scale, an important feature for the forensic investigator.

- *Citrus Technology Replay Professional* features a highly visual interface for quickly building a decision tree on any data set, from any database. One can explore, analyze, define, and reuse decision trees within minutes. As with many of these software tools, a free evaluation copy is available from their website.

- *DTREG* can generate both classification and regression decision trees, depending on whether the target variable is continuous or categorical; the software can find the optimal tree size automatically and supports variable costs, priors, and variable weights. A free download demo is available.

- *Palisade PrecisionTree* can generate decision trees and influence diagrams directly from Excel spreadsheets.

- *PolyAnalyst* includes an information gain decision tree among its 11 machine learning algorithms.
- *SPSS AnswerTree*, an easy-to-use package with CHAID and other decision tree algorithms, includes decision tree export in XML format.
- *XpertRule Miner* (Attar Software) provides graphical decision trees with the ability to embed as ActiveX components.

An XpertRule Case Study for Detecting In-Store Fraud at M+W Retailer

"Although many find the subject embarrassing or fear that it might upset staff, we feel that it is important to protect honest staff and safeguard the viability of each store. Ultimately, that protects everyone's jobs." That is how Les Mitchell Hynd, Information Systems Director at convenience store group M+W, describes the importance of measures to reduce fraud among staff. M+W has adopted a progressive approach to dealing with the problem and, among other measures, has recently implemented expert systems technology. It is a problem area that many retail and service companies are shy about acknowledging publicly. But, with in-store theft typically accounting for 1% of turnover and staff theft accounting for three quarters of this loss, it is a problem that begs for an effective solution.

M+W's reported turnover for 1995 was over UK £100m, and the company has seen rapid expansion over recent years. Although Frederick Misselbrook ("M") and Arthur W Weston ("W") opened their first shop in 1870, it was not until 1976 that the firm opened its first experimental convenience store in Southampton, England. Last year saw M+W open its 150th store, and there are now 170 spread between Bristol and the Wash, with a concentration in the South and London. The stores, which range from corner shops to small supermarkets, offer a wide range of merchandise and services and are open 7 days a week from early until late. As a result, there are temptations for dishonest employees—particularly, since quieter periods of trade may involve little in-store supervision of staff.

Les Mitchell Hynd comments: "Thankfully, most of our staff are very honest, but there is a significant percentage who could be subject to temptation. We ensure that, when staff are employed, they are made aware that we use sophisticated security methods to monitor their activity. Even if this discourages most from dishonest behavior, a single thief may take £1000 of goods in a single week." He also points out that, to some extent, in-store theft has almost become institutionalized: "It can be difficult to draw a clear line between the member of staff who takes a can of Coke on a hot day or a few sweets from the "Pick and Mix" and the one who carries out a series of thefts involving £3–£4000 worth of goods."

M+W has acquired a reputation for advanced thinking in the convenience store sector of the retail trade. The company began implementing EPoS (electronic point of sale) technology in 1989 across all stores—a process that was completed by 1992. Stores are now equipped with bar-code scanning equipment and PC tills that download data overnight to the Southampton head office. The value of M+W's EPoS experience is reflected in the fact that the firm is actively marketing its 7 years worth of EPoS data to suppliers and other operators in the sector. Les Mitchell Hynd believes that antifraud systems can have more immediate impact than EPoS sales data: "The gradual roll-out of EPoS systems means that early sales statistics are not 100% reliable. It takes time before the information has a real commercial value. By contrast, security measures have an immediate impact on the bottom line—even if only a fraction of the fraud cases are being detected at the outset."

M+W took the decision to introduce a so-called Son-of-EPoS system, which captured certain exceptional transactions from the till data at each store (low-value goods, voids, cancellations, refunds, and other transactions). Area managers, who were equipped with laptop PCs, were then able to capture this information and ask pertinent questions about the previous day's till activity. "As well as keeping staff on their toes, a steady stream of general assistants and store management left the company's employment—often in the back of a police car," recalls Les Mitchell Hynd. However, this approach required area managers (typically with responsibility for 10–12 stores) to trawl through the data looking for suspect transactions. "Although they were generally very diligent in carrying out this task, the additional pressures caused by the company's rapid expansion and increasingly high staff turnover meant that the system was not being used to its full effect."

Les Mitchell Hynd had previous experience of working with expert systems and was able to research the potential of this technology as part of his studies for an MSc qualification. By gathering knowledge from an expert—knowledge elicitation—a series of rules can be determined for analyzing till transactions, which help to highlight suspicious transactions. Knowledge elicitation involved a series of interviews with one of M+Ws security officers, who was also an ex-police officer and had a background in crime pattern analysis. He was asked to comment on a series of transaction details from the existing database and then on the database of rules that was determined by the system. The software chosen for the task was XpertRule—a PC and Windows-based software development tool capable of capturing domain knowledge and expressing this graphically as a series of structured decision tasks. "The system was easy to use, required very little programming, and allowed us to be up and running within a few weeks" says Les Mitchell Hynd.

The security officer who provided the initial knowledge for the system has since left the company to take up a more senior position elsewhere. M+W's operations director considered that the XpertRule system was sufficiently effective for the departing expert to be replaced by two part-time staff (both past store managers) who now run the system on a PC located in an office above one of M+W's Southampton outlets. Two-week batches of data from each store are fed into the system in the form of an ASCII file, and XpertRule runs the analysis in a matter of minutes. "Because the software is easy to use and graphical, it means we can make the most of staff knowledge about convenience store management and reduce the need for IT expertise," says Les Mitchell Hynd. Reports provided by the XpertRule system are followed up by M+W's one remaining security officer and the 15 area managers.

The XpertRule system identifies transactions that are potentially suspicious: Low-value transactions of one or two pence; refunds, voids, and cancellations equal to the selling price of popular brands of cigarettes; and high value, self-authorized refunds, for example. Les Mitchell Hynd comments: "Because of the nature of the business, it is impossible to look at any single transaction and declare that it is definitely fraudulent without corroborative evidence. This might take the form of videotape recordings, an interview with the till operator concerned or further manual checks carried out by a member of the management team."

Although the expert system may not be the final arbiter of guilt or innocence, it does focus M+W's investment of management time. Since the system was introduced in late 1995, around 150 cases of staff fraud have been identified. This compares with 25 more serious cases for a similar previous period. Les Mitchell Hynd comments: "We find that one thing can lead to another and that a simple mistake might encourage later dishonesty. By homing in on problems quickly, it allows us to give warnings early on and to prevent more serious problems."

Given the early results and the estimated scale of the problem (currently £750,000 per annum), the XpertRule system has been remarkably cost-effective. Les Mitchell Hynd recognizes that further work is required to refine the rules used by the system: "Just as a human expert continues to learn and improve with experience, it will be necessary to continue monitoring the expert system and use the results of evaluation exercises to feed back into improvements in the rule base." He also believes that expert systems technology has the potential to support other parts of the business, including evaluation of new sites: "Developing a new site is a high-risk decision that involves major investment. It also requires evaluation of socioeconomic data about the local community, details of competing and supporting stores in the area, and comparisons with other existing sites. Capturing knowledge about the results of this blend of factors could help to reduce the risk of future development work."

M+W is committed to a policy of expansion through new development, redevelopment of M+W's present sites, and acquisition of other stores. In parallel with this desire to grow, the number of retail outlets is a desire to avoid growing head office overheads. Home working and the use of field-based office space is encouraged, but efficient computer systems are seen as an essential part of achieving this objective: "Central command and control is vital," concludes Les Mitchell Hynd. "Systems provide the tools to control the business at a time of rapid growth, but they also allow us to provide information for area managers and other field-based staff to make effective business decisions."

5.5.1 Free and Shareware Decision Tree Tools

- *C4.5*—the "classic" decision-tree tool code, developed by J. R. Quinlan, with restricted distribution is available in gzipped tar file format.
- *GAtree*—this tool employs genetic induction and visualization in its free decision trees.
- *Mangrove*—a tool for the visualization of decision tree learning,
- *OC1*—decision tree system with continuous feature values; builds decision trees with linear combinations of attributes at each internal node; these trees then partition the space of examples with both oblique and axis-parallel hyper planes.
- *ODBCMINE*—analyzes ODBC databases using C4.5 and outputs simple conditional rules in ASCII. This tool is intended to be a simple and inexpensive, yet powerful, implementation of the classic machine learning decision tree technique.
- *PC4.5*—a parallel version of C4.5 built with Persistent Linda (PLinda) system, free from New York University.
- *SMILES*—advanced decision tree learner, with new splitting criteria, nongreedy search, extraction of different solutions, boosting, cost-sensitive learning, and more. Free to academia only.
- *Random Forests*—a combination of tree predictors such that each tree depends on the values of a random vector sampled independently and with the same distribution for all trees in the forest.

5.5.2 Rule Generator Tools

- *Compumine Rule Discovery System* (RDS) has a complete coverage of rule-based predictive modeling methods for both classification and regression, with a user-friendly interface. A free evaluation copy of the tool is available.

- *Datamite* enables rules and knowledge to be discovered in ODBC-compliant relational databases.
- *DMT Nuggets* suite of business and scientific solutions based on Sift Agent$^{(TM)}$ technology. What is Sift Agent Nuggets technology? This is how the firm explains it:
  1. A small number of predictor variables, often less than 10 or 15—Nuggets can handle up to 50,000 without attribute reduction methods.
  2. No mix of nominal and numeric—Nuggets can handle both.
  3. Predictor attributes must be uncorrelated—Correlation among predictor attributes is allowed with Nuggets.
  4. Missing values not allowed—Nuggets uses all data and ignores missing values. Noise generating imputation is avoided.
  5. Nonlinearities not allowed—Not an issue with Nuggets.
  6. Small patterns lost. Small patterns are not lost—Nuggets will generate rules for these.
  7. Need statistical and/or other specialized knowledge—Nuggets can be used by nontechnical people. Knowledge of the problem and data is still required.
  8. Numerical values need to be either linearized or have other transformations applied—Nuggets can use numerical values as they are given without user-supplied transformations.
  9. Building models is a slow hand-crafting exercise—Nuggets has a built-in "Autobuild" module that enables models to be built in minutes with a few keystrokes. Of course, you can also use many control parameters in the "Manual Build" mode if you wish to tweak the model.
  10. Accuracy is often low—Because of the lack of data restrictions in Nuggets, the accuracy of predictions is enhanced.
- *PolyAnalyst* supports decision tree, fuzzy logic rules, and other classification algorithms.
- *SuperQuery*, a business intelligence tool, works with Microsoft Access and Excel and many other databases. *WizWhy* automatically finds all the if-then rules in the data and uses them to summarize the data, identify exceptions, and generate

predictions for new cases. Their WizRule component can generate predictive rules.

A WizRule Case Study

Application: INSURANCE FRAUD DETECTION

Goal: REDUCE FRAUDULENT DEATH CLAIMS

A major insurance company is concerned with finding patterns in death claims, which occur within and shortly after the 2 years contestability period. During this time frame, the insurance company has the right to contest benefit payments. Therefore, it is imperative that fraudulent claims be detected in a timely fashion.

The company database consists of over 100,000 policies. A traditional auditing tool was first used as a preprocessor to manipulate the files and sort the data according to date clusters. The contestability date was selected, and the period 2 years before (back to the issuing date) and 2 years after formed the total 4 years period of interest. The data were sorted into 6 months clusters or a total of eight clusters over the 4 years, and the records containing death claims were selected. Each resulting cluster of interest consisted of an average of about 550 records.

Once the preliminary step was taken with a traditional auditing tool, WizRule was used to mine the data. Each cluster of interest was analyzed by WizRule for patterns in the data and for deviations. Since WizRule finds all the rules and relationships in the data without requiring preknowledge of the auditor, interesting and unexpected results were obtained.

Among the unusual patterns detected by WizRule were cases where the death occurred in a state other than either the state of insurance or the state the decedent lived in during the effect of the policy. In some cases, a pattern of foreign-issued death certificates pointed to potential fraud. These cases are currently under investigation by the appropriate agencies.

- *XpertRule Miner* (Attar Software) provides association rule discovery from any ODBC data source.

5.5.3 Free Rule Generator Tools

- *CBA* mines association rules and builds accurate classifiers using a subset of association rules.
- *PNC2 Rule Induction System* is a Windows software tool that induces rules using the PNC2 cluster algorithm.

An SPSS Case Study

Using a technology made familiar by Amazon and NetFlix's personalized recommendations, browsers have become accustomed to seeing, and even demand to see, similar books and movie titles to ones they purchased earlier. Through association algorithms or by looking at a user's click stream—the sequence of pages viewed from browsing to buying—the movie and e-commerce giants hope to predict what the user might buy next.

Traditionally, these tools have been adopted by retailers or merchants in order to make more sales. But more recently, predictive analytics is being leveraged by the public sector to provide better services and produce more efficient outcomes. By looking at historical data and using statistical algorithms, state and local governments can transform their seemingly infinite amount of latent data into meaningful, actionable information.

At the Florida State Department of Juvenile Justice, and in other segments of the detention system across the country, they are hoping to better understand and treat causes of recidivism, especially in young adults. The Florida Department of Juvenile Justice (DJJ) announced recently a partnership with SPSS, an IBM company, to identify high-risk youth and prescribe individualized rehabilitation programs to keep them from re-entering the system as adults.

CivSource spoke to Bill Haffey, predictive analytics strategist for the public sector at SPSS, about how DJJ is leveraging the technology and what kinds of predictors could indicate high- and low-risk offenders.

"At the Department of Juvenile Justice, their interest has always been the same—to identify offenders who are likely to accelerate, or graduate, into the adult court system," Mr. Haffey said. Generally, the juvenile justice system in the United States has taken a unidimensional analysis. "If a juvenile was in the system two or three times," Mr. Haffey said, "there was a knee-jerk reaction to 'watch out' for that person. But there are other pieces of information that haven't been fully exploited."

With the new IBM SPSS software, DJJ will move beyond Excel spreadsheets to analyze key predictors such as past offense history, home life environment, gang affiliation, and peer associations, predicting which youths have a higher likelihood of reoffending. But Mr. Haffey said it is often hard to look at any one of those factors because individually they mask the larger effects of their combined influence.

To paint a complete picture, and to understand who is more or less likely to reenter the system, Haffey said the technology could be used prescriptively and be built in as an operational process tool. Once you look at the juvenile offenses, and the various factors that might impact those offenses, you can begin to make sense of what is causing them, Haffey said. Over time, trends and patterns can be incorporated during the intake process, and indicators— such as education levels, parental status, working status, and other types of noncrime-related information—can be combined.

"[This information] can then predict the level of risk for an individual, and based on that assessment, a program can be designed."

DJJ officials plan to do exactly this. In a blog posting, Mark Greenwald, chief of research and planning at DJJ, said he hopes to improve existing screening and placement processes with evidence-based interventions. "We can [then] direct youth toward treatment that will address their specific criminogenic needs," Greenwald wrote. "This gives us the opportunity to place individuals in specific programs, such as combating substance abuse or addressing mental health issues, creating personalized—versus generic—rehabilitation programs."

This approach is not unique to DJJ, though. Mr. Haffey suggested there are a number of county and state parole boards that are also interested in using predictive analytics to assess risk of their parolees. Similar to the DJJ example, parole officers ask parolees specific questions, which are fed into a predictive model to decide how often a parolee should be required to check in.

More than 85,000 youth enter the juvenile justice system in Florida. Moving forward with predictive analytics, officials said they hope the first time is the last time.

Before selecting a decision tree or rule generator tool, the forensic investigator must conduct a data audit. That is, the investigator must perform an exhaustive inventory of all the different types of data collected by the client organization or department. The investigator should focus this audit on the fraudulent or suspected criminal behaviors the client feels is just "not right." Suspicions by humans can be verified by machine learning investigations, which quantify these "suspicious" behaviors and criminal profiles.

The investigator should consider what existing auditing, reporting, and analytics tools are being used to track these behaviors at the client call-site, website, CRM and ERP systems, and how to integrate them into a seamless map of behaviors "of interest" for forensic analysis. Careful negotiations and courtesies are at times very important in the assembly of data sets for investigations.

Do not discard the knowledge and expertise of clients and their data owners and keepers. The investigator needs to incorporate a "buy-in" from IT, security, web, and other departments during the development, and of ongoing investigations and subsequent detection systems. The knowledge of domain experts is vital to the development of accurate decision tree and rule generation analyses and systems. This is a very important forensic technique that needs to be implemented in a seamless and strategic manner: treat your client organization with respect and a sense of urgency by assisting them with machine learning technology.

5.6 The Streaming Analytical Forensic Processes

There is unique streaming analytical software that can be enlisted by forensic investigators. There are two main types of streaming analytical software products that react to real-time events using modeling predictive rules. The most prevalent are the deductive streaming group of software products that operate by user-defined rules, very similar to expert systems that were popular years ago.

These deductive streaming programs are used to monitor massive and multiple streams of data, reacting in real time to human or system events as they take place, such as when an application form is filled at a website, when a monetary transaction takes place, or when an e-mail is received—in fact, whenever a human or server event occurs—triggering an immediate reaction based on a preprogrammed rule monitoring this kind of activity.

These software products offer graphical interfaces for easy construction of behavioral analytics and forensic rules, functioning as event filters in the form of preventive rules placed for monitoring the processing of data streams for real-time triggering of specific actions for deterring fraud or criminal activities. The following are some of the deductive real-time streaming analytical software firms that work with user-defined preventive rules.

StreamBase provides software for rapidly building systems that analyze and act on real-time streaming data at a fraction of the cost of building a data warehouse. StreamBase uses what it calls complex event processing (CEP) technology for low-latency filtering of consumer event data. The academic origins of CEP began with research efforts at Cal Tech and Stanford University in the mid-1990s, with a focus on processing streaming data by identifying complex sequences of events within specified time intervals, and then triggering an appropriate action or alert as a result of these real-time behaviors.

The processing of messages for real-time analysis also involves access to "clouds" of data sources to enable the creation and maintenance of "behavioral analytical filters" for enterprises. With the increasing speed and amount of behavioral data being generated 24/7, this type of software can be leveraged by forensic investigators to improve an organization's reaction to threats, attacks, and criminal events.

StreamBase explains its streaming software solution in the following manner: data-gathering systems used for intelligence, security, and defense must be able to "sense and respond" to patterns of events that indicate pending threats. Traditional data management and analysis software architectures cannot keep pace with the volume and velocity of the data streaming into many of today's modern intelligence systems. This is certainly the case with forensic real-time preventive systems. StreamBase provides government agencies and system integrators with the ability to quickly solve real-time data processing and analytics challenges that previously have been time-consuming and often intractable.

StreamBase's powerful real-time processing architecture with StreamSQL enables users to consolidate data across multiple sources and formats, and monitor complex conditions to identify patterns of events that indicate a need for action. StreamBase is ideal for real-time message/text analysis, combat theatre surveillance and battalion monitoring, real-time surveillance and alerting, and network monitoring (Figure 5.5).

Complex event processing (CEP) is a technology for low-latency filtering, correlating, aggregating, and computing on real-world event data. Within the CEP industry, some event processing systems can only process events or messages as they pass by, without necessarily retaining and processing state. However, StreamBase's software for event processing handles the bulk, if not all, of traditional CEP. StreamBase in effect is a method by which certain conditional rules can be crafted by forensic investigators for monitoring and alerting an organization of possible server attacks, threats, fraud, or other criminal activity.

First, StreamBase believes it is critical to define several terms. The processing of messages as they arrive is called *real-time processing*, and the use of a sophisticated and optimized storage mechanism is called *historical processing*. Another term that shows up in the CEP literature is an *event cloud*, or *cloud* for short. StreamBase believes that a *cloud* is really a manifestation of historical processing coupled with real-time processing. The power of a good event processing platform is in how well it integrates real-time and historical processing. In other words, a cloud can be easily simulated by a modern stream processing system. Here are some further details on how the government and military sectors are leveraging StreamBase for security and intelligence:

- *Intelligence and surveillance*—A key challenge in providing watertight security is to effectively capture, filter, analyze, and act on flows of data from disparate sources in real time. Federal, state, and local law agencies are constantly generating related

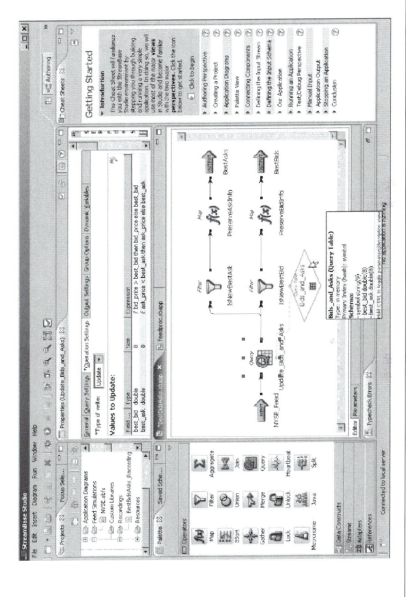

Figure 5.5 This is the StreamBase Studio interface for filtering streams of data.

information from monitoring of networks, e-mails, financial transactions, watch-lists, and other sources. As a result, it is increasingly difficult to aggregate this real-time data into a holistic view that can help identify imminent or potential threats. With StreamBase, these organizations are able to organize, filter, and interpret streams of high-volume information in real time. The forensic investigator can assist organizations in implementing this type of detective framework.

- *Intrusion detection and network monitoring*—Military and civilian agencies rely on their information systems and networks to execute their missions. These systems need to be protected from malicious attacks by hackers and terrorists. StreamBase is a tool that can be used to create applications to detect and shut down such attacks. By capturing and analyzing network traffic in real time—at data rates of tens to hundreds of thousands of messages per second—the software can be used to protect critical information infrastructure. Again, the forensic investigator can assist other types of organizations and enterprises in the creation of this type of continuous deterrence.

Progress and its Apama® software also enable real-time response to fast-changing business conditions in an event-driven service-oriented architecture (SOA). This streaming behavioral analytical software monitors human events, identifies patterns, and takes action instantly. Using Progress, an enterprise can achieve operational awareness with real-time and event-driven business activity monitoring (BAM).

Progress, another of these streaming behavioral analytical software providers, argues that by detecting criminal patterns in real time, it can help organizations to quickly respond to attacks, fraud, and assist in identifying threats wherever they may occur *and* while there is time to act. This type of event-driven software is being used across a wide range of applications in financial markets, manufacturing, and retail operations for fraud detection and prevention.

As Progress explains its solution to fraud, it points out that as the speed of transactions increases, so does the sophistication of the fraudulent activity that is under way across many industries, but specifically in financial and web commerce firms. Progress argues that, with this abundance of information flowing everywhere, it has become much more difficult to stop fraud, and that certain organizations are left vulnerable. Whether the crime is check, credit card, or corporate fraud and theft, the problem can be found in every industry. There is no end to the creativity of those who engage in fraudulent activity.

Their Apama® Event Processing Platform leverages the power of complex event processing to spot potential fraud patterns in real time, giving the forensic investigator the ability to construct a framework that can immediately act on that information. By identifying conditions that could negatively impact an organization, an investigator can assist the organization with the ability to intercede, providing them the capability to dramatically reduce risk. Furthermore, as fraud schemes change and evolve, Apama tools allow the forensic investigator to quickly create new detection rules or to alter the parameters of existing ones to keep pace with the perpetrators. Here are some more features of the Progress fraud prevention solution:

- Highly interactive dashboards that allow loss prevention professionals to view information in an intuitive real-time display that is easily customized to their requirements.
- An integration environment that allows monitoring data to be connected with different middleware systems, applications, and other endpoints without disrupting the current IT infrastructure.
- Development and testing tools that can rapidly create, test, and evolve monitoring scenarios, without lengthy development cycles that risk being too late.
- The ability to create customized capabilities like the correlation of real-time event data with video surveillance systems.

Yet another streaming analytical software provider is *Aleri*, and their streaming platform, which was recently acquired by *Sybase*, also supports complex event processing, allowing enterprises to react instantly to changing conditions by analyzing incoming data in real time. The software allows companies to rapidly build and deploy new applications that derive insight from streaming event data, letting them instantly respond to changing conditions. Sybase believes firms need to be event driven and that delayed response to changing conditions can mean missed opportunities to detect crimes while they take place and prevent overlooked threats.

5.7 Forensic Analysis of Streaming Behaviors

There are also inductive streaming analytical software in which rules are constructed from multiple analyses performed horizontally across structured databases and unstructured documents, clickstreams, and e-mails. The inductive streamer software can be used for behavioral analytics by forensic investigators by giving them the ability to analyze streams of data from call sites, websites, e-mail, and transactional legacy systems in order to develop global models. Once constructed, those behavior analytical filters—models and detective rules—can be deployed at websites, call sites, and other operational systems to react to human and server events as they occur enterprisewide for real-time reactions to them as they take place.

At the core of the inductive streaming analytical software, products such as *InferX* are advanced algorithms for clustering, text analysis, and the development of decision rules that can perform behavioral analytics for segmentation, classification, clustering, concept extraction, visualization, and prediction directly from data streams. This type of distributed analytical software supports the processes of analyzing an assortment of behaviors, demographics, lifestyle, transactional, Internet, and geospatial information for the detection of digital crimes at the various touch points as humans interact with an organization. With this type of inductive streaming analytical software, there is no latency between analysis and action—instead, it is one single-integrated continuous-networked forensic process.

In this new distributed forensic model, real-time streaming data analytics becomes a continuing and iterative process in which decisions and action are continuously refined and perfected over time. In the end, it is about creating self-adaptive and responsive organizations capable of reacting to threats and crimes in real time. Among the advantages of this kind of inductive streaming analytic software are the following:

- Empowers data owners with total control
- Provides near-real-time analysis and predictions
- Keeps the data concealed by encrypting the results
- Eliminates the need for creating data warehouses
- Works with multiple databases in different formats
- Predicts future risks and opportunities over networks

- Accesses and mines structured and unstructured data remotely
- Increases speed over conventional methods by employing parallel analysis

Deployment of this technology is typically accomplished in two stages: first, the software is "trained" or signatures are developed from the analysis of the data in the multiple databases that encompass the knowledge network. The second phase involves using the signatures developed from the first phase dynamically across the network of databases, continuously monitoring applications that include risk scoring, fraud and intrusion detection, and business intelligence.

5.8 Forensic Real-Time Modeling

Both deductive and inductive streaming analytic systems are "event driven" in that they respond to user interactions as they occur, reducing or eliminating the decays of data over time. This is a very important feature because the value of translating data directly into action is much higher. Reacting at the time to interactive "events" as they take place enables organizations to react to criminal activities in real time with no latency.

These real-time software analytical streamer products allow forensic investigators and their client organization to construct behavioral analytics detection systems on top of their existing IT investments and legacy systems while increasing their ability to react to attacks and crimes. Whether an inductive or deductive analytical streaming software is used or a combination of both, one common feature is that massive amounts of information can be leveraged from multiple data sources within an organization for behavioral analytics as criminal events take place.

A Real-Time Behavioral Analytics Checklist

1. Leverage dormant data assets into new untapped streams to improve security and intelligence
2. Leverage current IT investments and infrastructure "as is" for new untapped value
3. Tap into existing legacy databases despite their format, structure, or location

4. Achieve a global view of *all* their data assets for a new level of detection
5. Improve efficiencies at every level of security and intelligence operations
6. Reduce uncertainty, predict with precision, and optimize performance
7. Leverage all daily transactions into predictive protective models
8. Provide security and protection while preserving privacy
9. Gain insight, and find and detect crimes as they take place

Additional benefits to analyzing these data streams is that they can be used to trigger a response based on patterns of events, trends, missing events, etc.; analytical streamer software can also compute aggregate values from data flows that are constantly updated, and they can provide global views of users by combining data from multiple sources, both streaming and static. These real-time streaming software products can enable the leveraging of criminal behaviors, propensities, transaction, and other events to make forensic detection possible for organizations.

5.9 Deductive Forensics for Precrime

Many of the software products covered in this chapter are extremely fast, powerful, intuitive, and robust, and require no statistical background or training in the field of artificial intelligence or machine learning; all that law enforcement personnel need is a desire to apply these analytical tools to crime data. They are ideal tools for use in special task forces in which traditional methods of investigations are severely limited; they are also ideal for use in operational planning of manpower and resources. They can be used to predict where specific crimes are likely to occur by different parameters, such as time of day, day of the week, and probability of occurrences by specific type of perpetrators. They can put the police where the hockey puck is going to be, not where it was. Strategically used, they can be used for precrime.

Decision tree and rule generator tools enable local law enforcement personnel to be proactive in such areas as tactical crime analysis, risk and threat assessment, behavioral analysis of a variety of crimes, and telephone and web log files for the deployment of productive enforcement strategies. They go beyond criminal reporting in that the same data can now be leveraged to plan and anticipate criminal activity. These machine learning tools are relatively easy to use; they are relatively inexpensive and some are even free, yet they can potentially save hundreds of thousands of dollars for police departments throughout the world.

These same tools can be used by state and federal agencies, whose missions are highly specific, such as those responsible for security at border crossings. Using historical data of previous seizures, for example, models for automobiles and trailer trucks can be developed to profile high-risk vehicle likely to be used for smuggling operations. Border security personnel can use not only their internal seizures data but supplement it with external data sources to construct these predictive models by using such information as state vehicle registration records, insurance files, financials on vehicles, etc. The point is that criminal data can be leveraged to improve detection and reduce risk for border detection agencies and police departments at any level.

Deductive forensic software tools enable creative law enforcement personnel to merge and analyze data sources that traditionally did not coexist or have never been used to predict criminal activities. The creation of criminal models can be used to link unsolved cases to criminal and gang methods of operations, which can identify and apprehend suspects and prevent future crimes. For law enforcement departments and agencies, machine learning forensic tools can also be used to determine how to proactively use their limited manpower resources. The tools can be used to identify and characterize criminal patterns in order to reduce risk to its officers and the public. Normal activity can be baselined in order to rapidly identify unusual or suspicious activities warranting subsequent analysis and surveillance. Lastly, deductive forensic analysis can be used by police departments to identify and quantify actionable patterns and trends in criminal behaviors.

6

Fraud Detection

On the Web, Wireless, and in Real Time

6.1 Definition and Techniques: Where, Who, and How

Improving data effectiveness means obtaining a consistent version of the truth, and a strategy for achieving this starts with detecting fraud and theft. For the forensic investigator, this involves developing a strategy for enabling critical decisions to be made on accurate, concise, trustworthy information with swiftness, precision, and efficiency. Often, the most immediate challenge that the forensic investigator faces is that data systems containing information relevant to fraud, waste, and abuse detection cannot share information with one another. The forensic strategy must deal with assembling or having access via data pointers to relevant data sources impacted by criminals. This may involve a strategy by the forensic investigator of using analytical networks and systems developed for real-time marketing.

Unfortunately, the results are often incomplete and inaccurate views of the data that allow errors or fraudulent actions to slip through the cracks. However, by using data integration solutions along with sophisticated data matching and standardization routines that reach across multiple platforms and formats, forensic investigators can begin to create a single version of the truth so that the information on which analyses and decisions are based is accurate and complete. This requires the assembling of a fraud detection framework for merging information from diverse data sets and the use of multiple machine learning tools, such as those covered in prior chapters.

Another essential step in reducing error and fraud is to verify the identity, eligibility, and authentication of payees, shoppers, visitors, and other legal entities. This ensures that the right people are receiving the right services and products within a legal framework. Using data quality solutions, organizations can standardize and augment data while identifying duplicate names, addresses, and other identifying information, thereby validating key entity information. This process of authenticating the entities, whether humans or organizations, also reduces overpayments, underpayments, and duplicate billings.

Fraud can be found in a large array of products, services, and industries, ranging from financial mortgage, social networks, pirated software, insurance claims, IRS taxes, iTunes apps, to Facebook Credits. The important fact to forensic investigators is that a large percentage of these crimes are digital in nature and require the identification of digital fingerprints and behaviors. The second important issue for the forensic investigator is the need to quickly adapt to fast-evolving fraudulent schemes and cons.

For example, in the area of mortgage fraud, one common con was the use of "straw buyers" with good credit to apply for "no doc" loans, in which banks would rely solely on credit reports. However, with the financial meltdown of the Great Recession, such loans are a thing of the past. However, fraudsters adapt quickly, and criminals now rely on the falsifying of documents, the use of bank insiders, and identity theft. To fight mortgage fraud, some companies such as CoreLogic provide specific products such as their 4506-T Direct service, which provides a way to validate applicant information with IRS 1040 data, including wages, business income or loss, other income, and adjusted gross income. The report also calls attention to discrepancies between borrower-supplied data and the IRS-verified information by identifying suspect data.

A growing area of fraud is that of counterfeit drugs made in Asia. The Pharmaceutical Security Institute (PSI), a group funded by drug manufacturers, estimates fraud is costing their clients between $75 billion to $200 billion a year. Counterfeit medicine may include too much, too little, or none of the ingredients found in the real product, causing injury and in some instances death. Contributing to these types of frauds is the web and the popularity of some medicines, such as Pfizer's erectile dysfunction drug Viagra in the 1990s. To counter such crimes, investigators need to check to see if the site is located in the United States and licensed by a state board of pharmacy where it is operating. Again however, this type of crime is digital in nature and takes place almost exclusively online.

Another low-level type of fraud involves the failure to pay IRS payroll taxes by small firms' bookkeepers who are erroneously given the dual responsibilities of both receipts and disbursement. In fact, 31% of all business frauds nationally were in companies with fewer than 100 employees, and an additional 23% were suffered by those with fewer than 999 workers. Only 21% were committed in companies with more than 10,000 employees. The median loss for companies with fewer than 100 employees was about $150,000, compared with $84,000 in businesses with payrolls exceeding 10,000. Small businesses are relatively easy targets because of a lack of formal financial controls; to counter this, outside auditors should be periodically brought in to review business financial records.

Managing fraudulent claims is one of the biggest challenges facing the insurance industry. The National Insurance Crime Bureau (NICB) estimates that 10% of all claims are fraudulent. NICB estimates that property casualty insurance fraud alone cost insurers about $30 billion annually. Identification of even a few percentage points of these fraudulent claims will yield a significant payback to the insurers and policyholders. However, the claims-handling process in the insurance business is time consuming and labor intensive, typically involving an investigation, assessment, evaluation, negotiation, and settlement.

Fireman's Fund Insurance Company Case Study

To increase the overall effectiveness and efficiency of Claim Fraud Detection while minimizing the productivity impacts on claims adjusters, FFIC's Analytics group in Customer Research and Strategies (CRS), in partnership with the Claims organization, undertook a major initiative to create a technological solution for systematic fraud detection. Faced with a lack of structured data of predictive value in fraud detection, the focus of the initiative was the adoption of text analytics–based productivity solutions on adjuster notes to enable early fraud detection and create unique competitive advantages for FFIC.

After extensive vendor analysis, FFIC selected IxReveal's uReveal for its text extraction and mining needs. uReveal is IxReveal's flagship product built on the Microsoft .NET architecture, and is designed to read large volumes of unstructured data and generate meaningful intelligence in the form of hard-to-spot trends, patterns, and clues.

The decision to select uReveal was based on its superior feature set that perfectly matched FFIC's business needs. These included uReveal's user-friendly interface, its ability to allow the user to control the analysis process, its unique ability to handle synonyms of industry terms, the ability to identify negated concepts to differentiate whether an event occurred or not, and its powerful relationship discovery capabilities. In addition, the context analysis feature that provides causal, conditional, and temporal visibility to a specific concept was particularly valuable from a problem-solving perspective.

Recognizing that adjuster claims notes are an important, even vital, source of information, FFIC analysts used uReveal to extract key "suspicion" concepts from the text through an iterative refinement process.

The concepts thus extracted were then combined with other coded information such as claim date, location, amount, etc., to create patterns historically correlated with fraudulent claims. New claims were then evaluated against these patterns and scored for their fraud potential, with the adjusters being alerted if the system detected a strong presence of suspicion concepts.

The use of uReveal has the ability to transform the decision-making process at the claims adjuster and SIU levels to be driven increasingly by analytic insights and metrics. Some of the benefits of using unstructured text analysis in the claims investigation process are as follows:

- Identifying claims likely to result in fraud with speed and accuracy not systematically possible before
- Increased productivity of the SIU teams by minimizing the amount of time spent reading through claim details to pull together facts for analysis
- Reduced cycle time in enabling timely interventions on fraudulent claims
- Increased flexibility in monitoring and updating fraud profiles based on changing conditions

- Improved effectiveness in minimizing the impact of fraud through higher rates of SIU utilization (Assists and Consults)

The first Fraud Modeling initiative at FFIC was on General Liability Claims data, and the uReveal analysis was executed in less than four weeks. When tested on three months' worth of open claims, the model doubled the number of referrals to the SIU without compromising the hit rate (or accuracy) of the referrals.

uReveal's success in unstructured data analytics for claim fraud has opened new areas of opportunity at FFIC. One area that is actively being explored is to better understand the "Voice of the Customer." By analyzing customer feedback and open-ended survey responses, FFIC seeks to develop a deep understanding of customer sentiments and identify key areas of improvement in their delivery of a superior customer experience.

Increasingly, fraud is taking place on the web and wireless world; typically, this involves tiny amounts of theft; for example, as iTunes has grown into the world's biggest music retailer and a repository of more than 225,000 apps, it has also become a target for fraudsters, in which Apple consumers' iTunes accounts are hacked. Typically, criminals break into a person's iTune account, changing the owner's e-mail address and password on file with Apple, authorizing a new device, and then quickly downloading as many songs, videos, and apps as possible. To combat this type of fraud, victims need to cancel their debit or credit card as soon as possible because Apple has been slow to react to these crimes on their site. This type of iTune hacking underscores the risks of purchasing digital goods online, which is vulnerable and can take place very quickly by cyber criminals. Users may want to verify that their iTunes account has not been hacked. To do so, fire up iTunes, navigate to iTunes Store in the iTunes sidebar, click the Account link (on the right of the main iTunes Store page), log in when prompted, then click the Purchase History button.

Phishers have targeted users of the music store with sophisticated identity theft attacks: subscribers receive spammed messages telling them that they must correct a problem with their iTunes account.

A link in the spam leads to a site posing as an iTunes billing update page; that phony page asks for information, including credit card number and security code, Social Security number, and mother's maiden name. The identity thieves aimed the new attack at iTunes users because of the service's perceived demographics. iTunes users are younger than those for some of the other phished sites, such as banks and eBay. The way that teenagers and young adults use the Internet, they show a certain level of trust or openness when they post their name, age, school, music, etc., on social networks and thus tend to make easy targets for criminals.

A Checklist for Preventing Online Fraud

- Use a safe, strong password that includes a combination of upper-case and lowercase letters and numbers. Do not use the same password for every online account you have. That's basically like using the same key for your house, car, and office. If you lose that key, you're in trouble.
- Protect your computer: Use a modern, supported operating system such as Windows 7 or Apple's OS X Snow Leopard. You should also use an updated Internet browser that blocks fraudulent websites, such as the latest releases of Explorer, Safari, Firefox, or Chrome. Always, keep your antivirus software updated.
- Do not click on links in e-mail: Never click on links in e-mail, and then enter your username, password, or other sensitive information, even if the e-mail looks like it's from your bank, an e-commerce site, the IRS, or popular sites like PayPal, and Apple.
- Use common sense: If you would not do something in the offline world, do not assume it's safe online. If you get an e-mail, phone call, or some other unexpected message demanding that you turn over your username and password, do not do it.

Most online retail purchases at sites such as Amazon.com involve the shipment of physical goods, so there may be time for fraud to be detected and stopped even if a credit card is charged. However, with digital virtual goods, customers expect to immediately download their purchases, so there is not enough time to run a thorough check for fraud. Merchants such as Apple could easily detect these types of fraud by analyzing users' behaviors, preferences, and the types of music, movies, and apps they purchase. Sales of virtual objects and currency used in online games and social networks are taking off with consumers and criminals.

Worldwide sales of digital items in games and social networks reached $2.2 billion in 2009 and is expected to grow to $6 billion in 2013. Facebook, for instance, in 2009 unveiled its virtual currency called Credits, allowing users to spend it on Facebook games and other services. These virtual goods are often easier to obtain than physical goods, and criminals have learned that there are ways to convert them into cash. A common way criminals profit from digital objects' fraud is to buy the goods with a stolen card and then sell it for real money on a third party's site, often at a deep discount.

Digital goods pose unique challenges; an online merchant selling a book or a computer has a shipping address to compare with the billing one. This type of merchant has hours to review the order if a fraud is suspected. However, sellers of digital goods typically do not have such a luxury, and sales of virtual goods do not have a shipping address to help the merchant make such decisions. Another complication is that sales of digital goods are usually tiny, sometimes for one of two dollars, often hidden from consumers who miss the small charges on their credit and bank statements. The extent of fraud has penetrated not only the web but also mobile devices and popular services such as Twitter, which the Federal Trade Commission penalized and required the firm to perform independent security audits for 10 years. The FTC found that Twitter failed to do enough to secure its site, allowing hackers with password-guessing programs to commandeer thousands of customer accounts.

In the end, fraud is taking advantage of an organization through deception, which can result in the loss of not only revenue, but also brand value, proprietary innovation, and competitive advantage. Standards were established by the Auditing Standards Board of the American Institute of Certified Public Accountants (AICPA) in October 2002—commonly called SAS 99—on the "Consideration of Fraud in Financial Statement Audits." The key components are as follows:

- Describes fraud and its characteristics.
- Requires "brainstorming" sessions to discuss how and where the entity's financial statements might be susceptible to material misstatement due to fraud.
- Requires the auditor to use the information gathered to identify risks that may result in a material misstatement.

- Requires the auditor to evaluate the entity's programs and controls that address the identified risks of material misstatement.
- Requires the auditor to assess the risks of material misstatement due to fraud throughout the audit and to evaluate at the completion of the audit whether the accumulated results of auditing procedures and other observations affect the assessment.
- Provides guidance regarding the auditor's communications about fraud to management, the audit committee, and others.
- Describes documentation requirements.

It is important for the forensic investigator to understand that fraud occurs at different intervals and in different guises; for example, retail fraud differs from that in the financial sector, and so does healthcare fraud from that on the web and wireless sector. Investigators need to work closely with domain experts in each industry and organization. Fraud is perpetrated differently in small firms than in larger corporations; furthermore, in this global economy, traditions differ from one country to another, and the investigator needs to understand this. Investigators must be aware that asset misappropriation schemes often occur with low-level employees, while the misstatements and manipulation of financial statements occur at the executive levels. In the following, we list several areas a forensic investigator needs to be aware of.

A Fraud Detection Checklist

1. Creation of phantom sales
2. Fraudulent claims of customers
3. Recording of sales prematurely
4. Embezzlement by employees and executives
5. Intentional inflation of prices and units by vendors
6. Falsifying of expenses by employees and executives
7. Intentional misstatement of assets by an organization

6.2 The Interviews: The Owners, Victims, and Suspects

The interviewing of the owners of systems and victims of fraud involves a systemic gathering of knowledge and intelligence about the suspected crime. It requires their input about possible schemes and scenarios pointing to fraudulent behaviors. Their interviews often require talking to personnel from different functions and departments, including management, IT specialists, legal, human resources, operations, and security people. Fraud scenarios from similar firms in the same industry may point to current schemes being perpetrated, but historical patterns are not reliable, since this type of crime is really about staying ahead of the forensic investigators.

The forensic investigator interview of the fraud victims often involves two general types: owners who know criminal activity is taking place because "the numbers don't add up" and those who just suspect fraudulent activity is taking place in their organization or department. The interviews of these data owners should lead the forensic investigator to the use of strategies for the deployment of software tools to scan for discrepancies, relationships, and hidden patterns that are often impossible to perform manually.

Machine learning forensics relies on software tools capable of sorting, matching, and uncovering patterns too massive for a human investigator to perform without the aid of powerful analytics. These fraud discovery and prevention analytics can suggest wrongdoing and other issues worth investigation originating from the interviews of data owners and fraud victims. These forensic techniques and technologies can involve procurement and accounting fraud, money laundering, and fraudulent medical claims. These data interrogation techniques can lead to the interviews of internal and external fraud suspects.

Fraud Assessment Questioning (FAQ) is a nonaccusatory, structured interview method designed to elicit information about potential fraud matters. It operates on the theory that attitudes of individuals will provide the interviewer with good information to assess fraud risks, and to find specifics, if any. FAQ is based on the notion that telling lies is unnatural to most people. As a result, a good interviewer can structure questions so that the individual being questioned is not even aware of the significance of the information he or she is providing.

A forensic investigator should understand that one good way of uncovering hidden fraud utilizes the most direct approach possible: asking about it. FAQ relies on the time-proven method of beginning with general questions before proceeding to the specific. Understanding both the order in which to ask questions and also the reasoning behind the questions is a critical aspect of the interview technique. For example, a simple question designed to solicit a "yes" answer from the person being interviewed is something an investigator should strive for, such as question 1:

> I have been asked to make an inquiry about potential misdeeds by management and employees in this department. Do you understand that?

This question is used to approach the sensitive subject of fraud in the least offensive way. Fraud should be addressed only after rapport has been established with the person being interviewed. Soliciting a positive response is critical to creating that rapport and progressing to the next level of the interview. Pauses before answering simple direct questions such as this is sometimes an indication of deception. A "yes" or "maybe" response to this question will normally indicate general agreement with the fraud problem, and further discussion will be fruitful. An innocent person is much more likely to recognize and accept the problem than someone with something to hide, continuing with question 2:

> Do you think this company has any particular problem with fraud?

In accordance with FAQ methodology, the questioning is proceeding from the general to the specific, and the interviewer should proceed slowly, so that the interviewee does not feel intimidated or uncomfortable. Question 3 should be more specific:

> If you suspected someone of stealing from the company, what would you do?

This question again is put in hypothetical terms to reduce the possibility of offending the interviewee. Question 4 is intended to solicit an avoidance response and a list of possible suspects:

> In your opinion, who is beyond suspicion when it comes to committing fraud in your department?

Most guilty people and criminals will not give names. Fraud perpetrators become defensive at nonaccusatory questions and will want to hurry up and move on to the ultimate question: did you do it? But negative responses to any of these general questions are a sure sign of the identification of a fraud suspect, which can be confirmed by performing an audit of their assets and lifestyles. The use of machine learning forensics can also lead to the discovery of transactional information that points to avoidance behaviors by suspects who attempt to cover their tracks and their stolen assets and accomplices.

6.3 The Scene of the Crime: Search for Digital Evidence

Digital evidence is any information stored or transmitted in digital form that may be used in a court case trial. Before accepting digital evidence, a court will determine if the evidence is relevant, whether it is authentic, if it is hearsay, and whether a copy is acceptable or the original is required. The use of digital evidence in fraudulent and other criminal court cases has allowed the use of e-mails, digital photographs, Word documents, ATM transactions, Internet log files, instant message histories, cookies, Facebook pages, spreadsheets, browser histories, and all types of digital files, including in cases involving fraud and corruption.

The machine learning forensic investigator is likely to handle digital evidence in a manner that it is in compliance with existing policies and procedures that meet federal, state, and local law requirements. The following five steps describe the necessary actions for conducting a forensic examination involving digital evidence and suggest the order in which they should be conducted. Although documentation is listed as the last step, a forensic investigator must understand that the search for digital evidence documentation is a continuously ongoing process throughout the entire investigation.

A Digital Evidence Gathering Checklist

1. *Develop Policy and Procedure Standards*—Establish an effective way to conduct fraud investigations, evidence collection, and machine learning forensic analysis.
2. *Evidence Assessment*—The digital evidence should be thoroughly assessed with respect to the scope of the case to determine the course of action, consider legal authorization, case detail, and the circumstances surrounding the acquisition of the evidence to be examined.
3. *Evidence Acquisition*—Digital evidence is fragile and can be altered, damaged, or destroyed by improper handling or examination; failure to do so may render the evidence unusable or lead to an unsuccessful prosecution.

4. *Evidence Examination*—Different types of cases and media may require different methods of examination; the examination should *not* be conducted on original evidence.
5. *Documenting and Reporting*—The forensic investigator is responsible for completely and accurately reporting findings and the results of the analysis of the digital evidence examination.

When dealing with digital evidence, the following machine learning forensic should be applied by the investigator:

- Actions taken to secure and collect digital evidence should not affect its integrity.
- Persons conducting an examination of digital evidence should be trained for that purpose.
- Activity relating to the seizure, examination, storage, or transfer of digital evidence should be documented, preserved, and available for review.
- The investigator should be aware of the need to conduct an accurate and impartial examination of the digital evidence.

6.3.1 *Four Key Steps in Dealing with Digital Evidence*

1. *Assessment*: The machine learning forensic investigator should assess digital evidence thoroughly with respect to the scope of the fraudulent case to determine the course of action to be taken.
2. *Acquisition*: Digital evidence, by its very nature, is fragile and can be altered, damaged, or destroyed by improper handling or examination. The examination is best conducted on a copy of the original evidence. The original evidence should be acquired in a manner that protects and preserves the integrity of the contents.
3. *Examination*: The purpose of the forensic analysis is to extract relevant digital evidence. The extraction process refers to the recovery of data from its media. Analysis refers to the interpretation of the recovered data and putting it in a logical and useful format for legal use.
4. *Documenting*: Actions and observations should be documented throughout the forensic processing of evidence, including the preparation of a written report of its findings.

Finally, the machine learning investigator should describe in detail the results of the fraud investigation, which may include the following documentation:

- Specific files related to the request
- Machine learning forensic analysis and findings
- Description of relevant programs on the examined items
- String searches, keyword searches, and text string searches
- Graphic image analysis, such as link networks and clustering findings
- Indicators of ownership, which could include program registration data
- All files, including deleted files, which support the investigation's findings
- All web activities, cookies, log and cache files, e-mail, and social networking activity
- Techniques used to hide or mask data, such as encryption, steganographics, hidden attributes and partitions, all file name anomalies

6.4 Searches for Associations: Discovering Links and Text Concepts

A combination of link and text analyses—visualization and clustering techniques—can be used by the machine learning forensic investigator to determine unusual and isolated patterns and transaction aberrations. For example, an outlier analysis using a SOM software tool may be used to find unusual activities—such as billing discrepancies—that necessitate immediate perusal by the investigator. Inductive clustering analysis can lead to the discovery of these anomalies indicating potential fraudulent activity to the machine learning investigator.

Other techniques can add value in determining unusual patterns or practices. Sequence analysis and association analysis uncover events that tend to occur together or in sequence. Link analysis can identify relationships among citizens, organizations, and services, thereby uncovering interactions that might need closer inspection. For example, link analysis can uncover personal injury attorneys who repeatedly send clients to the same clinics or doctors for diagnosis. All of these techniques mentioned above are integral parts of an ongoing, continuously improving antifraudulent monitoring process.

With machine learning forensic analytical capabilities, fraud detection is taken one step further to improve audit and investigation effectiveness. A variety of advanced forensic techniques can be utilized depending on the client organization's data. If the organization has not captured the necessary data surrounding known fraud schemes, then cluster SOM analysis can be used. This unsupervised analysis determines unusual aberrations within the data autonomously; once unusual clusters are uncovered, further scrutiny may be required to deem them fraudulent or not. However, if an organization has documentation of known fraud patterns, then predictive analytics using decision trees can be used to identify and predict future fraud and associated risk scores. Organizations can ease the burden of validating false positives, maximizing recovery and prosecution while reducing processing time, improving efficiency, and limiting revenue loss.

6.5 Rules of Fraud: Conditions and Clues

Next, it is important for the investigator to monitor information to identify fraudulent activity. Once fraudulent activity is identified, organizations can institute machine learning predictive business rules to prevent the fraud from recurring. Many agencies and departments have IF/THEN rules associated with documented fraud schemes. As part of the antifraud strategy, these rules can be automated and scheduled to run in real time, monitoring for targeted crimes. These fraud-derived rules can be used to flag cases that need investigative follow-up. In addition, machine learning investigators can analyze data across peer groups to determine abnormalities. For instance, physician-billing practices can be compared with those of physicians in the same field for the same diagnostic codes to determine unusual practices indicating potential fraud.

Analyzing both structured and unstructured data with decision trees and text mining and clustering, respectively, helps organizations to use both their quantitative and qualitative data software tools to better identify fraudulent claims. By doing so, forensic investigators are able to stop fraudulent payments before they are made. Additionally, investigators can prioritize cases that appear to be improper for further investigation, and organizations can rapidly detect new fraud schemes and patterns before they cause major revenue losses.

Once machine learning investigators have determined a likely fraud scheme, the next steps are audit and investigation of suspects and their associates. After these crimes are determined, these new fraud schemes can then be incorporated into the known predictive detection business rules and incorporated into operational systems. But then the antifraud process begins again. Fraud detection is an ongoing, cyclical process of continuous analysis, forensic investigations, and refinement. Organizations are not only concerned with detecting and deterring fraud, they also want to ensure that their processes are effective in monitoring expenditures, allowing for tightened internal controls on costs. Machine learning forensics enable organizations to scrutinize financials across multiple operations and functions while assisting in creating a culture of accountability, compliance, efficiency, and deterrence.

6.6 A Forensic Investigation Methodology

The following machine learning forensic methodology is proposed for detecting and deterring digital fraud and related crimes. This may involve using multiple software tools requiring unsupervised and supervised techniques. Systemically, it is important for forensic investigators to consider the following steps during their inquiries and interrogation of the data.

6.6.1 Step One: Understand the Investigation Objective

Understand the insight or outcome sought by the client organization: for example, is it the detection of fraud, or the identification of the perpetrators, or both. Most likely an organization will want to develop predictive rules for thwarting future criminal activities. During the course of the forensic analysis, the investigators need to understand the type of fraud they are attempting to detect, the costs of positive and negative predictions, and the enforcement and pre-emptive actions that can be taken by the client organization in each case. This initial phase focuses on understanding the investigation objectives and requirements from a business or law enforcement perspective, and then converting this knowledge into a forensic problem definition and a preliminary plan designed to achieve these objectives. The overall costs and benefits of the entire machine learning forensic project should be estimated and quantified.

6.6.2 *Step Two: Understand the Data*

Understand the fraud or crime that needs to be detected. This will ensure that the appropriate data sets will be collected, assembled, and leveraged to achieve the desired objectives and predictions. During this phase, the investigator starts with an initial data collection and proceeds with exploratory activities necessary to get familiar with the data, to identify data quality problems, to gain an initial insight into the data or to detect interesting subsets, and to form hypotheses from the hidden information. During this phase, consideration is given to the quality of the data and how that will impact the results obtained. Consideration is also given to how the investigation will impact security, confidentiality, and privacy issues and concerns. At this juncture, the forensic investigator may consider appending additional information such as demographics or data sets from other departments, organizations, or commercial databases, if warranted.

6.6.3 *Step Three: Data Preparation Strategy*

The data preparation phase covers all related activities needed to construct the final data set, which will be used for the forensic analyses from the initial operational and transactional raw data sets. Data preparation tasks are most likely to be performed multiple times and not in any prescribed order or sequence. These forensic tasks may include table, record, and data attribute selection, as well as transformation and the cleaning of the data prior to their exposure to the modeling tools. In this phase, data quality issues must be addressed, and a determination of how much data will be needed and the format the forensic solution will take must be made. For example, decisions need to be taken on how to handle missing values, which in fraud detection takes on an especially important dimension. A process and a plan on how to obtain and prepare the data in the most efficient way possible must be made at this stage, with consideration given to other applications accessing the same operational data and to servers and network restrictions and permissions.

6.6.4 *Step Four: Forensic Modeling*

In this phase, various modeling and analyses are tested and selected, and their parameters are calibrated to optimize their value and accuracy. Typically, there are several approaches to the same fraud detection challenge. Some techniques and forensic tools have specific requirements, depending on the structure of the data; therefore, stepping back to the data preparation and data selection phases may be required. For example, some decision tree tools are superior in accuracy in the analysis of data sets with a large number of categorical attributes. During this phase, the construction of multiple models and approaches should take place to compare error rates. For fraud detection, it is essential that a number of techniques and models be tested and used in cooperation, via an ensemble of models. This is fundamental to a viable methodology and strategy for achieving a cost-effective fraud detection solution.

6.6.5 *Step Five: Investigation Evaluation*

At this stage in the forensic investigation, the models, clusters, or graphical networks have been constructed and appear to have a high degree of quality from an analysis perspective. However, before proceeding to final deployment, it is important to evaluate them thoroughly and review the steps executed to construct them to be certain they properly achieve the fraud detection objectives. A key goal for the investigator is to determine if there is some important issue that has not been sufficiently considered, such as a high number of false positives, which can impact the total cost of operational deployment. At the end of this phase, a decision on the use of forensic results and models should be reached with the client organization. The entire process is iterative, and this evaluation phase should ensure and validate the results before final deployment.

6.6.6 *Step Six: Detection Deployment*

The deployment of the fraud detection models and insight is often the neglected phase of most machine learning investigations. For fraud detection, this phase requires a commitment to continuous learning and improvement, automated monitoring, and error evaluation. This phase requires the refreshing of models to capture the ever-changing characteristics of criminal avoidance. Creation of clusters, graphs, or models is generally not the end of a fraud detection project. Even if the purpose of the investigation is to increase knowledge from the data, the knowledge gained will need to be organized and presented in such a way that it can be used in a production environment. Code or rules may need to be exported into production systems, such as a call site, website, or proprietary networks. Depending on the client organization's requirements, the deployment phase can be as simple as generating a report or as complex as implementing a repeatable forensic process with a stream of rules generated on a regular basis.

6.7 Forensic Ensemble Techniques

The optimal methodology for fraud detection is to avoid designing a system that is rigid and based on a set of rules, code, or thresholds that can be easily circumvented by knowledgeable perpetrators. In addition, the fraud detection systems and models cannot be based on a single algorithm or technique; instead, they should be based on a paradigm of a committee of models. The methodology should employ an ensemble of techniques and models, with each providing a vote of confidence regarding the legitimacy of any transaction, whether it is credit card purchases, insurance medical claims, website transactions, or any other type of events a forensic investigator is trying to detect. The following are some essential steps needed to execute this type of forensic investigation.

6.7.1 Stage One: Random Sampling

A random sample of fraudulent digital evidence should be collected and used in the construction of multiple graphs, clusters, and models. That is, fraudulent transactions need to be used in the development of very specific models along the lines of different product lines or services—since they are very unique in terms of the different types of schemes and the criminals they attract. Fraud detection models will require the sampling of legal and illegal transactions in order to discriminate between them.

6.7.2 Stage Two: Balance the Data

Another important step is having an adequate sampling of all types of fraudulent transactions along with an equal number of legal ones. The point is to develop rules and code to distinguish between the two; this is especially important when developing predictive rules via symbolic classifiers such as decision trees, which require an adequate number of observations to be able to recognize the unique features of the phenomena of fraud they are attempting to recognize and detect.

6.7.3 Stage Three: Split the Data

It is a common and standard practice in advanced predictive analytics to split the data into at least two parts, a training data set for the constructing of models and a testing data set for evaluation and calibration of error rates. However, due to the nature of criminal detection and infrequency of fraud, where samples tend to be tiny, an extra step should be taken: data should be split into three segments: training, testing, and validating data sets.

6.7.4 Stage Four: Rotate the Data

As an extra precaution and to ensure the optimization of the fraud detection effort, aside from splitting the data into three segments for training, testing, and validating, the data sets should also be rotated—again, this is done because of the relative scarcity of fraud sample data sets. The rotation of the data can be structured as follows:

Training	Data Set 1	Data Set 2	Data Set 3	Results A
Testing	Data Set 2	Data Set 3	Data Set 1	Results B
Validating	Data Set 3	Data Set 1	Data Set 2	Results C
	Results A	Results B	Results C	**Final Solution**

6.7.5 Stage Five: Evaluate Multiple Models

The optimum method for ensuring the best possible detection system is through the use and comparison of multiple models created with Self-Organizing Map (SOM) clustering, decision trees, and rule generators. If time permits, multiple software tools should be downloaded for evaluation and tested to optimize the performance and the lowering of error rates. An additional step is the testing of a neural network using a genetic algorithm for optimization; it should be noted that such tools are readily available in analytical sites for free evaluation. A good site where such tools are available is http://www.kdnuggets.com.

6.7.6 *Stage Six: Create an Ensemble Model*

After splitting, rotation of the data, and the evaluation of multiple models, an ensemble of models can be created with the following methodology:

SOM Clustering	Data Set 1	Data Set 2	Data Set 3	Results A
Decision Tree	Data Set 2	Data Set 3	Data Set 1	Results B
Rule Generator	Data Set 3	Data Set 1	Data Set 2	Results C
	Results A	Results B	Results C	**Final Solution**

The model ensemble combines the results from the best-performing analytical processes for the forensic investigator; it optimizes the detection capabilities and completely saturates the search space via clustering, segmentation, classification, and prediction. This machine learning forensic methodology and scheme is also known as the statistical technique of *bagging* or the voting by multiple classification technologies for combining the prediction results from an assortment of models. This machine learning forensic methodology is used to address the inherent instability of results when applying complex multiple models to relatively small data sets, as is often the case with fraud investigations. Another technique, called *boosting*, is to derive weights to combine the prediction from those models in which greater weights are assigned to those observations that are difficult to classify (fraud events) and lower weights are given to those that are easy to classify (legal transactions).

6.7.7 Stage Seven: Measure False Positives and Negatives

Consideration should be given to the overall performance of the model ensemble—especially to cost of misclassifications errors—that is, the wrong fraud alerts (false positives) and undiscovered cases (false negatives):

	Crime	No Crime	
Alert	Correct	False Positive	Alert
No Alert	False Negatives	Correct	No Alert

Cost considerations are different for both of these misclassification errors. For false positives, for example, there is the manpower consideration for checking on a potential criminal case that turns out to be legal. For false negatives, the cost is the potential loss of revenue by not identifying a criminal incident. This may turn out to be the more expensive of both errors.

The biggest obstacle in any fraud detection system is the prediction of false positives. This is where a legitimate transaction, conducted by a legal consumer, be it a credit card owner, insurance policy holder, or any other legitimate customer, is misclassified as potentially fraudulent. There are two problems with false positives.

If the misclassification of legal transactions happens too often, a valuable legitimate customer is likely to get upset by the intrusion and delay this error creates. Worse yet is the implication that these consumers are labeled as criminals. Also, if the numbers of false positives are large, the business process may be erroneously delayed due to these misclassification errors.

6.7.8 Stage Eight: Deploy and Monitor

Once the fraud detection model ensemble has been built and tested, it must be deployed in a real-time business environment. This can be accomplished by the export of its rules, formulas, clusters, and assorted code from the models that most software tools support. The continuously changing environment and skewed distribution of data—coupled with the cost-sensitive requirements—complicate the evaluation of the performance of a fraud detection system. However, any adaptive fraud detection system must be continuously evaluated, monitored, and improved on a regular basis, as the methods and techniques of fraud behavior change and attempts to escape detection will no doubt continue. Crime and criminals do not stop, nor should the forensic investigation efforts to stop fraud and criminal behaviors. The investigator should strive to find solutions that automate this process of refreshing behavioral patterns.

6.7.9 *Stage Nine: Anomaly Detection*

Compounding the challenge to constructing an accurate fraud detection adaptive system is the reliance on historical fraud examples, which means they can only detect those patterns that were used to create the models. The ensemble and stages discussed in this section provide an optimum method for making the best possible decision on the predicted legitimacy of the system, along with a measure of confidence to support these detection alerts. Finally, as a means of identifying new fraud patterns, the forensic investigator should periodically perform a completely new clustering analysis using a SOM neural network and new data. The objective is to look for potentially fraudulent transactions that fall out of the patterns of normal transactions; this is a search for outliers. These are transactions that do not adhere to the way most business activities are carried out in a 24/7 business environment.

6.8 Fraud Detection Forensic Solutions

The following is a list of fraud detection services and software; they provide a diverse source of approaches for the forensic investigator. Some solutions are proprietary and industry specific, and may be leveraged by organizations with limited resources for developing their own machine learning forensic investigative team:

- *Alaric Fractals Systems* uses their proprietary inference techniques based on Bayesian methods to detect credit and debit card fraud. Alaric licenses its state-of-the-art payment software to banks, retailers, issuers, acquirers, and service providers. Alaric's products and expertise cover card fraud detection, card fraud prevention, and enterprise risk management, as well as EFT switching and authorization, solutions for ATM management, POS payments, web, wireless, and other payment channels. Fractals is a Java-based card fraud detection framework that uses easily configured rules and intelligent detection scoring to achieve high rates of fraud detection and fraud prevention.

Alaric Fractals Case Study

Swisscard faced a significant challenge from the ever-increasing problem of credit card fraud. Switzerland has continued to experience significant growth in both domestic and international fraud, mainly due to counterfeit, skimming, and card-not-present fraud, and BIN range attacks were becoming increasingly more prevalent. Swisscard's Risk Policies Department decided that a sophisticated fraud detection solution was required that not only would help Swisscard accurately differentiate fraudulent transactions from genuine ones but also would enable the business to decline or refer transactions as soon as the first fraudulent transaction was detected.

Swisscard was also implementing a new authorization system (CAMS2) and wished to introduce the new fraud detection capability at the same time. Swisscard already had use of Aristion from MasterCard—a rules-based fraud detection system—and the models maintained by American Express for detecting fraudulent transactions on American Express cards. However, the fraudsters' patterns changed too rapidly for a purely rules-based approach to be effective, and Swisscard required a system that could automatically identify fraudulent patterns across all card products while allowing it to apply its own well-established rules to check for known fraudulent behaviors.

Swisscard also realized that it needed a solution that was customized to the fraud patterns within its own card base and which would adaptively track card usage patterns. After an initial analysis, Swisscard's impression was that the only solutions in the marketplace that could meet these requirements were neural-network-based systems. Swisscard was concerned that the infrequent retraining process necessary to enable neural systems to keep up to date with changing fraud patterns would mean that a neural solution would not be sufficiently dynamic and adaptive for their needs. Swisscard decided that it needed a system that would:

- Be capable of maintaining its detection effectiveness continually with regular model updates that could be performed economically
- Operate in real time with CAMS2; provide detection strategies customized to the usage and fraud patterns specific to Swisscard
- Detect a high level of fraud with low false positives (good transactions flagged as fraud)
- Allow Swisscard to easily incorporate its own rules via a GUI-based interface
- Provide intelligible alerts that could easily be investigated (not a black box solution)
- Permit inclusion of third-party alerts to further enhance the detection capability
- Permit profile cardholder usage
- Operate on an open database to allow extensive management information to be extracted

Fractals' core technologies are probability theory and Bayesian inference to deliver its fraud detection performance while having an easy-to-use and open framework.

- *Analyst's Notebook 6*, from i2 Inc., conducts sophisticated link analysis, timeline analysis, and data visualization for complex investigations. This is the most popular, robust, and powerful link analysis tool in the market. It is used by defense, homeland security, and law enforcement agencies worldwide. Their i2 Fraud solution simultaneously collects and analyzes data from multiple sources and incorporates data acquisition tools for simultaneous searches over multiple databases. Filters and histograms show patterns and anomalies in data,

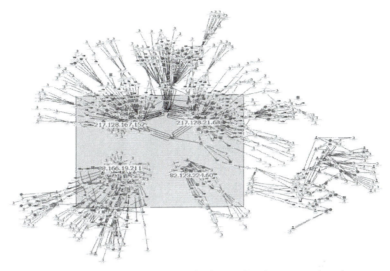

Visualize fraud from any medium: Internet, bank networks, telecom networks and more

Figure 6.1   An i2 link analysis fraud network.

with the ability to drill down queries. It can perform geospatial mapping of fraudsters by numerous types of data points (Figure 6.1).

An i2 Case Study

In a time of global financial crisis, CPPGroup Plc (CPP), a provider of card, identity protection, and mobile phone insurance, understood that it was imperative to detect and prevent fraud. With thousands of mobile insurance claims, CPP chose i2's *Analyst's Notebook* and *iBase* for its ability to visualize previously unknown fraudulent connections.

CPP has the daunting task of processing thousands of mobile insurance claims. In the midst of an economic downturn, it became even more critical for the CPP to be able to distinguish between legitimate and fraudulent claims. CPP created a Fraud Investigation Unit (FIU) with eight analysts to find, stop, and prevent fraud.

The FIU was instantly able to connect 5,000 previous fraud alerts to well over 100,000 customers through *Analyst's Notebook*.

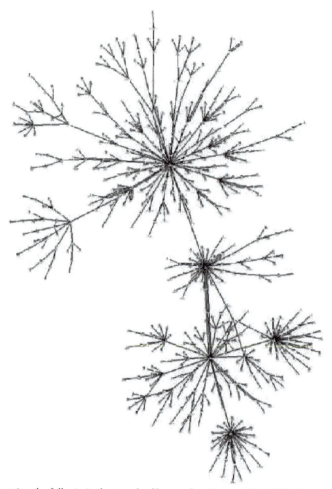

Exposing the full criminal network of known fraudsters within CPP's data would
have been previously undetectable without i2's Analyst's Notebook and iBase.

Figure 6.2   A CPP network of fraudsters exposed by i2 software.

They were able to visualize both organized networks of fraud as
well as individual customers. *iBase* recognized repeat claim sub-
missions from known fraudsters and blacklisted individuals who
were changing minor details such as surnames, bank accounts,
mobile phone numbers, or addresses to avoid detection, which
allowed CPP to save money by stopping these policies before further claims could be made. Over the initial three month period of
deployment, CPP identified over 1500 individuals connected to
false claims (Figure 6.2).

- *ALI Solutions* for collections, marketing, and risk management for consumer credit and Internet transactions. Their ActionOptimizer for Early Detection is a predictive analytic solution that provides a competitive edge to risk managers by delivering preemptive risk decision for Early-Month-on-Books ("EMOB") and semiactive account portfolios.
- *ArcSight AntiFraud Accelerator Solution* ArcSight FraudView detects and prevents online fraud by evaluating and scoring financial transactions in real time. Unlike legacy fraud prevention technologies, ArcSight FraudView can correlate activity across multiple banking channels to detect sophisticated fraud schemes that span online, ATM, telephone, and bank branch activity.
- *Centrifuge* offers analysts and investigators an integrated suite of capabilities that can help them rapidly understand and glean insight from new data sources. Centrifuge Systems uses advanced link analysis—complemented by charts, timelines, and geospatial views—with which investigative analysts can discover nonobvious relationships and significant insights. It allows analysts to easily combine disparate data sources and explore multiple visualizations in a single integrated workspace, all through a standard web browser.
- *Dinkla Artificial Intelligence and Fraud Detection* site contains links to white papers and other fraud detection sites.
- *Equifax Fraudscan* detects, validates, and verifies potentially fraudulent information automatically and simultaneously at the time of credit card application. Equifax is one of the three major credit bureaus in the United States, and it uses HNC's fraud-control program to offer an identity authentication score.
- *FICO* (formerly Fair, Isaac), offers Falcon and other tools for risk management systems, including credit card fraud detection.
- *Fraud Wiki, Fraud Detection and Prevention Wiki* Oscar Kilo consultancy offers customized Complex Event Processing (CEP) streaming analytic software and services.

- *FraudBreaker* CONECTYS web-based fraud detection software captures transaction data and performs real-time checks on a wide range of risk factors.
- *Friss Fraud Solutions* offers fraud and risk detection and settlement delivered with best practice fraud indicators in standard interfaces.
- *IDES technologies* introduces eyeDES, a next-generation customized analytical technology for accurate and efficient enterprise fraud management solutions.

An IDES Case Study

A bank facing growing losses from credit card fraudulent transactions decided to incorporate a more efficient solution in a cost-effective manner. The bank had an extensive portfolio in the credit card (CC) market, having hundreds of thousands of CC transactions occurring each day. Even though their percentage was very small, the fraudulent transactions were resulting in large amounts of losses every year. In an attempt to reduce the losses due to fraud, the bank had been using a market-established fraud detection system. The system had a rule-based component that used some knowledge of the typical types of pre-fraud or fraud transactions and/or some information on stolen or copied cards. The second component was the statistical component where the personal profiles of card holders were determined and the deviations from their profiles were evaluated to determine the possibility of fraud.

eyeDES solution was tested for its performance as a statistical component. For this test, the IDES team had access to the full bank card data mart containing 279 variables. The number of variables selected from the data mart was 72, where some of them were based on other variable combinations. After applying feature reduction and selection techniques, the team ended up with 17 variables to be used in the eyeDES model. Using this strategy, eyeDES solution increased the detection rate of the fraud transactions that were identified as fraudulent and, at the same time, decreased the number of total fraud alerts produced daily.

IDES Technologies' team worked on fine-tuning eyeDES model parameters and ended up with twice the number of identified frauds with even 5% less number of alerts. The IDES solution doubled the fraud hit rate and reduced the number of fraud alerts. Based on these results, eye DES solution was chosen to replace the statistical component that was used by the bank in their credit card fraud management system.

- *InferX* remote distributed analytic solutions for law enforcement, intrusion detection, and related fraud detection applications.
- *Infoglide* are developers of the patented Similarity Search Engine (SSE) for finding fraud in the insurance industry. It includes a function for screening and detecting common employee fraud problems, such as policy violations, embezzlement, theft of customer or bank assets, and theft of customer data. It enables organizations to screen, investigate, and monitor fraudulent activities across multiple data sources, geolocations, and delivery channels. It exposes fraudulent social networks though identity matching and nonobvious relationship analytics.
- *International Compliance Association* supports and educates compliance professionals in the fight against terrorist financing, corruption, money laundering, and financial crime (Figure 6.3).
- *LEADMiner* offers a refinement of Numerically Integrated Profiling System (NIPS) developed for US government fraud detection and trade analysis. Data Mining International, Inc. (DMI), a private company, develops tools and technologies to identify risk patterns of illicit activity within global trade and financial transactions. DMI is the sole software and services supplier to the Trade Transparency Initiative. Its units are currently being deployed worldwide.
- *Magnify PATTERN:Detect™* is used for uncovering fraud and anomalies, such as fraudulent credit card transactions or network intrusions. It is now part of LexisNexis Insurance Claim Solution.

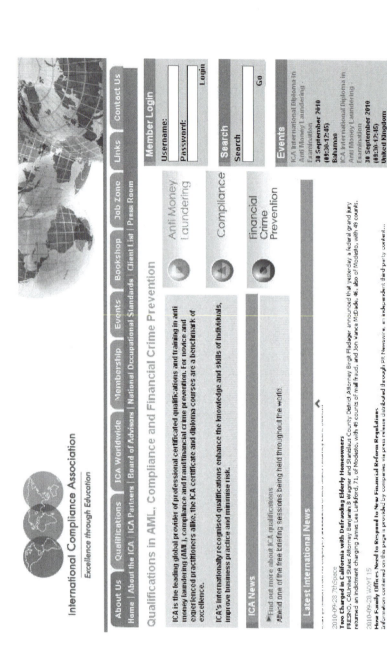

Figure 6.3   ICA provides a wide range of news and training in fraud detection.

- *Neural Technologies Decider* Neuralt offers a suite of solutions, Minotaur, for the finance industry for modeling and score-card development for detecting bad debt and application fraud.

A Neuralt Case Study

At the beginning of 2006, DIRECTV decided that it needed to look for a partner organization to assist it with its increasing fraud problem. The types of fraud the company was experiencing were varied and included

Commercial Misuse—Fraudsters activate a residential account at a commercial establishment (for example, at a bar or a tavern).

Mirroring—Fraudsters establish an account, or multiple accounts, with several receivers and sell the receivers to be used at another address.

Repeat Debtor—A previous customer who owes money attempts to set up a new account.

Account Flipping—Accounts that are shut down after a certain number of months and then reactivated, resulting in another commission payment for the dealer for the same customer.

ID Theft/Manipulation—Fraudsters misrepresent their identity in an effort to obtain services without paying.

Neural Technologies worked with DIRECTV's Fraud and Finance departments to identify several key metrics that enabled the success of the project to be measured. Within seven months, all the financial metrics were met, demonstrating complete system investment payback, which included the total cost of purchase, inclusive of all installation, lifetime product license costs, and internal IT costs.

In the period January to October 2009, DIRECTV saved more than $60 million through the identification of fraudulent subscriptions. This healthy return on investment is calculated on the savings made by DIRECTV relating to the substantial up-front costs it faces each time it activates a new account. Kent Mader, Senior Director of Fraud Management for DIRECTV, explained, "The cost of activating a new subscription amounts to around $700; therefore, the ability to identify suspicious applications at the outset helps us to make serious savings. Neural Technologies' Minotaur software not only helps us identify individual fraudulent applications, it also enables us to identify fraud rings, that is, multiple fraudulent accounts with linking account information. It enables DIRECTV to be tough on fraudsters—50% of the fraud rings we identify are presented to law enforcement for criminal prosecution."

Further benefits for DIRECTV include the following:

- Automation of manual fraud processes and improved staff efficiency
- Earlier identification of fraud abuse; identification time reduced from around one month to several days
- Significant increase in volume of fraud abuse identified
- Ability to make changes to fraud configuration/models "post go-live"

The last point is extremely important because fraud is an ever-moving target. Therefore, it is essential for DIRECTV to be able to make quick system changes without Neural Technologies' help. This has led to ongoing system performance improvement and the ability to adapt to ever-changing business models' challenges.

- *Plug&Score*, scorecard development software that can be used with any phase in the loan cycle from loan origination to fraud detection and prevention
- *Searchspace*, now NICE Actimize, is a fraud prevention solution to detect, prevent, and identify card, employee, deposit, and employee trading fraud.
- *Svivot SN-Sphere™* creates effective intelligence related to networks, associations of people and organizations working together in a particular context.
- *The Modeling Agency* offers PiCard(SM) Intelligent Procurement Card Monitoring System, designed to actively

detect misuse, target auditing team effort, reduce risk when moving from a purchase order system to credit cards, promote higher purchase card volume sooner, and forecast usage trends. Consulting and training is also provided by this agency.

- *StatConsulting* offers fraud detection based on customer behavior modeling using the latest data mining methods together with traditional statistics.
- *Xtract Fraud Detector* uses adaptive neural nets to analyze customer behavior and detect insurance claims fraud, payment card fraud, and more.

6.9 Assembling an Evolving Fraud Detection Framework

The rise of the web and wireless has impacted every organization, with each transaction bringing with it a challenge for the forensic investigator and team to detect potential fraud, which can occur in microseconds over a vast number of individual accounts. Driven to cut operational costs, organizations have evolved into centers of self-service, where consumers can create, modify, and operate accounts for purchases, payments, orders, transfers, and millions of other transactions every second of every day. Increasingly, this attracts criminals, hackers, and malware designed to perpetuate organized fraud, which increasingly has grown to be highly sophisticated. The overall result for organizations and machine learning forensic investigators is that they must constantly devise detection methods that are smart, numerous, and constantly evolving with new schemes of deterrence.

The effects of online and mobile fraud are enormous, resulting in millions of lost revenue, high operating costs, delays in service, inconvenience for consumers, and large penalty fees. Criminals use an assortment of modus operandi to instigate fraud, including the following three criminal schemes:

1. Using phishing attacks to steal and capture legal authentic credentials from unsuspecting consumers
2. Using stolen payment account numbers to make illegal purchases of products and services, which are quickly sold for cash

3. Using sophisticated bots executing "man in the browser" (MITB) attacks to steal funds and identities during fully authenticated sessions

The result for forensic investigators is that they must concentrate their efforts to combat these fraudulent criminal acts in the following areas:

1. Continuously monitor and detect account takeovers
2. Monitor and detect suspicious account creation and modifications
3. Develop an ensemble of antifraud rules for detecting suspicious transactions

The forensic investigator must be alert and monitor such factors as the normal time frames between account creation and the use of suspicious machine IP addresses and normal usage patterns to determine the likelihood of unauthorized access due to account takeover. Rules need to be created by the forensic investigator for benchmarking normal behavior versus abnormal behaviors, which could indicate potential cyber attacks by criminals. The investigator needs to use a variety of Internet mechanisms, such as log files, JavaScript, and cookies, to determine the difference between normal and abnormal behaviors in an organization's servers and website.

Usage patterns, destination country, and requester IP address are all clues for the forensic investigator that can indicate potential fraud attacks. The machine learning investigation can lead to the development of dynamic rules to analyze these factors, such as destination addresses, web page usages, and database actions requests. The investigator is responsible for developing rules to analyze these factors and patterns, which may indicate a high level of risk and potential fraud.

A common method of account takeovers is via the use of bots, which are also known as web robots. They are software applications that run automated tasks over the web. Typically, bots perform tasks, both simple and structurally repetitive, at a much higher rate than would be possible for a human alone. The largest use of bots is in spidering, in which an automated script fetches, analyzes, and files information from web servers instantly, including the stealing of identities and funds. In a "man in the browser" (MITB) attack, the bot program sits between the user and an organization server, and displays what appears to be a normal page to the customer, while actually creating transactions designed to steal funds, products, and services.

The consumer is kept in the dark about the transactions invoked by the MITB bot, and the organization is also blind to the account takeover, unless predictive rules are in place to issue immediate alerts. To thwart such takeovers, the forensic investigator needs to develop and apply machine learning rules to monitor account activities, such as an unusual amount of transactions by the minute. For example, if the bot creates a barrage of transactions invoked multiple times in a very short time frame, then the likelihood of an MITB takeover is imminent. Multiple low-level transactions might be deemed a low risk, but if they all happen within a few minutes, then rules should be deployed to issue alerts. These antifraud rules should be designed to become active as trends and suspicious activities are detected.

For example, machine learning rules developed by the forensic investigator can rate and score each account or transaction on a risk scale of, say, 1 to 100, with a cutoff behavior score of, say, 70, causing an alert to be generated for immediate counteraction and the opening of an active investigation. Simultaneously, an automated detection of a pattern may find that such activity, when analyzed with other activities and in conjunction with other events, matches a particular pattern warranting a fraudulent alert. These high-risk alerts allow investigators to focus and respond to transactions indicating a possible theft and fraudulent activities.

The risk model also allows for the import of attributes from external sources, such as a blacklist feed from previously detected fraudulent activities. The capability of matching external feeds allows investigators to identify gangs of criminals by networking them to known hostile IP addresses, or to compare a user's host machine to lists of suspicious payees, countries, or fraudulent identification numbers. There are also commercial demographics that can be enlisted to develop robust profiles of criminal hackers for investigative triangulation.

Similarly, suspiciously rapid movements and behaviors can trigger high-risk alerts; for example, when an account deviates from normal behavior, machine learning rules developed by investigators can detect the patterns of activity that can be marked as fraudulent, and attributes that indicate high risk. These high-risk behaviors may include rapid money movement or purchases, payee manipulations, change of account addresses and passwords, and other account administration activities. The forensic investigator must tier these activities into a detection network of predictive rules and conditions, so that, for example, (1) destination, (2) transaction, and (3) device risk scores are generated as these activities take place.

Destination risk scores can be applied when a payment country, foreign address, or suspicious payee or recipient are involved. Transaction risk scores apply when suspicious orders of purchases take place in odd amounts, and at strange times of day and day of the week. Device risk scores apply on the basis of suspicious account geolocation, IP address, system alterations, and previous attack histories. The investigator should also consider developing a tier of watch lists, so that as suspicious behavior takes place, that account will come under additional scrutiny. If the suspicious behavior continues, the account is elevated to a suspicious watch list and is closely monitored, investigated thoroughly, and eventually closed.

Finally, the forensic investigator should monitor potential fraud activities by developing several levels of risk from Low, to Medium, to High. A built-in case management system should be developed either by issuing regular reports or by the development of a dashboard to monitor cases and accounts as these predictive rules are triggered. Notifications or risk scores and alerts need to be issued on a 24/7 basis for an adaptive fraud detection system to succeed and be effective. Once a pattern has been determined to be indicative of fraudulent activity, it can be marked as such, and a new rule can be created to detect future instances of attacks.

The point of the detection system is to be adaptive and creative in its search for deviations while at the same time evaluating transactions as they occur in real time against a network of fraud detection rules developed by multiple machine learning forensic investigations. As each correlation rule is triggered, the system can have a series of actions associated with it, and an evolving method of adapting is developed over time so that an organization can "learn" the patterns of fraud activities and criminal attacks by individuals and organized groups of hackers.

New detection rules of fraud behaviors can be used for analysis against historical transactions to see if similarities exist with other accounts; thus, networks of suspicious IP addresses, machines, and geolocations can be uncovered, and the system can eventually become smarter. One clear example of how real-time demographic and geolocation could be leveraged to target perpetrators is by identifying users from suspect countries such as those from Ukraine, Latvia, Estonia, Belarus, and Georgia.

7

CYBERSECURITY INVESTIGATIONS

Self-Organizing and Evolving Analyses

7.1 What Is Cybersecurity Forensics?

As with other types of machine learning forensic investigations, with cybersecurity crimes one needs to follow methodical techniques to solve crimes involving machines attacking other machines. It requires the application of human skills and experience, coupled with pattern recognition software and a precise investigative methodology. Such investigations involves sifting through gigabytes of data and server log files looking for specific clues to discover what happened at certain times and locations over networks, server farms, and the Internet. This usually involves remote digital attacks on machines, networks, and websites that are commonly referred to as an incident breach, which is followed by an incident response.

An incident response involves forensic investigations requiring the preservation, identification, extraction, documentation, and interpretation of digital evidence. The forensic investigator needs to understand from the start of a cybersecurity case that the preservation of intent, evidence, and other digital clues may end up in a courtroom. The key mission of the investigator in this type of digital crime is timely and precise documentation throughout the entire process.

A Cybersecurity Investigation Methodology Checklist

1. The investigator needs to acquire the digital evidence without altering or damaging it in its original format from its original location.
2. The investigator needs to authenticate how the evidence was recovered:
   a. When: precise time and date.

    b. Where: exact location of servers, machines, logs, and data.

    c. What: evidence recovered with detailed information about its format.

    d. Why: how did the digital investigation lead to perpetrators.

3. Lastly, the investigator needs to use an assortment of machine learning forensic tools to analyze the data evidence without modifying it; these analyses can also lead to the identification of other perpetrators.

However, a cybersecurity investigation is much more than simply detecting and prosecuting digital crimes and hackers. More importantly, it is about ensuring that such attacks cannot take place again. This type of investigation is more about security than convictions, although the latter is a good deterrent and thus helps ensure security. Cybersecurity forensic methods consist of multidisciplinary approaches, including the following tasks:

1. Investigate a crime or a scene of an incident
2. Reconstruct the scene or incident
3. Collect the digital evidence, and make a copy of the original data
4. Analyze the evidence using inductive and deductive forensic tools
5. Establish linkages, associations, and reconstructions
6. Use the evidence for the prosecution of perpetrators

7.2 Cybersecurity and Risk

Emerging technologies such as cloud computing, mobile devices, and social networks are expanding the risk horizon for many organizations. No longer can the IT and security departments within those organizations rely solely on firewalls, antivirus programs, and other cyber fences. Increasingly, these emerging technologies elevate the level of risk for all organizations and their employees. For an organization, a new cybersecurity strategy needs to be developed in which the focus is clearly on the security of *data* rather than only physical networks or servers. Employees within these organizations need to be briefed or restricted on how they use social media and personal mobile devices, for they provide new attack points for increasingly sophisticated data thieves.

Cloud computing is fraught with security risks; organizations and forensic investigators need to ask tough questions and consider getting a security assessment from a neutral third party before committing to a cloud vendor. Cloud computing requires risk assessment in areas such as data integrity, recovery, and privacy; and it requires an evaluation of legal issues in areas such as e-discovery, regulatory compliance, and auditing by forensic investigators. Amazon's EC2 service and Google's Google App Engine are prime examples of cloud computing, in which massively scalable IT-enabled capabilities are delivered "as a utility service" to external customers using Internet technologies.

Cloud computing offers enticing economies of scale, promising organizations a dramatic reduction in spending on technology infrastructure, but they also put their crown jewels—their data—in the hands of a remote storage vendor. Forensic investigators and their clients must demand transparency, and request detailed information on security programs from cloud vendors. Investigators need to know about the qualifications of policy makers, architects, coders, and operators; they need to know about risk-control processes and technical mechanisms; and the level of testing that has been done to verify that service and control processes are functioning as intended, and that vendors can identify unanticipated vulnerabilities.

A Forensic Investigator Cloud Checklist

1. Who are the technicians and administrators, what background investigations were conducted when they were hired, and what oversight and controls does the vendor have in place over their access, privileges, tracking histories, and contracts?
2. Demand the right to conduct external audits of their storing system and request to view security certifications of their employees.
3. Ask that your data be stored and processed in specific jurisdictions, and demand contractual commitment to obey local privacy requirements; for example, Europe is different from Asia.
4. How is the data segregated, replicated, and encrypted? Ask to see evidence that encryption schemes were designed and tested by experienced specialists.
5. Get a contractual commitment allowing for forensic investigations to be conducted in the event of intrusion attacks or compromises of their cloud.

Social network risk comes in the form of potential damage to an organization's reputation. There is an emerging risk in the social network environment called niche social bookmarking, where users can "tag" or associate organizations to specific content. The iPhone antennae comes to mind; once unleashed the damage is done, and it is fast and vast, and so counterintelligence strategies need to be planned and kept ready for execution. Forensic investigators need to keep an eye on Facebook to make sure no one is posting damaging content on the client organization, and Google Alerts can also pick up stuff from blogs and other periodicals. Organizations need to put policies and technologies in place to minimize the risk of employees damaging the company's reputation on social networking sites.

Today, many workers are carrying mobile devices that contain at least some business data, such as contact lists, account passwords, confidential e-mails, phone numbers, and file attachments. Increasingly, this means organizations are being exposed to attack points they have no control of when these devices are lost, or worse, stolen by knowledgeable perpetrators. While these devices are increasingly well connected, they are largely unsecured and can pose a significant risk to organizations. Reducing that risk starts with establishing an information security policy that deals with both employee-purchased and company-owned mobile devices. However, periodic audits by forensic investigators should be conducted randomly on staff personnel devices, under contractual employee agreements; the focus of the audits is the location of proprietary and confidential information from the client organization, which the employee may not realize could be a security compromise breach.

7.3 Machine Learning Forensics for Cybersecurity

Machine learning for cybersecurity is the task of taking a forensic discipline approach using computers—with the primary goal of discovering how intrusions have taken place—and how they can be protected from future attacks. This involves the modeling and simulation of computer behaviors and attacks against other computer systems, servers, and networks. Machine learning forensics involves combating cybersecurity intrusions by observing, capturing, and modeling how, where, and when digital crimes takes place.

This type of digital forensics relies on machine learning pattern recognition technology to study digital evidence as it relates to criminal events and scenes involving illegal intrusions and thefts via the analysis of file systems, mobile devices, log files, and other digital depositories as they relate to web and wireless systems. Cybersecurity forensics relies on a hybrid of intelligence from humans and machines; today, most intrusion detection systems (IDSs) are one of the core technologies of computer security. The goal of intrusion detection is the identification of malicious activity in a stream of monitored data, which can be network traffic, operating system events, or log entries.

However, most current IDSs rely on a signature-based approach in which, similar to virus scanners, events are detected that match specific predetermined patterns known as signatures, which are created manually by IT security personnel. The main limitation of these signature-based IDSs is their failure to identify novel attacks, and sometimes even minor variations of known patterns. Besides, a significant administrative overhead is incurred by the need to maintain signature databases. Machine learning forensics provides a different approach to improve quality and to facilitate administration of these rigid rule-based IDSs.

IDSs are usually deployed along with other preventive security mechanisms, such as access control and authentication, as a second line of defense that protects information systems. IDSs are traditionally categorized into two methodologies: anomaly detection and misuse detection. Anomaly detection is based on the normal behavior of a subject (e.g., a user or a system); any action that significantly deviates from normal behavior is considered intrusive. Misuse detection catches intrusions in terms of the characteristics of known attacks or system vulnerabilities; any action that conforms to the pattern of a known attack or vulnerability is considered intrusive.

IDSs can also be classified into host-based, distributed, and network-based. A host-based IDS gets audit data from host audit trails and usually aims at detecting attacks against a single host; a distributed IDS gathers audit data from multiple hosts and possibly the network that connects the hosts, aiming at detecting attacks involving multiple hosts. A network-based IDS uses network traffic as the audit data source, relieving the burden on the hosts that usually provide normal computing services. These IDSs do not employ machine learning algorithms and thus are in effect expert system utilizing human-generated rules.

On the other hand, an unsupervised analysis using a SOM could be developed that is capable of issuing alerts to these exclusively human-developed rule-based IDSs. For example, SOM clusters would be based on different system parameters such as

1. Central processing unit (CPU) usage
2. Paging activity
3. Mailer activity
4. Disk accesses
5. Memory usage
6. Average session time
7. Number of users
8. Absentee jobs
9. Reads of "help" files
10. Failed log-ins
11. Multiple log-ins

Deviation from normal network activities would be displayed by the SOM in graphical maps; these deviations could identify specific attack attempts and could be used to target remote perpetrators' machines, geographic locations, and IP addresses. From this unsupervised clustering analysis, machine learning forensic investigators could next move to develop predictive rules via the use of deductive tools.

Supervised learning via decision trees can be used for automatically generating a set of conditional detectors without the need to manually define and update signatures. In addition, anomaly detection and other unsupervised learning techniques using neural network self-organizing maps can detect new kinds of attacks, provided they exhibit unusual characteristics in some feature space. Several studies indicate that the use of an ensemble of algorithms is the optimum approach to detecting different types of cyber intrusions, including (1) probing attacks; these are information-gathering intrusions, (2) denial-of-service (DoS) attacks; these are intrusions that deny legitimate requests to a system, (3) user-to-root (U2R) attacks, which are unauthorized accesses to local super-user or root, and (4) remote-to-local (R2L) attacks, which are unauthorized local accesses from a remote machine.

Machine learning rules can be created on the basis of different network behaviors. For example, rules can be created on the basis of sequential patterns that represent highly repetitive activities and are expected to provide predication. The temporal patterns, which are represented in the form of rules, are generated and modified from the input data using a logical inference for inductive generalization. When applied to intrusion detection, the rules describe the behavior patterns of either a user or a group of users based on past audit history. Each rule describes a sequential event pattern that predicts the next event from a given sequence of events. An optional approach to generating machine learning rules is instance-based learning, to learn entities' (e.g., users) normal behavior from temporal sequence data.

7.4 Deep Packet Inspection (DPI)

Another limitation of IDSs is that they cannot block attacks effectively, only detect them. In addition, their detection capabilities are also limited, with a high number of false positives and negatives, since they lack the machine learning capabilities discussed here. Because they rely on static rules, their management burden is huge, theoretically demanding 24-hour monitoring of their functioning.

However, a newer technology can be enlisted by forensic investigators to supplement the limitations of IDS, and that is deep packet inspection (DPI). DPI is normally referred to as a technology that allows packet-inspecting devices, such as firewalls and IPS, to deeply analyze packet contents, including information from all seven layers of the Open Systems Interconnection (OSI) model. The OSI model is a way of subdividing a communications system into smaller parts called *layers*. The following is the hierarchy of the OSI model (Figure 7.1).

7.4.1 Layer 7: Application

This layer supports application and end-user processes. Communication partners are identified, quality of service is identified, user authentication and privacy are considered, and any constraints on data syntax are identified. Everything at this layer is application specific. This layer provides application services for file transfers, e-mail, and other network software services.

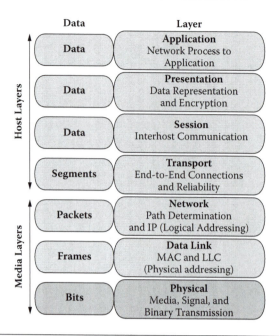

Figure 7.1   The OSI Model and its seven packet layers.

7.4.2 Layer 6: Presentation

This layer provides independence from differences in data representation, such as encryption by translating from application to network format, and vice versa. The presentation layer works to transform data into a form that the application layer can accept. It is sometimes called the *syntax layer*.

7.4.3 Layer 5: Session

This layer establishes, manages, and terminates connections between applications. The session layer sets up, coordinates, and terminates conversations, exchanges, and dialogues between the applications at each end. It deals with session and connection coordination.

7.4.4 Layer 4: Transport

This layer provides transparent transfer of data between end systems, or hosts, and is responsible for end-to-end error recovery and flow control. It ensures complete data transfer.

7.4.5 Layer 3: Network

This layer provides switching and routing technologies, creating logical paths, known as *virtual circuits*, for transmitting data from node to node. Routing, forwarding, addressing, internetworking, error handling, congestion control, and packet sequencing takes place at this layer.

7.4.6 Layer 2: Data Link

At this layer, data packets are encoded and decoded into bits. It furnishes transmission protocol knowledge and management and handles errors in the physical layer, flow control, and frame synchronization.

7.4.7 Layer 1: Physical

This layer conveys the bit stream—electrical impulse, light or radio signal—through the network at the electrical and mechanical level. It provides the hardware means of sending and receiving data on a carrier.

7.4.8 Software Tools Using DPI

There are two types of network security software tools using DPI technology. First, there are firewalls that have implemented content-inspection features present in IDS systems. Second, there are IDS systems working with an in-line positioning approach, intended to protect the networks instead of just detecting attacks against them.

First, with regard to analyzing firewalls that have incorporated IDS features, there are two key technologies making this possible: pattern (signature) rule-matching and protocol anomaly (clustering). The first approach incorporates a database of known network attacks and analyzes each packet against it. The limitation to this approach, however, is that success in the protection of a network is normally obtained only for known attacks, which have signatures (rules) previously stored in a database. Machine learning forensic investigators can supplement these static rules by conducting deductive analyses to develop new dynamic rules using decision tree and rule-generating software.

The second approach, protocol anomaly, incorporates a key security principle known as *default deny*. The idea is to, instead of allowing all packets in which content does not match the signatures database, define what should be allowed, based on the definitions of how the protocol works. The main benefit is to block even unknown attacks. Because the time window between the discovery of a new vulnerability and their exploitation by tools or worms has dramatically decreased, this ability can be considered almost indispensable nowadays. As with the first approach, machine learning forensic investigators can supplement this type of anomaly detection via the analysis of traffic using neural network self-organizing map (SOM) software. These analyses go beyond the common approaches, because they combine both IDS, DPI, and machine learning techniques and technologies for protocol anomaly detection and signature scanning.

7.5 Network Security Tools

Network security software prevents unauthorized access to a computer network. Organizations use these applications to prevent unauthorized, malicious, or inadvertent intrusions into or usage of secure systems. Network security solutions are designed to recognize legitimate traffic over today's complex enterprise networks and isolate abnormal events for further investigation as well as to perform key security audit and regulatory compliance functions. Features can include antispam, antivirus, and intrusion detection; the following list gives the most popular network security products.

Active Network—Active Wall: Provides continuous enterprisewide protection against the full range of Internet threats.

Astaro Internet Security—Astaro Security Gateway: Unified threat management solution providing complete e-mail, web, and network protection.

COMDOM Software—COMDOM Antispam for Servers: Antispam system operating as a stand-alone mail gateway with relay control, authentication, and load-balancing support.

CrossTec—Activeworx Enterprise: Secure, cross-platform, remote support, management, inventory, file transfer, and scripting software.

Cyber Operations—ACL Manager: Centrally managing thousands of router ACLs from a single software application.

Data Infocom—SpamJadoo: Antispam service that eliminates spam at the protocol level.

DragonSoft Security Associates—DragonSoft Vulnerability Management: Vulnerability assessment software with network scanning, vulnerabilities evaluation, risk assessment, reporting, and remediation.

ExaProtect—Solsoft Policy Server: Solution for the unified management of network security that meets the challenges of today's IT infrastructures.

FreeStone Software—SafeInternetEmail: E-mail virus protection, spam, and server-based website content filtering.

Grisoft—AVG Internet Security: Centrally controlled complete protection for networks.

Grove Group—Business E-mail Security: Secure boundary services that protect e-mail communications by providing complete e-mail intrusion prevention.

Intelliden—Intelliden R-Series: Enables network-driven organizations to control, manage, and scale their networks.

Kaspersky Lab—Kaspersky Anti-Virus Business Optimal: Protects users against malicious programs such as viruses, worms, Trojans, hackers, spam, and other forms of intrusion.

MailCleaner—MailCleaner: Professional antispam server protection for ISP SME SMI and large companies.

Netcore Solutions—Emergic CleanMail: Provides comprehensive, secure, and reliable e-mail protection using multilayered proprietary technology.

Netsweeper—Netsweeper: Web content filtering specialist, focusing on protecting networks from spam, phishing, spyware, and other malicious applications.

PKWARE—SecureZIP: Provides practical, reliable data encryption and protection that is easy to deploy, maintain, and use.

Qualys—QualysGuard Enterprise: Monitors the vulnerability management process, tracks remediation, and ensures policy compliance.

ScanSafe Services—Web Security-as-a-Service: Ensures a safe web environment for businesses, keeping viruses and spyware off networks and ensuring secure web and instant messaging.

Software602—602LAN SUITE: Secure mail server with antivirus and antispam, built-in firewall with NAT and web content filter proxy.

SpectorSoft—Spector Pro: Desktop, Internet, and wireless monitoring and surveillance software for organizations concerned about inappropriate use of devices and the web.

TeleMate.Net Software—NetSpective Content Filter: Passive, deep packet inspection identifies URL, VoIP, and P2P signatures regardless of port with unprecedented scalability.

Utimaco—SafeGuard: A comprehensive solution portfolio that guarantees your organization protection from all data security requirements the way you want.

Zada Partners—Zada Suite: Wide array of solutions for various industries and government agencies.

Most of these high-end network security products provide the following types of functions and features:

- Custom user interface
- Customizable fields
- Customizable functionality
- Customizable reporting
- Data import/export
- E-mail attachment protection
- Event correlation
- Event relationship diagrams
- Event tracking
- Internet usage monitoring
- Intrusion detection system
- IP protection
- Legacy system integration
- Mobile access
- Multi-currency
- Multi-language
- Packet analyzer
- Reporting

- Software development kit
- Vulnerability scanning
- Web traffic reporting

We next move to another type of electronic crime that has become very problematic and common—phishing—which is the criminally fraudulent process of attempting to acquire sensitive information such as usernames, passwords, and credit card details by masquerading as a trustworthy entity in an e-mail or instant message. It is the type of cybercrime that involves rings of criminals using viruses to steal and loot money from unsuspecting victims. Phishing typically involves both humans and malicious code to steal money and identities.

7.6 Combating Phishing

Phishing takes place when communications, via e-mail usually, purporting to be from popular social networking sites, auction sites, online payment processors, gaming websites, online banking sites, or IT administrators are commonly used to lure unsuspecting online users. Phishing often directs users to enter details at a fake website whose look and feel are almost identical to the legitimate one, or by requesting information via an e-mail. Phishing is an example of social engineering techniques used to fool users, and is the act of manipulating people into performing actions or divulging confidential information, rather than by breaking in or using technical cracking techniques.

Zeus, which is also known as Zbot, PRG, Wsnpoem, Gorhax, and Kneber, is a phishing Trojan horse, which appears to perform a desirable function for the user prior to run or install but instead facilitates unauthorized access of the user's computer system. Zeus steals banking information by keystroke logging, which is the action of tracking (or logging) the keys struck on a keyboard, typically in a covert manner so that the person using the keyboard is unaware that his or her actions are being monitored.

Most recently, the FBI announced it had discovered a major international cyber crime network which had used Zeus to hack into US computers and steal around $70 million. More than 90 suspected members of the ring were arrested in the United States. Phishing usually targets individuals, but this gang targeted small businesses and municipalities. These latest bank heists involved criminals from Russia, Moldova, Ukraine, Kazakhstan, and Belarus in Eastern Europe; arrests were also made in the United Kingdom and the Ukraine. This is how it worked.

1. Criminals in Eastern Europe send seemingly innocent e-mails to small businesses and municipalities in the United States.
2. These e-mails contain the Zeus Trojan malware. Once the e-mails are opened, the malware embeds itself into the victims' computers.
3. The malware records the victims' keystrokes, which give the cyber criminals access to account numbers, passwords, and other personal data.
4. The cyber criminal uses the information to take over the victims' bank accounts.
5. The cyber criminal transfers money to accounts set up with fake IDs by "mules": people traveling in the United States or in the country on student visas.
6. The mules keep a percentage of the money—typically 10%—and transfer the rest to the cyber criminals.

Combating these types of phishing attacks takes collaborative effort by the forensic investigators involving both trace-back techniques and machine learning analyses involving such tools as link analysis. First, phishing domain take down procedures involve identifying the phishing hosting system via a trace-back routine. Traditional phishing hosting machines can be identified relatively quickly by their public DNS name or directly if their IP address is embedded within their spam e-mail. Phishers, however, are using a newer technique known as *fast-flux* networks, which use a pool of compromised machines to hide their phishing website hosting system, making phishing website trace-back difficult and impractical. However, discovering these fast-flux networks is possible via the use of a triangulation strategy using a collaborative intrusion detection system (CIDS) architecture.

In this scenario the participating CIDS are from different ISPs, which allows the fast-flux machines to be monitored via triangulation across different ISPs on the web. The suspicious communication pattern of fast-flux machines can thus be correlated across different

ISPs in a multistage manner, to trace-back the actual phishing website hosting machine. This CIDS architecture is highly scalable and self-healing through its use of a structured peer-to-peer network, and also enables the participants to be self-protecting; these decentralized remote CIDS are more effective than a fully centralized system.

Secondly, forensic investigators can perform link analyses to identify associations between ISPs, e-mail accounts, as well as the identification of associates and members of the phishing gang participants, such as the mules being used. To combat phishing, the strategy is one of collaboration—such as the CIDS and the collaboration of ISPs—along with forensic investigators performing analyses with the goal of identifying associations and relations of both machines and individuals. Once individuals have been identified, physical inspection of their machine by forensic investigators can identify hostile code.

7.7 Hostile Code

A great deal of software has been created to enable criminals to break in, steal, and take over machines remotely over the Internet. Some are benign, such as system administration suites, access control programs, and forensic utilities; while others are hacking tools designed to enable one person to exercise electronic superiority at the expense of someone else—these types of programs, such as Ataka, can be considered to be hostile code, and forensic investigators should be on the lookout for them.

Any code that can be used to destroy or steal information, or gain unauthorized access, must be treated as potentially hostile code. The presence of such hacking tools tells forensic investigators that the system being examined has been involved in a cyber attack. Consideration must be given, of course, that, cyber criminals do not need access to a machine in order to harm it; they can do it remotely over the Internet using their software agents.

There are four types of hostile code: (1) internally directed, (2) externally directed, (3) manual, and (4) autonomous. Of these, the most destructive are those that are self-replicating, such as viruses and worms. Viruses are not stand-alone programs; instead, they are code fragments that must ride piggyback within other programs, such as Word documents. Worms, on the other hand, are discrete programs that copy themselves to other computers over a network or the Internet. Worms are always stand-alone executable files.

Both viruses and worms, however, spread their self-replicating destruction most of the time randomly; in most cases, their attacks are not target specific. For example, in the Zeus attacks mentioned in this chapter, the targets were small firms and municipalities; however, the banks they stole money from were not the original targets, but instead were randomly selected. Whatever format these hostile code programs have, their goals are usually the following:

- Circumvent access control mechanisms
- Remote access
- Denial of service
- Elude detection
- Resources theft
- Data gathering
- Self-fulfillment
- Social status
- Sabotage
- Theft

More specifically, there are different types of hostile code for information gathering and stealing. First, there are vulnerability scanning active programs externally directed. They primarily map networks and locate hosts, identifying their characteristics. Second, there are sniffers; they are also externally directed, but they are passive. A sniffer collects all of the network traffic visible to it on a specific network segment, which is what network administrators need to perform their diagnostics.

Sniffers are usually application specific and are designed to collect logon and password pairs. One of the most dangerous sniffers is the Web_sniff, which is designed to sniff passwords from logons to password-protected Internet pages; the program sniffs packets destined for web servers and scans for headers with basic authentication, then automatically decodes the authentication string giving up username and password pairs in clear text.

Another type of hostile code is one designed specifically to steal passwords for digital identity theft; the following is a list of the most popular:

CODE NAME	PURPOSE
Gammaprog	Cracks passwords of web-based e-mail, such as Hotmail and Post Office Protocol (POP) an application-layer standard protocol
Hypnopaedia	Remotely connects to POP3 mail servers for passwords
John the Ripper	UNIX based; can attack UNIX and NT systems
Mssqlpwd	Cracks Microsoft SQL server passwords
PGPPASS	Cracks PGP key rings
Slurpie	UNIX-distributed password cracker
Webcracker	Remote brute force tool to crack passwords from Internet sites
Zipercrack	Cracks ZIP files
Cain	Can locate and retrieve cached passwords in the registry of PC machines or in .pwl files for Microsoft Windows. Cryptanalysis attacks are done via rainbow tables, which can be generated with the winrtgen.exe program provided with the program.

While knowledge of these tools is important, their use by forensic investigators is critical, and they need to use the Internet sites of antivirus software vendors as well as the CERT (United States Computer Emergency Readiness Team) to monitor for security alerts, as well as SANS for training and certification. These websites can also provide additional assistance:

- packetstormsecurity.org
- f-secure.com
- faqs.org
- iss.net

The more skilled the forensic investigator becomes, the more motivated criminals are to conceal their activities and attacks, encouraging the use of encryption. Encryption is the process of obscuring the content of messages and the obscuring of behavior. This can include the use of ciphers, which involve the use of mathematical techniques to alter data so that its meaning is not discernible unless an additional mathematical technique is applied. There are a number of ways of attacking encrypted text; the most common is a brute force technique in which a methodical attempt to substitute every possible key until the correct one is discovered. For example, the L0phtCrack or the Cain tool are password cracking tools that use cryptanalytic techniques to effectively reduce the potential keys and then offers the investigator a choice of potential passwords.

7.8 The Foreign Threat

Increasingly, organizations and government agencies are targets of organized attacks from foreign entities. The President of the United States Barack Obama recently said a cyber threat exists, which he described as one of the most serious economic and national security challenges we face as a nation. This threat, the president said, includes acts of terror that could come not only from a few extremists in suicide vests but from a few keystrokes on the computer.

The United States federal government is launching a program dubbed Perfect Citizen to detect cyber assaults on private companies and government agencies running critical infrastructure such as the electricity grid and nuclear power plants. These organized attacks may come 90% of the time come from locations where US laws do not apply—originating in foreign countries—and because these intrusions are international, forensic investigators must be aware of foreign laws and regulations.

Perfect Citizen would enlist the surveillance by the National Security Agency (NSA), the government's chief eavesdropping agency, and would rely on a set of sensors deployed in computer networks for critical infrastructure that would be triggered by unusual activity suggesting an impending cyber attack. The defense contractor Raytheon recently won a classified contract for the initial phase of the surveillance effort that is valued at over $100 million. Perfect Citizen is an important program to combat an emerging security threat that only the NSA is equipped to provide.

The overall purpose of Perfect Citizen is to ensure the protection of the public sector from foreign organized attacks and the security of the national infrastructure. US intelligence officials have grown increasingly alarmed about what they believe to be Chinese and Russia surveillance of computer systems that control the electric grid and other US infrastructure. Perfect Citizen will look at large, typically older computer control systems that were often designed without Internet connectivity or security in mind. Many of those systems—which run everything from subway systems to air traffic control networks—have since been linked to the Internet, making them more efficient but also exposing them to massive organized foreign cyber attacks.

The goal of Perfect Citizen is to close the big glaring holes in the US infrastructure and help US companies that could call on the NSA for assistance in future organized foreign cyber attacks, such as the one Google encountered from China. The US government has for more than a decade claimed a national security interest in privately owned critical infrastructure that, if attacked, could cause significant damage to the government or the economy. Initially, it established relationships with utility companies so it could, for instance, request that a power company seal a manhole that provides access to a key power line for a government agency. However, with the growth in concern about cyber attacks, these relationships began to extend into the electronic arena, and the only US agency equipped to manage electronic assessments of critical infrastructure vulnerabilities is the NSA.

The NSA years ago began a small-scale effort code-named April Strawberry to address this problem; the program researched vulnerabilities in critical infrastructure and sought ways to close security holes. The prototype of April Strawberry eventually led to initial work on Perfect Citizen, which was an effort to forge working relationships with energy companies whose infrastructure is widely used across the country. The classified program is now being expanded with funding from the multibillion dollar Comprehensive National Cybersecurity Initiative. The CNCI consists of a number of mutually reinforcing initiatives with the following major goals designed to help secure the United States in cyberspace:

- To establish a front line of defense against today's immediate threats by creating or enhancing shared situational awareness of network vulnerabilities, threats, and events within the federal government—and ultimately with state, local, and tribal governments and private sector partners—and the ability to act quickly to reduce our current vulnerabilities and prevent intrusions.
- To defend against the full spectrum of threats by enhancing US counterintelligence capabilities and increasing the security of the supply chain for key information technologies.
- To strengthen the future cybersecurity environment by expanding cyber education; coordinating and redirecting research and development efforts across the federal

government; and working to define and develop strategies to deter hostile or malicious activity in cyberspace.

7.8.1 The CNCI Initiative Details

Initiative 1: Manage the Federal Enterprise Network as a single network enterprise with Trusted Internet Connections. The Trusted Internet Connections (TIC) initiative, headed by the Office of Management and Budget and the Department of Homeland Security, covers the consolidation of the federal government's external access points (including those to the Internet). This consolidation will result in a common security solution that includes facilitating the reduction of external access points, establishing baseline security capabilities, and validating agency adherence to those security capabilities.

Initiative 2: Deploy an intrusion detection system of sensors across the Federal enterprise. Intrusion Detection Systems using passive sensors form a vital part of US government network defenses by identifying when unauthorized users attempt to gain access to those networks. DHS is deploying, as part of its EINSTEIN 2 activities, signature-based sensors capable of inspecting Internet traffic entering federal systems for unauthorized accesses and malicious content. The EINSTEIN 2 capability enables analysis of network flow information to identify potential malicious activity while conducting automatic full packet inspection of traffic entering or exiting US government networks for malicious activity using signature-based intrusion detection technology.

Initiative 3: Pursue deployment of intrusion prevention systems across the Federal enterprise. This Initiative represents the next evolution of protection for civilian departments and agencies of the Federal Executive Branch. This approach, called EINSTEIN 3, will draw on commercial technology and specialized government technology to conduct real-time full packet inspection and threat-based decision-making on network traffic entering or leaving these Executive Branch networks. The goal of EINSTEIN 3 is to identify and characterize malicious network traffic to enhance cybersecurity analysis, situational awareness, and security response. It will have the ability to automatically detect and respond appropriately to cyber threats before harm is done, providing an intrusion prevention system supporting dynamic defense.

Initiative 4: Coordinate and redirect research and development (R&D) efforts. No single individual or organization is aware of all of the cyber-related R&D activities being funded by the government. This initiative is developing strategies and structures for coordinating all cyber R&D sponsored or conducted by the US government, both classified and unclassified, and to redirect that R&D where needed. This initiative is critical to eliminate redundancies in federally funded cybersecurity research, and to identify research gaps, prioritize R&D efforts, and ensure the taxpayers are getting full value for their money as we shape our strategic investments.

Initiative 5: Connect current cyber ops centers to enhance situational awareness. There is a pressing need to ensure that government information security offices and strategic operations centers share data regarding malicious activities against federal systems, consistent with privacy protections for personally identifiable and other protected information and as legally appropriate, in order to have a better understanding of the entire threat to government systems and to take maximum advantage of each organization's unique capabilities to produce the best overall national cyber defense possible. This initiative provides the key means necessary to enable and support shared situational awareness and collaboration across six centers that are responsible for carrying out US cyber activities.

Initiative 6: Develop and implement a governmentwide cyber counterintelligence (CI) plan. A governmentwide cyber counterintelligence plan is necessary to coordinate activities across all federal agencies to detect, deter, and mitigate the foreign-sponsored cyber intelligence threat to US and private sector information systems.

Initiative 7: Increase the security of our classified networks. Classified networks house the federal government's most sensitive information and enable crucial war-fighting, diplomatic, counterterrorism, law enforcement, intelligence, and homeland security operations. Successful penetration or disruption of these networks could cause exceptionally grave damage to our national security. We need to exercise due diligence in ensuring the integrity of these networks and the data they contain.

Initiative 8: Expand cyber education. While billions of dollars are being spent on new technologies to secure the US government in cyberspace, it is the people with the right knowledge, skills, and abilities to implement those technologies who will determine success. In order to effectively ensure our continued technical advantage and future cybersecurity, we must develop a technologically skilled and cyber-savvy workforce and an effective pipeline of future employees.

Initiative 9: Define and develop enduring "leap-ahead" technology, strategies, and programs. One goal of the CNCI is to develop technologies that provide increases in cybersecurity by orders of magnitude above current systems and which can be deployed within 5 to 10 years. This initiative seeks to develop strategies and programs to enhance the component of the government R&D portfolio that pursues high-risk/high-payoff solutions to critical cybersecurity problems.

Initiative 10: Define and develop enduring deterrence strategies and programs. Our nation's senior policymakers must think through the long-range strategic options available to the United States in a world that depends on assuring the use of cyberspace. To date, the US government has been implementing traditional approaches to the cybersecurity problem—and these measures have not achieved the level of security needed.

Initiative 11: Develop a multi-pronged approach for global supply chain risk management. Globalization of the commercial information and communications technology marketplace provides increased opportunities for those intent on harming the United States by penetrating the supply chain to gain unauthorized access to data, alter data, or interrupt communications. Risks stemming from both the domestic and globalized supply chain must be managed in a strategic and comprehensive way over the entire lifecycle of products, systems, and services.

Initiative 12: Define the federal role for extending cybersecurity into critical infrastructure domains. The US government depends on a variety of privately owned and operated critical infrastructures to carry out the public's business. In turn, these critical infrastructures rely on the efficient operation of information systems and networks that are vulnerable to malicious cyber threats.

The CNCI is critical because cyber espionage has surged against governments and companies around the world, and cyber attacks have become common among states. US military and civilian networks are probed thousands of times a day; and the systems of the North Atlantic Treaty Organization (NATO) headquarters are attacked at least 100 times a day. These cyber attacks have become a new form of permanent, low-level warfare. More than 100 countries are currently trying to break into US networks, with China and Russia being the source of the greatest concentration of these attacks. For this reason, the administration has designated cyber security as a critical national asset. Cyber weapons are being developed at a rapid pace. Many countries—including the United States, Russia, China, Israel, the United Kingdom, Pakistan, India, and North and South Korea—have developed sophisticated cyber weapons that can repeatedly penetrate and destroy computer networks.

Already, scrimmages between countries are occurring; as tensions rose between China and Japan, hackers in both countries lobbed cyber attacks at each other, with Chinese denial-of-service attacks on Japan's Defense Ministry being a case in point. A Kuwaiti hacker recently attacked some Israeli banks. The Stuxnet worm—the first known worm to target critical industrial infrastructure—has been used to target the computer control systems of Iran's Bushehr nuclear facility. These types of attacks can inflict severe damage that is difficult to reverse and cannot be fixed by blocking Internet traffic and destroying computers and other automated devices connected to the Internet before the governments or companies can respond. Cyber security is a new major challenge to the intelligence community. Agreements among countries are needed to establish thresholds beyond which cyber attacks would be deemed to constitute an outright act of aggression.

7.9 Forensic Investigator Toolkit

Often, the forensic investigator must engage with physical machines and server systems to identify, extract, preserve, and document computer data; this requires special software to deal with computers. As previously mentioned, the investigator should avoid working directly with the original media. It is very important also for the investigator to know whether any of the tools being used are going to store data temporarily or permanently within the file systems they are examining.

The investigators need to constantly verify the integrity of the data that they are examining, and the way to do so is by creating a cryptographic hash value from the media both before and after the examination. Maresware's Disk_crc can be used by the investigator for this task. Disk_crc reads the contents of a disk, floppy, or hard disk and produces a 32-bit CRC, 128-bit MD5, or 160-bit SHA representing the hash of that disk. This value can be used later as a reference to verify that the contents of the disk have/have not been changed.

The forensic investigator needs to rely on mathematical validation to verify that the restored mirror image of a computer disk drive and relevant files exactly matches the contents of the original computer. Such comparisons help resolve questions that might be raised during litigation about the accuracy of the restored mirror image. They also act as a means of protection for the forensic investigator concerning allegations that files were altered or planted by law enforcement officials during the processing of the computer evidence. More recently, it has become necessary to use more accurate mathematical calculations for this purpose, that is, 128-bit hashes. The reasons are tied to the potential for brute force attacks using today's machines; it is not uncommon to find over 100,000 files stored on computer hard disk drives. New Technology International has adopted the use of the RSA MD5 algorithm for this purpose, and it has been incorporated in its forensic tool.

The forensic investigator will also require the services of a "viewer" utility tool, such as Quick View Plus (QVP), for opening various files without having to import them into another application. QVP can recognize over 200 file types, including PC, Mac, and UNIX machines formats; files are opened for viewing almost immediately. Another tool for the forensic investigator is DataViz, which also can work with Mac, PC, and UNIX files. It has the ability to open e-mail and attachments without having to copy or extract the attachments from the e-mail messages; the findings can also be sent to wireless devices such as iPhone, Android, and BlackBerry.

Many cases involve thumbing through stacks of images, documents, and e-mails, looking for something incriminating or relevant. Instead of having to go through all of the images one at a time on a large workstation or server, with tools such as ThumbsPlus, the investigators can simply pick a drive or directory and the software catalogs and displays all the image files on them. ThumbsPlus displays a directory listing of the drive so that the investigator can visually scan a directory or the entire drive for relevant images (Figure 7.2).

Text analytics tools, such as those mentioned in Chapter 3, Section 3.5, can also be used to search for incriminating content from documents and e-mails. Tools such as dtSearch can be used to index, or perform fuzzy searches on thousands of documents and e-mail instantly. Tools such as these can find words even when misspelled; they contain a thesaurus that can be used to automatically include synonyms in their free-form searches. One of the good feature of dtSearch is the capability to search Microsoft Outlook .pst files,

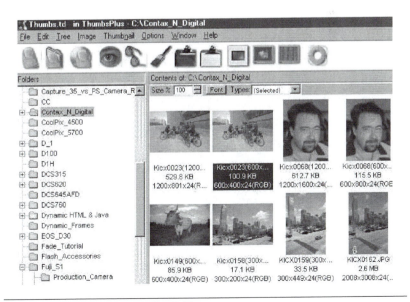

Figure 7.2 An image scan using ThumbsPlus.

which facilitates investigations involving e-mails for large organizations. Some of these text mining tools provide synonyms of keywords or values such as names, ID numbers, e-mail addresses, domains, etc.

Forensic suites also exist that provide multiple utilities that can both collect and analyze data. For example, Forensic Toolkit is a court-validated digital investigations platform with decryption and password-cracking capabilities all within an intuitive and customizable interface. This toolkit can provide a list of files by their last access times, and it does not change the directory's access times. It also can scan a disk for files that either have the hidden attribute sets or use Windows NT's directory and system attributes to hide files. Forensic Toolkit can also scan an entire disk for hidden data streams and report all of the attributes of a single file.

Yet another forensic suite is The Coroner's Toolkit (TCT), which is designed primarily to investigate a hacked UNIX host. TCT has the ability to analyze activities on a live host and capture current state information that would be impractical to capture manually. The capability of analyzing a running system contains a great deal of volatile information that isn't necessarily on the hard drive and disappears in a short amount of time. Accessing this information is the best way to know what kinds of unauthorized activities are taking place and may well be the only way to find out what is happening on a particular system and where attacks are originating. The front-end tool graverobber collects information on running processes, network connections, and the contents of hard drives.

ForensiX is an all-purpose set of data collection and analysis tools that run on Linux, which supports a greater number of file systems than any other OS. The tool allows investigators to perform searches for a simple string or more complex Boolean operation that include proximity searches. ForensiX has several unusual capabilities, such as a function to check a UNIX system for known vulnerabilities.

New Technologies Incorporated (NTI) is one of the most established vendors of forensic software; the company provides custom software suites for incident response, corporate and government evidence protection, disk wiping, electronic document discovery, internal audit, and several other purposes. NTI supports the following utilities:

CRCMD5: A CRC (cyclic redundancy checksum) program that validates the contents of one or more files.

DiskScrub: A hard disk drive utility used to eliminate all data.

DiskSig: A CRC program that validates mirror image backup accuracy.

FileList: A disk catalog tool that creates a list of the files on a system that is sorted by their last time of use.

Filter_we: A fuzzy logic filter for use with ambient data.

GetFree: An ambient data-collecting tool used to capture unallocated data.

GetSlack: An ambient data collection utility used to capture file slack.

GetTime: A program used to document the CMOS system time and date on a computer seized as evidence.

M-Sweep: An ambient data security scrubbing utility.

NTI-Doc: Can record file dates, times, and attributes.

PTables: Used to analyze and document hard disk drive partitions.

Seized: A utility used to lock and secure evidence computers.

TextSearch Plus: A text mining utility to locate strings of text and graphic files.

Another tool is EnCase, which is widely used by corporate and government investigators. Its functions include preview a volume, search grep and text expressions, and view disks and volumes. EnCase has the ability to perform regular expression searches on evidence. This feature is handy when the investigator is trying to locate numbers, such as phone numbers, social security numbers, IP addresses, and birth dates to identify a suspect or associate. For a more extensive list of forensic software suites, go to http://www.forensix.org/toolkits.

7.10 Wireless Hacks

Hackers found private information about iPad users through a security hole in AT&T's website shortly after the release of the mobile device from Apple. The hack compromised the users' e-mail addresses and an obscured number called the ICC-ID. The ICC-ID is the Integrated Circuit Card ID, a 19-digit serial number of the SIM card on all mobile devices. ICC-IDs are stored in the SIM cards and are also engraved or printed on the SIM card body during a process called personalization. The ICC-ID number is composed of the following subparts:

1. The issuer identification number (IIN), with a maximum of seven digits, including a major industry identifier (MII), 2 digits, (89 for telecommunication purposes)
2. The country code, 1–3 digits
3. The issuer identifier, 1–4 digits
4. The individual account identification number; its length is variable, 9–10 digits, but every number under one IIN will have the same length
5. The check digit, which is a single digit calculated from the other digits using the Luhn algorithm

The ICC-ID is basically a serial number for every mobile device SIM card. They are often written inside a device or printed on the boxes in which they are shipped. The ICC-ID number could help hackers learn another more critical piece of the wireless security puzzle known as the international mobile subscriber identity, or IMSI, number. IMSI numbers, usually 15 digits, are like a use's driver license on wireless networks and are used in part so carriers know whom to bill and restrict access internationally. The IMSI identify users' home networks and link to databases containing billing information, such as name, address, and phone number, and a device's latest location on the network.

Carriers consider the IMSI number so sensitive that they are transmitted from devices to cell towers as infrequently as possible. To protect subscriber confidentiality, network operators instead generate temporary IMSI numbers to place calls, and send data or update a subscriber's location when they move to a new area. The TIMSI (Temporary IMSI) number is a pseudo-random number generated from the IMSI number and is utilized to remove the need to transmit the IMSI over the air and enhance security.

Theft of an ICC-ID is troubling, as it is the starting point for tracking a user's rough location and intercepting encrypted data. Here is how the wireless hack works:

1. Obtain the ICC-ID; this number is the serial for the SIM card, which is the chip that enables wireless service. It is often written on the SIM card itself.

2. The hacker uses the ICC-ID to rearrange some numbers in order to get the IMSI number, which is the main subscriber identifier in phone carrier databases.

3. Using the IMSI number, hackers can now access the carriers' network to query the subscriber database.

4. The hacker can now triangulate the device since the carrier databases can provide the location of a device down to the level of a city or area of a city.

By using the ICC-ID, program routines can be used to discover the IMSI numbers simply by rearranging the ICC-ID digits. Here is a program found on the Internet to do so:

1. Read off the first 2 digits as the system code (all the ones we care about start with 89 for GSM).

2. Read the ITU dialing prefix out of the next 2 or 3 digits. Make sure to match the longest prefix first.

3. After parsing out the ITU prefix, parse the next three digits as the Mobile Network Code (MNC).

4. Match the MNC with the ITU prefix country to find the Mobile Country Code (MCC).

For example, if I have an ITU prefix of 01, meaning the United States, I then look at the list of MNCs for that country and find the corresponding MCC to get the MCC for the IMSI.

- So at this point we have the MCC, the MNC, and are only missing the subscriber number to form an IMSI. Getting the subscriber number out of an ICC-ID is vendor specific, so it's different between AT&T and T-Mobile.

- To get an AT&T subscriber number, simply take the next 9 digits after the MNC.

Example: If I have a ICC-ID of 89014101234567891, the subscriber number is 123456789.

- To get a T-Mobile subscriber number you need the take the two digits before the double 00 and concatenate them with the seven digits following the zero.

Example: If I have an ICC-ID 0f 8901260390012345679, the subscriber number is 391234567.

And here is some code to convert the IMSI back into the ICC-ID, also found on the Web:

```
<DllImport("cellcore.dll")> _
Shared Function SimInitialize( _
 ByVal dwFlags As Integer, _
 ByVal lpfnCallback As IntPtr, _
 ByVal dwParam As Integer, _
 ByRef lphSim As IntPtr) As Integer
End Function
<DllImport("cellcore.dll")> _
Shared Function SimDeinitialize( _
 ByVal hSim As IntPtr) As Integer
End Function
<DllImport("cellcore.dll")> _
Shared Function SimReadRecord( _
 ByVal hSim As IntPtr, _
 ByVal dwAddress As Integer, _
 ByVal dwRecordType As Integer, _
 ByVal dwIndex As Integer, _
 ByVal lpData() As Byte, _
 ByVal dwBufferSize As Integer, _
 ByRef dwSize As Integer) As Integer
End Function
```

The IMSI number is a critical piece of data that helps law enforcement and intelligence agencies work backward from mobile devices to identify the suspects who use them. They can also be used to track suspects and listen in to their communications. With the IMSI number, however, a hacker can do the same and track a person down to an area of a city.

Another source for obtaining IMSIs is by accessing SS7 networks. The Signaling System No. 7 (SS7) is a set of telephony signaling protocols used to set up most of the world's public switched telephone network telephone calls. Several text messaging marketing and mobile service retailing firms have access to SS7 networks, which can be used to identify the area of a city where a device last pinged a cell tower. There are ways to manipulate protocols within the telephony network to subvert access.

7.11 Incident Response Check-Off Checklists

Computers, e-mail, websites, the Internet, and mobile devices are essential tools for all organizations; however, these same tools can also expose a firm to embarrassing, expensive, and damaging security breaches. The following are a group of checklists for dealing with intrusions, attacks, and incident response reports.

Reasons for Countering Cyber Attacks Checklist

1. Prohibit unauthorized access to or modification of network systems or data.
2. Stop disruption or distributed denial of service (DoS).
3. Prevent electronic theft of confidential information.
4. Counter interception of internal communications.
5. Stop viruses, worms, and Trojan infections.
6. Prevent malicious probes or scans.
7. Detect computer-facilitated fraud.
8. Prevent website defacement.

A serious breach can cause irreparable harm to an organization; for this reason, organizations need to formulate an incident response plan (IRP).

An Effective IRP Checklist

1. Understand the extent and source of a breach.
2. Effectively and efficiently manage a breach.
3. Isolate and recover compromised systems.
4. Return to normal operations ASAP.
5. Protect systems and networks.
6. Protect sensitive data.

Organizations without a formal IRP may be poorly prepared to respond to and deal with a breach, which can lead to damage to systems and networks, increased costs and losses, disruptions of operations, and damage to their reputations. An organization should have a system IRP in place capable of the following tasks and processes.

A Systemic IRP Checklist

1. Preparation
2. Detection
3. Containment
4. Eradication
5. Recovery
6. Closure
7. Follow-up

A forensic investigator needs to inform client organizations about how to detect a breach and what indicators to look for, such as the following systemic symptoms.

Indicators of a Breach Checklist

1. Unexplained system slowdown of systems, network, and website
2. Unexplained filing of file systems
3. New or unfamiliar filenames
4. Unusual off-site access
5. Denial of service
6. System crashes

In addition, a forensic investigator should assist organizations in drafting a plan to be better prepared to respond to a breach.

A Preparing to Respond Checklist

1. Create a detailed inventory of all computing resources.
2. Build a resource kit of tools and hardware devices.
3. Make full daily backups of all systems and data.
4. Implement a configuration redundancy policy.
5. Use secure mechanism for communication.
6. Conduct IRP team training and testing.
7. Conduct periodic forensic audits.
8. Turn on auditing and logging.
9. Create a software archive.
10. Use an automated ISD.

Should a suspected breach occur, steps need to be taken to contain and measure its impact. Some of the questions an IRP team or a forensic investigator need to know are as follows.

A Post-Breach Questions Checklist

1. Does the compromised machine have network shares with any other machine?
2. Is sensitive information held on the compromised machine?
3. What resources could be required to handle the incident?
4. What is the potential damage of the incident in dollars?
5. How many machines have been compromised?
6. What is the entry point of the incident?
7. Is the compromised machine critical?
8. Is this a multisite incident?

When an incident has been detected and confirmed, steps must be taken to stop or limit its damage.

A Containment Intrusion Checklist

1. Shut down the system.
2. Isolate the affected systems.
3. Disable system services.
4. Change passwords.
5. Disable accounts.
6. Monitor systems and network activities.

Next the forensic investigator needs to eliminate the means of attacks and vulnerabilities; the investigator needs to stop the ways intruders gained access.

A Recovery Intrusion Checklist

1. Reinstall a trusted version of the affected software, servers, and network.
2. Reinstall trusted versions of files executed at boot time.
3. Reinstall a trusted version of your authorized user file.
4. Reinstall a trusted version of the password file.
5. Update the procedures and enforce them.

Lastly, a forensic investigator needs to follow up on intrusions and document as precisely and accurately as possible why, when, how and, most importantly, what recommendation to make to prevent future attacks.

An Intrusion Follow-Up Checklist

1. What can be done to improve communications in the detection and response process?

2. What can be done to improve user and system administrator preparedness?
3. Are there methods of discovery or monitoring that would improve detection?
4. Did detection and response processes and procedures work as intended?
5. What can be done to improve the ability to contain an incident?
6. What updates to policies and practices need to be executed?
7. If they failed, where did they fail and why?

For cyber security purposes, documentation of intrusion is vital for the forensic investigator, and the following form or similar versions designed to capture as much evidence (information) as possible must be followed. These reports are organization specific, often dealing with proprietary networks and systems.

Incident Response Report

1. What site is under attack?
2. Point of intrude contact?
3. Type of incident?
4. Date and time of incident?
5. Type of service, information, or process compromised?
6. Damage assessment?
7. Suspected attack source?
8. Primary system and networks attacked and damaged?
9. Type of malicious code, virus, worm, or Trojan?
10. Suspected method of entry and attack?
11. How was the incident detected?
12. Description and analysis of unauthorized access?
13. Remediation recommendations?

Many books have been written about computer forensics. How this one is different is that it suggests the use of machine learning techniques and technologies—coupled with traditional ISP and DPI technologies—and IRP techniques to improve security and detection for organizations and their networks.

The convergence of these technologies and techniques will require skill and effort on the part of machine learning forensic investigators, but the rewards will be huge. For the investigator, the objective is to know, as does a carpenter, what tool to use for what job. Do not use a hammer when a SOM or a decision tree will do the job faster and better. In addition, the investigator needs to be aware of new evolving technologies and techniques, including the digitization of all types of devices, such as computers, mobile phones, and other digital platforms.

7.12 Digital Fingerprinting

A relatively new technology has evolved that is designed to create distinct signatures of all types of devices, whether stationary machines or mobile devices. Digital fingerprinting creates a single "reputation" (profile) based on several factors. Fingerprinting is being used to prevent illegal copying of computer software or to thwart credit card fraud. New companies such as BlueCava are racing to collect digital fingerprints from every computer and cell phone in the world to perform "device identification" for forensic investigations. So far, BlueCava has identified 200 million devices, with hopes that by the end of 2012 it will have cataloged 1 billion of the world's estimated 10 billion devices. Aside from Gravity, there are a couple of other firms offering fingerprinting technology: Iovation and 41st Parameter.

Digital fingerprinting is a superior method of tracking all types of devices since it is anonymous, very robust, and more accurate than traditional Internet and wireless cookies, beacons, and other targeting mechanisms. Fingerprinting (Figure 7.3) involves capturing and modeling devices based on several parameters, including but not limited to the following attributes:

1. *Fonts*—It looks to see what fonts were installed and used on a device.
2. *Screen Size*—It looks to check the screen size and the color setting of the device.
3. *Time Stamp*—It compares the time a device logs on to a server, down to the millisecond.
4. *User ID*—It assigns a unique "token" that can be used to track all activities for that device.
5. *Browser Plug-ins*—It looks for and maps what optional software a device has, such as Flash.
6. *User Agent*—As with cookies, it identifies what type of operating system the device is using.

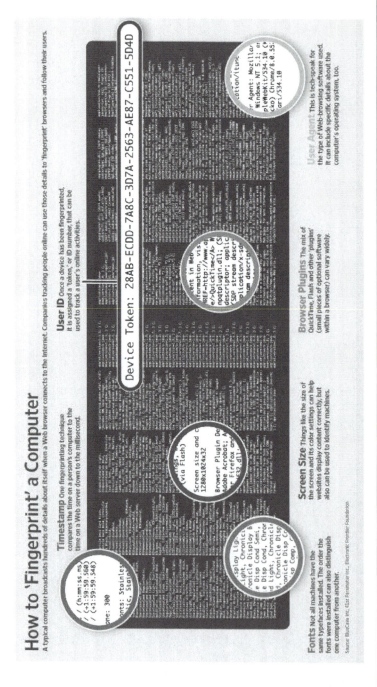

Figure 7.3   The features captured in a digital fingerprint.

BlueCava is actually a spin-off from an Australian anti-piracy company, Uniloc, which holds US patent 5,490,216. Its abstract is as follows:

A registration system allows digital data or software to run in a use mode on a platform if and only if an appropriate licensing procedure has been followed. Preferably, the system detects when part of the platform on which the digital data has been loaded has changed in part or in entirety, as compared with the platform parameters, when the software or digital data to be protected was last booted or run. The system relies on a portion of digital data or code that is integral to the digital data to be protected by the system. This integral portion is termed the code portion and may include an algorithm that generates a registration number unique to an intending licensee of the digital data based on information supplied by the licensee which characterizes the licensee. The algorithm in the code portion is duplicated at a remote location on a platform under the control of the licensor or its agents, and communication between the intending licensee and the licensor or its agent is required so that a matching registration number can be generated at the remote location for subsequent communication to the intending licensee as a permit to licensed operation of the digital data in a use mode. The code portion can be identical for all copies of the digital data. The algorithm provides a registration number which can be "unique" if the details provided by the intending licenses upon which the algorithm relies when executed upon the platform are themselves "unique."

And thus digital fingerprinting has evolved for machine-learning forensic purposes designed to prevent fraud and the theft of software and content.

8

CORPORATE COUNTERINTELLIGENCE

Litigation and Competitive Investigations

8.1 Corporate Counterintelligence

Intelligence is not information but the end product of evaluated information, valued for its currency value and timely relevance rather than for its detail or accuracy. Counterintelligence is the interpretation of corporate information, which must be treated as a constantly mutable component or variable within a larger equation of understanding a secret, covert or otherwise, involving private "intelligence" about an opponent or competitor.

For the forensic investigator, the objective is to answer questions or obtain advance warning of events and movements deemed to be important or otherwise relevant to his or her organization. This can include intelligence monitoring analysis of a rival's websites by mapping all the rival's web pages and links. The "crawling" of a competitor's site can uncover links and derive a list of terms, filings, and documents to quickly determine competitive intelligence about their activities, intents, focus, patents, and strategies.

Yet another technique is that of electronic discovery via *scraping*, which monitors and captures all instances of when a product or company appears on a social network site or blog. Scraping is a software technique of extracting information from websites. Usually, such programs simulate human exploration; in contrast, scraping focuses more on the transformation of unstructured web content into structured data that can be stored and analyzed by forensic investigators using machine learning tools. Scraping simulates human browsing behavior; however, it can also be used for competitive intelligence applications, such as online price comparison, buzz activity on blogs, product popularity, website change detection, and competitor monitoring.

Some scraping firms offer what is known as listening services, which monitor in real time thousands of news sources, blogs, and websites to see what people are saying about specific products or topics. Scraping providers vary from Dow Jones & Co. and Nielsen to start-ups such as screen-scraper.com and Infinigraph, which concentrate on a "social intelligence service" to help companies understand the likes and dislikes of online customers, by scraping social network sites. Nielsen combined CIA-funded technology from Intelliseek, which it bought with another start-up BuzzMetrics to monitor 130 million blogs, 8,000 message boards, Twitter, and Facebook to sell "ThreatTracker," which alerts a company if its brand is being discussed in a negative light. Corporate counterintelligence is a reverse form of competitive intelligence and could be described as a strategy to protect business information assets, corporate knowledge and reputation, via aggresive crawling and scraping for destructive information about an enterprise.

Forensic investigators can use the same tool used to detect crimes to ensure that internal operations are not being compromised. They can take a proactive role in assisting internal audits and investigations involving legal issues, such as insider trading, illegal disclosure, internal fraud, competitive intelligence, and counterintelligence. The forensic investigator can help an organization's clients identify potential relevant data, trends, or patterns, and assemble it, and then assist it and its litigators by supporting or defending facts and allegations of a legal case. This may well be the most important task for investigators, in which a multimillion dollar litigation case can revolve around the forensic findings of when data was generated, altered, deleted, and communicated by whom, when, and where, and under what circumstances.

Investigators should be prepared to use their skill, knowledge, and tools to assist clients by helping them better manage their data, intelligence, resources, and personnel in monetizing opportunities and understanding their security risks. The machine learning forensic investigator should use an array of technologies and techniques in support of an organization—in electronic evidence recovery and analysis, forensic investigations, anomaly detection, and business rule generation, utilizing encryption and security to preserve digital evidence.

Forensic investigators can combine their knowledge of machine learning and their potential output of data matching and discovery, pattern recognition, predictive modeling, and data forensics and accounting capabilities. The investigator is the lead coordinator and manager of investigations into fraudulent behavior by combining data from disparate sources and the development of fraud profiles and behaviors. One of the most difficult tasks for an investigator is performing an internal audit of an organization for the discovery of thefts, fraud, and other crimes.

A most important first step for forensic investigators is the location and preservation of digital data evidence. Most investigations begin in the accounting or financial departments, but incriminating evidence may also reside in sales, warehousing, shipping, and purchasing, and IT and HR departments within an organization. Today, the majority of this digital evidence resides in computer servers and networks. Fraud investigations, for instance, reflect this trend; they require skilled and knowledgeable forensic investigators using sophisticated techniques and powerful machine learning software capable of assembling hundreds of thousands of documents, e-mails, and other data captured in server log files and backup systems.

Quick action by the forensic team is essential in securing this type of digital evidence. Individuals or gangs who commit fraud and theft may seek to cover their tracks by destroying evidence that might incriminate them. What these perpetrators sometimes do not realize is that simply erasing this evidence does not make it go away. Security and retrieving this evidence by the forensic investigator requires special skills and tools for retrieving, organizing, and analyzing this recovered evidence. However, securing this critical evidence requires quick action on the part of the client organization and the investigators.

As previously mentioned, criminals often do not really delete digital data; they may just remove pointers to it. The investigator can use his or her forensic tool box to search and retrieve key evidence from hard drives, and search for incriminating text strings, such as names, addresses, e-mails, and other digital evidence. Investigators working with computer forensic tools can identify and collect vital evidence in a manner that preserves its integrity and its admissibility in legal proceedings. Care must be taken to not work with the original version of the evidence. Investigators do not want to find that their critical evidence is deemed inadmissible in court because it was mishandled and got corrupted or destroyed.

As the relevant documents are collected and analyzed, the investigator can move ahead with the case by conducting structured interviews. Typically, investigators begin this process by starting with those closest to the data, and are the most junior, prior to moving up the corporate structure. As suspects are identified, the investigator may move to analyze their communications, from web server files, e-mails, instant messages, tweets, spreadsheets, bookmarks, voicemail, etc. These communications archives can develop into information threads that can implicate accomplices within and outside a company. Fortunately, machine learning and cyber security tools are available to assist the forensic investigators in dealing with this evidence, which is typically scattered across a sprawling enterprise in multiple locations.

8.2 Ratio, Trending, and Anomaly Analyses

One of the basic types of investigative audits is trend analysis for evaluating fiscal ratios, such as balance sheets, income statements, statements of cash flows, and ratios. Ideally, several months should be used to profile the trend. The objective for the investigator is comparing key ratios against industry norms to pinpoint movement toward improvement or decline in a business and to identify unusual items indicating potential theft. Below are ratios forensic investigators can use for identifying trending and profiles, and for evaluating unsecured trade creditors, along with an indication of what the risk ratio signifies:

1. Quick ratio defines the degree to which a company's current liabilities are covered by the most liquid current assets.
2. Accounts payable turnover shows the average number of days that it takes the customer to collect its receivables.
3. Inventory turnover shows the average days that the customer takes to turn its inventory once.
4. Debt to tangible net worth indicates the ability of a firm to leverage itself. It shows how much the owners and creditors have invested in the firm. A high number reflects a potential danger to all creditors.

5. Gross profit margin is only meaningful when compared to the industry norm.

6. Return on investment reflects the efficiency of management's performance.

Yet another technique for financial analysis is unsupervised anomaly detection using a neural network Self-Organizing Map (SOM). This type of financial discovery is also referred to as outlier detection, and it refers to detecting patterns in a given data set that do not conform to an established normal behavior. These outlier patterns—detected autonomously by the neural network—are called *anomalies*, and often translate to critical and actionable information in several application financial and operational domains. Anomalies are also referred to as outliers, aberrations, deviations, spikes, peculiarities, etc. From trending profiling and anomaly detection, the forensic investigator can next move to the discovery of fraud attributes.

There are two methods by which fraud attributes can be discovered. The first and most common is by manually creating them in the form of business rules gleaned from domain experts and developed from investigations. As investigations move ahead, certain conditions indicative of potential fraudulent transactions in the future may be found. This can be anything like a large number of transactions in a limited time frame to other abnormal and deviant types of behaviors. This is the manual, top-down approach to fraud attribute discovery—an expert system populated by rules designed to detect fraud—where normally one or more human experts would need to be consulted. It is the codifying of human knowledge discovered via forensic investigations. The rules are crafted based on the conditions discovered by investigators.

The second method of fraud attribute discovery is by using machine learning to generate rules from historical data patterns. This is the automated, bottom-up approach to rule discovery. These rules are generated by the data itself and are at times more accurate than top-down rules because they have no bias. Because criminals tend to change their patterns of theft, one approach a forensic investigator might take is to construct a model of "normal behavior," enabling the client organization to flag records or accounts that vary from the norm by more than some threshold. For example, credit card companies immediately flag cards that deviate from normal location, amount, or type of purchases; their models use machine learning rules that examine consumer normal behavior, and the same strategy can be used by forensic investigators.

The ideal forensic solution is, of course, a hybrid fraud detection system that incorporates both top-down and bottom-up rules combining human expertise with machine learning brute computing power. This is where the forensic investigator needs to incorporate and blend both rules for an adaptive, flexible, and accurate fraud detection strategy and system (see Figure 8.1).

One thing the forensic investigator must be aware of is that even this hybrid detection system needs periodic maintenance. Criminal and fraud investigations need to take place periodically to ensure that new patterns of criminal behavior are being monitored, and new detection rules need to be generated via both bottom-up and top-down approaches. Crime and fraud is a highly dynamic activity, and the forensic investigator must be constantly updating new detection rules. Depending on the industry and type of client organization, these new rules must be repeatedly revised and updated, and new ones added. If human investigators are not improving in the detection of crimes, machine learning can help in this endeavor.

8.3 E-Mail Investigations

An important task for the forensic investigator is the protection of internal e-mail, which potentially could be used to damage the

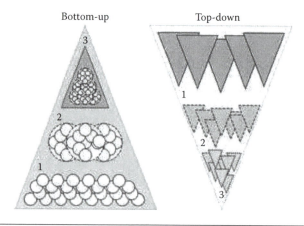

Figure 8.1   A hybrid detection system with human and machine rules.

reputation and activities of an organization. At a recent Congressional hearing, lawmakers asked a large pharmaceutical firm to explain its hiring of a contractor to buy defective children's medicine from store shelves, rather than conducting a recall. E-mails obtained during the committee's investigation raised the question of why the multinational corporation sought to avoid recalling the children's medicine. E-mail is Exhibit A in many of today's most high-profile legal investigations and court cases. Despite so many highly publicized legal cases involving e-mail, only 35% of companies have e-mail retention policies and 37% of employees say they don't know which messages should be retained and which purged, according to recent surveys by the American Management Association.

Most companies do not realize they are sitting ducks; they do not realize that e-mail is the electronic equivalent of DNA evidence. Even top technologists and software giants are in peril when it comes to what e-mail disclosures can lead to. When Bill Gates sent out an e-mail to Microsoft executives about the need for the company to increase its share of the web browser market, he had to explain this to Congressional investigators 2 years later. Watching Gates squirm in a court case involving e-mail should have been fair warning to business executives and other high-ranking officials to exercise greater caution when sending out e-mail.

Failure to gain control of e-mail, instant messages, blogs, and other business communications can cost organizations money and, more importantly, their reputations. Morgan Stanley recently was hit with million-dollar fines by the Securities and Exchange Commission and court fines, as well as legal judgments for violating e-mail retention rules; the firm was also embarrassed by archived e-mail introduced in a wrongful termination case. A host of companies have seen internal e-mail used in a variety of legal actions ranging from sexual harassment to software piracy, collusion, price fixing, and data theft. Some have been penalized with fines for failing to produce e-mail in court cases.

Additionally, many industries have regulations such as the Health Insurance Portability and Accountability Act in health care, and all public companies are governed by Sarbanes–Oxley and other rules requiring companies to retain and archive e-mail for 3–7 years. Even in industries that do not have e-mail retention rules, companies involved in legal disputes can expect to get subpoenas for e-mail.

Sometimes, for some law firms, that is the only evidence they require: e-mail and their attachments. Legal battles involving e-mail can be costly. A paralegal or attorney can review only a few e-mails per minute looking for evidence. If a company needs to manually review millions of pages of e-mail, legal fees can quickly add up to hundreds of thousands of dollars.

The average company creates at least a million e-mails each day, Forrester Research estimates. But technology tools, software, and services can assist organizations and law firms to monitor and manage e-mail, including specialized archiving, retrieval, and discovery software.

E-mail Analytics from Xerox is designed to be utilized in complex litigation or investigative matters; law firms and in-house counsel can use it to search for and identify key individuals and assess their relationships and communication patterns (see Figure 8.2). The user can select any individual involved in an investigation, choose a time frame, and get an instant graphical representation of all e-mails sent and received by that person; dates, frequency, quantity, and e-mail addresses are all accessible. Multiple views are available to allow for flexibility in how the investigators choose to dissect the data.

Some of the top e-mail security software tools are as follows:

1. *IronPort*—Its Intelligent Messaging Gateway appliances monitor and manage messaging and e-mail flow, and enforce corporate e-mail policies.
2. *Trend Micro*—InterScan Messaging Hosted Security package guards against malware and targeted spyware attacks sent by e-mail, while providing antispam and antiphishing protection.
3. *Postini*—It is an on-demand service; there is no software or hardware to buy. Administrators use standard web browsers to manage the system.
4. *Mirapoint*—Makes network appliances designed to route, store, and process incoming and outgoing e-mail for viruses, spam, and user access policies.
5. *Symantec*—Provides flexible quarantine management, graphical reporting, and protection against directory harvest attacks and other e-mail-borne threats.

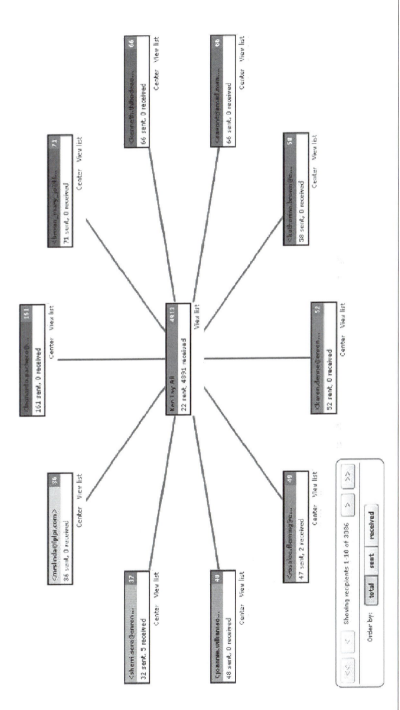

Figure 8.2 E-mail Analytics software from Xerox Litigation services.

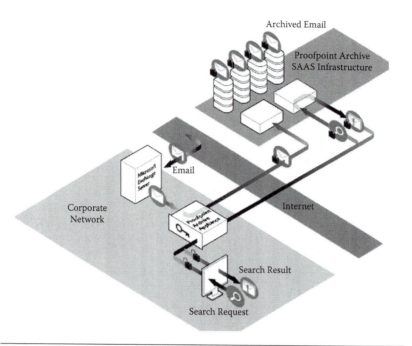

Figure 8.3   Proofpoint configuration for archiving and searching e-mail.

6. *Secure Computing*—Its TrustedSource eliminates numerous risks from data leakage, compliance violations, and messaging-borne malware.

7. *BorderWare*—Its Security Gateway is an appliance-based e-mail security, privacy, and compliance solution to control outbound information to enforce compliance regulations.

8. *Barracuda*—It deploys 12 comprehensive defense layers to deliver industry-leading defense capabilities for any e-mail server within large corporate or small business environments.

9. *Proofpoint*—Provides data loss prevention solutions for enterprises, prevents leaks of confidential and private information across all protocols, and encrypts sensitive e-mails (see Figure 8.3).

10. *Tumbleweed*—E-mail Security family of products is optimized for network defense, e-mail encryption, content filtering, and data integrity.

Some firms have created retention policies that called for the eradication of all e-mail more than 60 or 90 days old to eliminate evidence that could be used against them. However, these policies are difficult to enforce and generally are ineffective because once an e-mail goes out, it is out. Meaning it could be lurking on some user machine, forwarded to others, and so on. Some companies have little choice but to retain e-mail—for example, financial and insurance organizations operate within a very litigious environment that is heavily regulated and highly scrutinized. In addition, some organizations in these industries have federal and state regulators monitoring their activities constantly.

Some software can be used to discover and extract relevant e-mail by analyzing unique properties such as recipients, replies, forwards, CCs, and subject headers, which with a combination of organization data can be used to derive specific e-mail communication patterns. Linguistics and analytic algorithms can be employed to create rankings and discussion threads, and provide each e-mail with a relevancy score for potential review by forensic investigators. For example, software from Clearwell can identify and collect data from across an organization. The software sucks data from desktops, laptops, network shares, and applications in the cloud without requiring agents to be deployed, and allows data to be available for case assessments and review by investigators. Structured queries and keyword searches can be performed on all e-mails from the organization by forensic investigators.

Software from EMC eDiscovery can enforce litigation retention requirements and maintain a chain of custody as e-mails are sent for legal review. Such programs can assist organizations on e-mail archiving assessment and data erasure. For example, software from Proofpoint can assist attorneys in storing and searching e-mail records quickly during the legal hold stage at the beginning of the litigation process. The software uses an appliance that resides inside a customer's firewall, integrating directly with Exchange and Active Directory servers.

The Proofpoint appliance encrypts and transmits e-mail to storage facilities where all archived data is stored. Individual departments can perform e-mail searches themselves or by their investigators and attorneys. IntelliReach messaging management software uses a graphical interface to create and manage rules on how to handle messages and is designed to integrate policies for compliance, filtering, encryption, discovery, and archiving. These software packages assist investigators and organizations when hit with a lawsuit or subpoena, but advanced planning may be the best strategy for dealing with e-mail investigations.

While technology can help organizations manage their e-mail, what is really crucial is to set policies that are understood throughout a company. E-mail has become one of the most common forms of business communication, and executives need to understand that every click of the Send button creates a potential risk for an organization. In the end, it is better to deal with these issues in advance than to confront them on the witness stand, because e-mails are potential gold mines of electronic evidence. To have an effective e-mail policy, an organization should follow the three Es, as given in the following text.

E-Mail Policy Checklist

1. Establish a written policy that governs content and usage, and sets policies on retention and deletion.
2. Educate employees about the policy, and require them to read and understand it.
3. Enforce the policy with penalties for violations, up to and including dismissal.

For firms with policies, it is important to continue to apply them to periodically audit, review, and update them, and to conduct ongoing training. For organizations, the challenges include maintaining productivity and efficiency, and avoiding potential liability for improper and illegal conduct such as workplace harassment, defamation, and infringement on intellectual property rights. E-mail has been used for sexual harassment and racial discrimination and to create a hostile work environment.

E-Mail Risks Checklist

- *Lack of confidentiality*—Risk of interception by third parties
- *Permanence*—Risk of its becoming a permanent record
- *Forwarding*—Risk of misdirection to third parties
- *Integrity*—Risk of tampering and alteration
- *Authenticity*—Risk of forgery or spooking

E-mails can also serve as instruments of defamation. Another area of concern is employee infringement of intellectual property rights.

Finally, misuse of e-mail can damage an organization's reputation and professional image, even when it does not lead to liability. Adverse publicity from employee digital misconduct can be very damaging, particularly to professional firms. At the same time, e-mail can be useful in conducting forensic investigation.

E-mail is now the most common form of communication in modern business and commerce. As such, it often forms a significant part of investigations and litigations, in large-scale exercises such as discovery or disclosure. E-mail does, however, have an important place in machine learning forensics, and is a regular method for communicating sensitive, protected, or confidential information. An e-mail trail is often illuminating in demonstrating who knew what and when. It is also a very common method of distributing intellectual property such as client lists or copyrighted material.

An e-mail investigation, whether corporate e-mail or web-based mail (e.g., Hotmail), can be invaluable in determining a course of conduct, and in providing enough evidence to show that other systems, possibly in the control of a third party, may need to be investigated. In addition, received e-mail can often be the subject of an investigation as its source or author may need to be traced. Forensic investigators need to be creative in the use of text analytics, clustering, and e-mail tools during the course of their investigations in order to automate and expedite their search for digital evidence.

E-Mail Forensic Investigation Checklist

- What are the costs of the e-mail tool, and is it scalable to the organization's needs?
- What is the cost associated with retrieving the data for the investigation?
- Is the investigation a repeatable process that can be documented?
- What are the investigators' skills in conducting the investigation?
- What can actually be provided to the legal department when it requests data?
- What expectations does the legal department have?

8.4 Legal Risk Assessment Audit

Closely aligned to e-mail investigations are litigation lead inquiries dealing with risk. Risk is the uncertain possibility of suffering harm or loss. The forensic investigator will commonly work with attorneys and legal firms, and must be aware that risk is central to many industries and activities. Risk abounds in industries such as gambling, financial investments and trading, insurance, lending money and property, engineering and design, military operations, public and occupational health and safety, and security from crimes and terrorism. Lawyers consider and deal with risk on a daily basis in the substantive aspect of their practices, particularly those who represent clients in litigation. Text analytic software can be used by legal firms to organize and cluster their cases more efficiently and effectively. dtSearch allows legal firms to find a wide variety of documents quickly and easily in many different languages and writing systems.

---

dtSearch Case Study

Intellectual property departments and attorneys are being tasked with better intellectual property management practices. They are being asked to help the organization make better decisions, secure IP assets more completely, and process more documents in less time and with fewer people. InnovationQ from dtSearch helps corporations do all that while providing an enriched environment for creating even more intellectual property safety.

By applying collaboration, document management, and workflows to the problems of intellectual property management, InnovationQ helps corporations to secure their IP assets more thoroughly. At the same time, it helps streamline processes and remove bottlenecks that can result in lost or leaked IP and delayed product launches.

InnovationQ is an enterprise software solution for intellectual property and innovation management. It solves complex document, collaboration, and process management problems associated with managing intellectual property assets. With InnovationQ, companies can routinely safeguard their intellectual property while deriving the maximum value from their portfolios.

InnovationQ modules automate typical intellectual property and innovation processes including Invention Review and Disclosure, Freedom to Operate, Publication Clearance, R&D Collaboration,

Trade Secret Management, and Standards Management. With InnovationQ, customers can release new products faster, find new ideas, and participate in marketing activities without fear of leaking valuable intellectual property.

Since legal firms work closely with the forensic investigator, it will be useful to review some models of risk assessment that consider what risk assessment strategies and best practices might be useful for reducing the information security risk encountered today in the legal industry. The following checklist focuses on the five major risk assessment processes.

Legal Risk Processes Checklist

1. Inventory and identification of external inputs and requirements
2. Identifying assets and threats
3. Listing the risk tolerance of information assets
4. Listing and evaluating current protection mechanisms
5. Assessing under-protected assets and unaddressed threats

The forensic investigator can assist legal firms during this risk assessment process. An investigator can document all discoveries and issues uncovered. The documentation and careful collection of insights and issues are valuable as a tool for cataloging all relevant information as the risk assessment process proceeds.

8.4.2 Inventory of External Inputs to the Process

Before a detailed analysis begins, it is necessary to determine special needs; for example, for a legal practice that handles medical information, the risk assessment must address concerns raised by HIPAA security and privacy regulations. Applicable to all legal practices are the confidentiality and accounting requirements from various state rules governing legal professional conduct. Beside applicable federal and state regulations, there may be insurance policies, lender agreements, equipment leases, or customer-specific contracts that require protection of certain assets or data at a level not otherwise undertaken.

The next step of the risk assessment process involves gathering diagrams and information about physical buildings; wired, wireless, and data networks; and company policies. The goal of this step is not to evaluate or judge the worthiness of the network and physical space but to assemble hard-to-find documentation before it is needed. Next, the topology of all Internet connections should be identified. Where are desktops, routers, printers, and other equipment on the local network physically located? Who has the access controls on local file servers? An inventory of all laptops and other wireless devices need to be accounted for and included at this stage.

8.4.3 Identify Assets and Threats

From the inventory made in the previous step, the assets of the practice that require protection are identified, in addition to the consequences if the assets become corrupted or damaged, or get stolen. Next, think of all the critical information assets that the practice itself uses or stores. The audit at this juncture should adhere to the standard set by the International Organization for Standardization (ISO) 27002:

a. Information assets: Databases and data files, system documentation, user manuals, training material, operational or support procedures, continuity plans, fallback arrangements, and archived information
b. Software assets: Application software, system software, development tools, and utilities
c. Physical assets: Computer equipment, processors, monitors, laptops, modems, routers, servers, magnetic media, and other technical equipment
d. Services: Computing and communication services, general utilities, heating, lighting, power, and air conditioning

8.4.4 List Risk Tolerance for Major Events

For consistency, the levels of impact can be described as detailed as possible:

Catastrophic: There is a probability that the business will collapse if this event happens to this asset.

Major: There will be a major financial, criminal, or personnel impact if this event happens to this asset.

Minor: There is a minor impact to the business, mostly record-keeping, and the business will not suffer any revenue loss related to damage if this event happens to this asset.

None: There is no impact to the business if this event happens to this asset.

8.4.5 List and Evaluate Existing Protection Mechanisms

In this step, existing risk reduction mechanisms are identified that reduce the exposure of the practice to each event. For example, the risk that someone will gain access to customer records stored on an organization's computer can be mitigated by the following measures:

1. Computer access requires a frequently changed password.
2. The computer is protected by a correctly configured network firewall.
3. Highly sensitive data on the computer's hard drive is routinely encrypted.

8.4.6 List and Assess Underprotected Assets and Unaddressed Threats

The last step in the risk assessment process is to identify and assess all underprotected assets and unaddressed threats or residual risks so that they can be addressed in the subsequent risk response that follows.

A risk assessment is a living process; all relevant documentation generated during the process should be retained for future assessments. The risk assessment process should be performed periodically to make sure that the assessments are consistent with the current risk profile of a legal practice. A fundamental goal of risk assessment is to avoid the catastrophic impacts to a legal firm. It is important to note that legal firms and attorneys are different from managers of private and public organizations in that they are legally and ethically responsible for protecting client and investigation information, failure to do so will defeat the purpose of forensic investigation and their findings.

Machine learning text mining software can assist legal firms in the organization of its information assets, which can create clusters of concepts on the basis of the nature of the legal case.

A Recommind Case Study

As e-discovery practitioners, the goal of Recommind is to make the process for our clients more manageable and as cost-effective as possible. We sought to automate and streamline the process through the application of strategic technology and well-developed workflows. The firm of Fulbright & Jaworski L.L.P., was an early adopter of Recommind's Axcelerate™ eDiscovery platform, having implemented the solution internally in early 2008. Fulbright's strategic deployment of Axcelerate eDiscovery—especially the firm's use of Predictive Coding™ functionality—combined with concept clustering and data analytics has revolutionized document review, thereby reducing time and costs.

In 2007, we recognized the need to acquire new technology to help address our clients' increasing e-discovery costs, driven by growing volumes of electronic data. One of the first law firms in the country to implement a web-based litigation support system, Fulbright has long hosted large data volumes for the purpose of conducting linear document review, performing complex searches, and preparing electronic document productions. Meanwhile, we recognized the need to leverage advanced technology to more effectively analyze, filter, and strategically organize large document populations, while reducing document review costs.

In a typical e-discovery project, data would routinely be culled and filtered using file types, date ranges, and keywords, followed by a linear, eyes-on attorney review. This approach to document review has been a generally accepted practice for years, and works relatively well for many cases. As client data volumes continued to increase in size and complexity, and strategic search methodologies began to emerge and evolve, the opportunity for a new strategy was apparent.

The benefits and necessity of an alternative approach to document review can be easily demonstrated using a recent experience.

One of our clients was performing an internal review and engaged the firm to conduct an early case assessment to determine the validity and severity of the matter. The case team's objective was to quickly identify documents that would help senior attorneys, assess the scope of the matter, and prepare for custodian interviews. The client provided an unfiltered universe of approximately 500,000 documents, including e-mails and attachments. The corpus of data was expected to contain relevant material, but the issues did not lend themselves to traditional keyword searching.

Using a linear approach to review this volume at a rate of 50 documents per hour would require a minimum of 10,000 review hours and incur hundreds of thousands of dollars in attorney fees, even with contract attorneys to conduct a first-pass review.

In this example, our legal team needed to prioritize and review highly relevant material within two weeks. Without the appropriate technology, identifying and prioritizing all of the key documents among a highly diverse data set in a timely and cost-effective manner would be very challenging and imprecise. This challenge is not unlike the vast majority of cases today.

As we started to evaluate the e-discovery technology industry, meet with software providers, and test potential solutions to problems such as the example mentioned above, three distinct selection criteria were defined: supportability, efficiency, and defensibility. After examining four leading systems and conducting a proof of concept, Recommind's Axcelerate eDiscovery system best met the selection criteria, while also working with existing technologies.

From the outset of our internal deployment of Axcelerate eDiscovery, attorneys began to recognize how this technology could help bring greater transparency into client data, thereby innovating their approach to e-discovery and enhancing their practice by enabling them to (1) quickly identify highly relevant material; (2) more thoroughly evaluate the scope of discovery; and (3) define key issues early. For the first time, data began to truly reveal itself to attorneys through concept clusters and Predictive Coding. This type of functionality is a game changer in the e-discovery industry. It has altered the way our teams approach litigation and investigations, while substantially reducing client review costs.

Fulbright takes a multifaceted approach to its application of Axcelerate eDiscovery's functionality. When data is first loaded into Axcelerate eDiscovery, documents are automatically sorted into concept groups. Legal teams leverage concept groups to identify a key set of documents based on their knowledge of the case. The majority of relevant documents are often concentrated within just a few concept groups. The Smart Filters® functionality helps to direct reviewers toward relevant documents before the review starts. Attorneys then begin to review and code presorted documents, prioritizing those that are clearly important and deferring those that are obviously irrelevant or ancillary. This process improves the quality and efficiency of the document review. It also provides an intelligent and adaptable guide to formulating additional search criteria.

As the initial sets of documents are tagged by reviewers, the results are analyzed using Axcelerate's Predictive Coding feature, which (1) learns from actual attorney decisions; (2) trains the system to identify similar documents; and (3) presents reviewers with additional unreviewed documents that are most likely to match the attorneys' coding criteria.

As attorneys continue to analyze and code additional documents, we use the system to iteratively identify additional material until there is a high level of confidence that the system is no longer returning new relevant material. This process allows attorneys to apply critical thinking to highly relevant material without being significantly distracted by irrelevant content, thereby eliminating the most tedious and costly elements of document review.

Document review is further enhanced through Axcelerate eDiscovery's near duplicate and thread detection. By streamlining reviewer access to duplicative content and messages from the same thread, an attorney's attention is better concentrated on documents related to similar issues.

The result is a more accurate and consistent review, which can be completed far more quickly and much more cost-effectively. As Axcelerate eDiscovery is being deployed throughout our practice areas, document review rates have improved by an average of 60%. Using Axcelerate eDiscovery, attorneys are able to achieve an

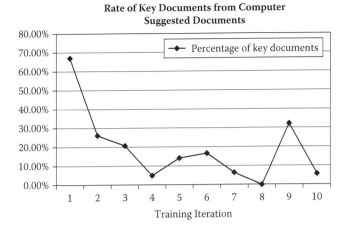

Figure 8.4 Machine learning software aids this legal firm in indexing its documents.

average rate of review of 80 documents per hour, and have reached rates as high as 120 documents per hour (Figure 8.4).

To put the benefits of this strategy in context, consider the actual outcome of the early case assessment mentioned earlier. After coding an initial "seed set" of key documents, 67% of the records suggested through the first round of Predictive Coding were determined to be accurate suggestions based on attorney review. Additional reviews and computer training were conducted, yielding fewer and fewer additional documents. The chart below illustrates the number of actual key documents returned by the system.

After approximately 12 days of review and 10 training iterations, the firm's legal team was confident that the results of the review were sufficient for their early case assessment. By leveraging all of the functionality of the system, they reviewed 38,000 documents out of 500,000 (less than 8%), using only eight document reviewers. By putting over 460,000 unfiltered documents aside for later analysis, our team was able to accomplish the task at hand and save thousands of hours of document review.

Axcelerate's Predictive Coding, combined with its strong feature set, help reveal highly relevant material early and efficiently. No technology can replace critical legal thinking, but this technology helps our attorneys make the most of the information they have and bring greater focus to substantive legal issues on behalf of their clients. With Axcelerate eDiscovery, we are doing more than lowering costs and improving the overall effectiveness of document review; we are also building a defensible next-generation process that will be standardized throughout the firm. At this point, the technology has been employed enough to establish workflow guidelines and benchmarks that we are in the process of formalizing and rolling out internationally.

8.5 Competitive Intelligence Investigations

Much of the competitive intelligence (CI) that a firm needs lies within the organization itself, primarily in its employees and operations. The forensic investigators with their unique skills and software tools can assist an enterprise in locating, retrieving, and organizing this internal knowledge for competitive advantage. The challenge lies in how to gather and synthesize this knowledge into a workable format that can benefit the planning and operations of the organization. However, as the previous case study demonstrated, text mining software can be enlisted to automate and organize key concepts from hundreds of thousands of unstructured content, such as e-mail and its attachments. The forensic investigator can be enlisted for using various machine learning software tools for linking, analysis, clustering, visualizing, and generating business rules, making an organization more competitive and intelligent.

Web-based tools can be used by the investigator to gather data from a dispersed sales force or other dispersed areas of the company. In addition, the forensic investigator can assist in the analysis of publicly available information to fill in existing gaps in the firm's knowledge base; this may provide a viable substitute when these difficulties arise. There are several methods for extrapolating data from a known external set as part of the effort to supplement an organization's internal knowledge base.

Established organizational competitive intelligence processes, however, often suffer from holes in data or data integrity, causing errors in the interpretation of that data for intelligence purposes. A variety of advanced behavioral analytic techniques as practiced by forensic investigators can, however, be used to fill in these gaps within an organization. Just as these investigators are deployed in combating fraud, crime, and intrusions, and in improving security, they can also assist their company in leveraging internal and external intelligence.

In today's world, the phrase "knowledge is power" is the essence of competitive intelligence activities within any organization. For clarification, competitive intelligence is the process of using legal and ethical means for discovering, developing, and delivering timely, relevant intelligence needed by decision makers wanting to make their organization more competitive. It is used for strategic decisions, such as product development, mergers, acquisitions and alliances, as well as tactical initiatives such as anticipating and preempting likely moves by customers, competitors, or regulators.

Competitive intelligence investigations are the processes supporting both strategic and tactical decisions. To accomplish this, forensic investigators need to enlist software that can enable them to gather and analyze reliable, relevant, and timely information that is available in vast amounts about competitors and markets. Competitive intelligence is important for several reasons; by learning about the competition, a firm is able to benchmark its own performance and predict competitors' activities to defend or enhance its own position. More importantly, competitive intelligence creates a knowledge asymmetry that enables an organization to emphasize its strengths over its competitors' weaknesses through viable and transparent product and/or service differentiation.

The Strategic and Competitive Intelligence Professional (SCIP) organization estimates that as much as 80% of the competitive intelligence and organization needs lies within the firm itself, primarily and principally with in its own employees. The problem lies, however, in how to gather and synthesize the knowledge into a workable format that can benefit the planning and operations of the organization. There is special collection and collaboration software that can be enlisted to automate this process of locating domain experts within and outside an organization. For example, Oracle Beehive is collaboration platform software developed by Oracle Corporation that combines e-mail, team collaboration, instant messaging, and conferencing in a single solution. It can be deployed on the premises as licensed software or as software as a service (Figure 8.5).

Figure 8.5   The Oracle collaboration software for competitive intelligence.

Oracle Beehive includes a platform along with several main components:

1. Beehive Platform: Unified architecture and data store for collaboration and communication services. Includes restricted-use licenses for Oracle Database and Oracle Fusion Middleware.
2. Enterprise Messaging: E-mail, calendar, address book, and task management accessible via Microsoft Outlook, Zimbra web client, and a selection of mobile phones.
3. Team Collaboration: Team workspaces with document library, team wiki, team calendar, team announcements, RSS, and contextual search.
4. Synchronous Collaboration: web conferencing and VoIP audio conferencing via the Beehive Conferencing Client.

There are other collaboration software vendors for expertise identification using search and discover technologies. There is software designed specifically for the location of experts within an organization. One such product is Kamoon, which connects a customer's needs to the right expert either inside or across an extended enterprise network, whether it is for a fee-based or a value-added service. Another product, Sopheon, enables manufacturers and service providers to achieve market differentiation by synchronizing strategic road mapping, idea development, and process execution.

The United States Central Intelligence Agency (CIA) defines the competitive intelligence process into six distinct steps:

1. The Destination Phase addresses the preparedness and capability to perform the task.

2. The Demand Phase identifies the information needs and determines the approach to be taken.
3. The Discovery Phase involves seeking out and collecting the information sources by legal means.
4. The Development Phase puts together a meaningful picture from the pieces of data that have been discovered and analyzed.
5. The Delivery Phase communicates the resulting intelligence to the right people at the right time.
6. The Disengagement Phase involves debriefing clients and reflecting to improve the process.

In the destination phase, the processes and systems are put in place to support competitive intelligence activities. The demand phase identifies the decisions to be supported by the activities and research. In the discovery phase, the company must identify the sources of information as well as how to gather the intelligence internally and externally. The development phase is primarily concerned with synthesizing the information and making sense out of it, which is the primary focus of the forensic investigator. Closely following the development phase, the delivery phase determines the best manner of selecting what intelligence to share and with whom to share it. The disengagement phase involves closing the feedback loop with the decision makers of the competitive intelligence to ensure their needs are met.

Despite the belief that 80% of the competitive intelligence that a firm needs is present within the organization, several specific industries can greatly benefit from external data sources. While most competitive intelligence groups in firms will rely heavily on external data sources such as the Internet and other media, industries that are regulated often have an additional amount of external data available for analysis from company filings with government agencies. Regardless, external data sources may also include patent searches, chemical abstracts, financial data from SEC filings as well as firms such as Dun & Bradstreet, and a variety of other databanks. The data available in these databanks tend to be organized in a way that facilitates integration into an analytical process.

A new source firms may want to monitor is what people are saying about their company and that of competitors on social networks such as Facebook, YouTube, and Twitter. Software such as Social Sentry provides corporations the ability to monitor the social networking communications of their employees and consumers. Delivered as a software as a service offering, Social Sentry provides granular and real-time tracking to eliminate significant corporate risks related to

- Compliance issues
- Leakage of sensitive information
- HR issues
- Legal exposure
- Brand damage
- Financial impact

One of the goals of competitive intelligence is to synthesize the information from a variety of resources and structures in order to discover the potential meaning and implications of the information. Of the two primary tasks of forensic analytics—predicting trends and behavior and discovering previously unknown patterns—competitive intelligence focuses primarily on the former: the ability to predict what the firm's competitors will do in a given situation. To form the prediction, the competitive knowledge process must be developed: a process that involves a set of behavioral activities that will, in turn, generate knowledge about the competitor's products and strategies. As discussed in previous chapters, this is best done using deductive software tools such as decision trees and rule generators.

Organizations recognize that their transactional data contains untapped knowledge about themselves and their customers, intelligence capable of giving them a competitive edge in a market-saturated world. Aside from consolidating information from multiple and diverse databases, they can be used by firms to drive decisions and improve business processes, such as

- Identify new clients likely to buy their products and/or services
- Anticipate demands on inventory
- Predict customer buying habits
- Map market developments
- Improve competitiveness

Savvy organizations are beginning to use this intelligence to develop marketing strategies, target web and wireless offerings, adjust inventories, minimize risk, and eliminate wasteful spending on an analysis of their internal data and that of their competitors. They are increasing the return on investment on current resources and improving their business intelligence. The discovery of information found hidden in internal corporate and customer data sets can reveal assets a firm did not know it had. However, in order to gain true competitive insight, organizations must be able to make sense of the data they are generating and storing, beyond simple graphs, reports, and manual queries. The methodology for discovering this type of strategic intelligence is best achieved via machine learning forensics, more specifically, rule induction software.

Rule induction is the essence of constructing the IF-THEN statements to predict the base price for the competition by calculation of the weights of the other variables after they are transformed into discriminate values. Decision trees are a graphical representation of the rules applied to the situation. To develop the rules and classifications needed for the tree structure, two of the most common methods are the use of the CART and CHAID algorithms.

The CART method (Classification and Regression Trees) was developed in 1984, and has quickly become a staple of machine-learning experiments. In this method, an initial training set of preclassified records is used to split the records at binary nodes according to single input fields. Since not all independent variables will be appropriate splitters, a diversity measure is used to indicate those independent variables with the greatest difference in the resulting records sets after the split. After the full tree is expanded and only "leaf" nodes remain, calculating the error rate at each node is necessary to determine inappropriate splits. Using the constructed tree applied to the training set, examining the records remaining at each leaf node, the percentage of records correctly classified is calculated and subtracted from 100% to find the error rate. If the error rate is too high, the tree must be "pruned" to avoid overclassification.

Another algorithm, CHAID (Chi-square Automatic Interaction Detector), was developed in the 1970s to detect statistical relationships between variables. One of the benefits of CHAID over CART is that it attempts to stop growing the tree before overclassification occurs, thus avoiding the pruning exercise. CHAID achieves this by analyzing the statistical difference between the proposed subcategories after the decision node, and if there is no significant statistical difference, the split is not made, and a leaf node is created instead. CHAID, unlike CART, is restricted to categorical variables, and continuous variables must be categorized to be used in the tree.

The delivering of the intelligence to those users identified in the demand phase is as important as in any other part of the process. Without proper presentation or visualization of the data, the users of the competitive intelligence are not able to apply the intelligence to their business decisions, and the work done is essentially worthless. Knowing the role of each of the employees involved in the competitive intelligence process is the key to identifying which method of delivery is best, and the forensic investigator needs to resolve this. Additionally, translating the data from a tree, cluster diagram, or discovered business rules is often necessary when presenting the results to employees not familiar with the machine learning techniques and technologies.

In the discovery phase of the competitive intelligence process, the collection of data, particularly internal data, is complicated by the complexity of and lack of incentive for collection. When the sales force or other employees are not encouraged or rewarded for their contributions to the competitive intelligence effort, the data become sparse, and the firm must rely on external data, which may not meet the needs of the firm. Likewise, if the results of the development phase are not expressed properly in the delivery phase, the value of competitive intelligence may not be recognized. All of these elements are complicated by the expanding breadth and focus of the type of information needed. The focus of competitive intelligence for short-term decisions, say, for six months to one year, is very tactical. As the time frame for future decisions expands to a long-term view of up to five years, the focus becomes more strategic, and the breadth of information increases dramatically.

Competitive intelligence is a very "now" knowledge type, and often requires real-time access to data, which can lead to rejection of the data warehouse concept of duplication. In these cases, the operational systems need to be the source of the analyzed and modeled data, which can lead to problems with data integrity and integration of external sources. The short shelf life of competitive intelligence, combined with its predictive nature, makes application difficult, particularly when it becomes actionable only when there is a knowledge gap between the firm and the competition.

The use of key indicators from the data elements as a means of predicting changes in competitor strategy is an important functionality of the data mining process. For example, knowledge of a competitor's plans to increase or decrease the size of its warehouse or sales force can provide the data necessary to ward off the effects of increased competition for the firm. Unfortunately, much of the information about a competitor is not easily classified. In most of these cases, the time frame is for strategic decisions, where market uncertainty and unpredictability preclude accurate forecasting.

Internally, an organization can leverage induction-based analysis designed to predict future trends, allowing a firm to make proactive, knowledge-driven decisions. Decision trees and rule generators can be used to assist in forecasting, classification, and association, such as the identification of unrelated purchasing patterns of products and services. The forensic investigator can assist a firm in answering business questions that traditionally were too time consuming to resolve, or find predictive information that was once overlooked because it lay outside the framework of traditional business expectations. Using rule induction software, a forensic investigator can discover for a firm return on investment (ROI) knowledge in the following format:

```
IF    is conjunction of a CONDITION
AND   is conjunction of a CONDITION
THEN  is a CLASS with a PROBABILITY VALUE
```

The forensic investigator can help a firm discover what customer attributes or combinations of attributes differentiate profitable buyers from unprofitable shoppers of its products and services. These business rules can also identify key intervals (ranges) and variables (attributes) in a data set relevant to classification. By analyzing existing customers, an organization can discover competitive intelligence rules such as the following:

```
IF    Customer Since       = 1998 through 2007
AND   Revolving Limit      = 5130 through 8900
AND   Credit/Debit Ratio   = 67
THEN  Lifetime Value       = $879.00
```

In this example, the forensic investigator can assist an organization with the value of certain customers; it can also discover time and dollar ranges that are important influences on the outcome for targeting potential buyers of new company products and services. Another way of viewing machine learning technology is as a simplifier. It enables the compression of large, diverse, distributed data sets with hundreds and even thousands of variables to only a few significant ones, such as Revolving Limit for predicting the outcome for a company such as the lifetime value of its customers.

As far as competitive intelligence is concerned, machine learning rules can discover time or dollar values of potential prospects. The technology can also indicate when a customer may be expected to go from poor to good for a specific product or service, based on historical trends and transaction patterns. Machine learning analyses by forensic investigators can literally provide answers to decision makers on key competitive intelligence business questions:

- Which customers are likely to respond positively to our next e-mail marketing campaign, and why?
- Which products will be the biggest sellers in our Western region next year, and why?
- Which consumers are likely to stop buying our premium service, and why?

Other uses of these business rules include identifying new customers, predicting customer buying habits, confirming suitable loan applicants, revealing fraud, indicating potentially rewarding investments, managing equity portfolios, diagnosing business problems, managing inventory, and conducting certain aspects of marketing. The forensic investigator can assist the company by discovering these "build for business" competitive intelligence rules, with the following features:

- Exportable solutions in multiple formats: C code, JAVA, and SQL syntax for decision support systems and management
- Robustness for handling any kind of data: noisy, skewed, missing, mixed, etc.
- Easy-to-understand results in IF/THEN formats with graphical decision trees
- Accurate results, especially with categorical and operational data sets
- Ability to analyze large data sets instantly as is

As demonstrated, a key advantage of machine learning algorithms over statistics and neural networks, which come from yet another branch of artificial intelligence, is that they formulate their solutions as plain statements. As rule induction programs, they are able to extract business rules directly from the data based on automatic tests they conduct for statistical significance. Their findings are easy to understand and can quickly be applied to real-world situations, so that:

```
IF     87% Income above $60,000
AND    ZIP 94502
THEN   $80 monthly service
```

The preceding rule, generated from a predictive model, can be used by a company to target a potential new group of consumers. In this way, machine learning analyses not only automatically find trends in large data sets—they can also generate usable competitive intelligence—that lead to specific areas of new strategic opportunities. Through an analysis of transactional data, customers can be identified for segmented offers of new products or services.

Data from consumer panels, shipments, and competitor activity can be applied to understand the reasons for brand and store switching. A firm can select promotional strategies that best reach the target customer segments. In doing so, a company can reduce overall costs, improve customer service, and expand its market by leveraging technology and its existing data resources to be more efficient and competitive.

A clear business objective needs to be identified prior to embarking on a forensic analysis project. What are the goals of the analysis? To identify potential new customers, increase market share, find product sale trends, etc. Once an objective is identified, the next question should be: "Is the data available to predict and model this outcome?"

Internal information can be enhanced by merging it with external demographics, Internet, lifestyle, social networking, and wireless data prior to a competitive intelligence analysis. Marketing data is also available by industry, region, and other data points. In the end, this type of forensic analysis is about a strategic partnership between a firm's business objectives (competitive intelligence) and advanced analytics and modeling (artificial intelligence).

8.5 Triangulation Investigations

No e-crime is more difficult to detect than money laundering, which can be masked as political contributions, fees for consulting or instructional services, or outright bribes. The forensic investigator may at times be called to detect such schemes. He should be aware of how the field has evolved: first, expert systems were used that employed rules developed by domain experts (FINCEN, FBI, Secret Service, IRS); next came neural networks and the development of alerts based on suspicious patterns of behaviors (Falcon from Fair Isaac); and then a third methodology from such AI firms as Fiserve and Actimize to outsource the problem using their own unique pattern recognition techniques and technologies focusing on clustering activities by specific industries and markets. The banking sector is required by law to monitor and report suspicious transactions indicating the possibility of money laundering, which forensic investigators can assist in detecting using their machine learning tools.

Prior to the USA PATRIOT Act, a report had to be filed for transactions over US $10,000; now, transactions must also be reported at adjustable limits. Under the act, a financial institution can be held liable—and punishable by both monetary fines and criminal indictment—if the institution is found to have handled illicit funds either knowingly or unknowingly. While it is virtually impossible to completely block the movement of illicit funds through a financial institution, banks find it necessary to implement more thorough monitoring programs in order to comply with this new regulatory stringency. In order to thoroughly monitor customer transactions, new account openings, and complex relationships between accounts for possible money laundering activity, large financial institutions have started to use machine learning forensic technologies capable of handling high volumes of transactions and multiple relational categories.

The act also affects various bank monetary services, such as check cashing, payment of government entitlements, and international money transfers to individuals with no formal account relationships, or the unbanked sector. Because unbanked customers do not necessarily pass through a know-your-customer account opening procedure, banks may need to institute special monitoring procedures for unbanked service customers, particularly in regard to money transfers.

These various factors affect other financial institutions as well with an even greater initial impact, because most of these organizations are starting from zero and must build their money laundering systems from scratch.

Information technology systems capable of storing and analyzing massive amounts of data, coupled with machine learning, have led to advances in the fight against money laundering in recent years. Under the 1996 Bank Secrecy Act, banks have long had to report suspicious deposits and transfers above $10,000 to the Treasury Department. The events of 9/11 changed that; under the PATRIOT Act there is currently an aggressive enforcement of anti–money laundering laws, which widened the reporting requirements to security brokers, insurers, car dealers, and travel agents. However, many of these businesses now operate on the web, meaning money laundering detection analyses have to be focused on the Internet and wireless transactions.

Money laundering has gone through several stages, evolving into techniques that focus on monitoring individual behaviors and the creation of unique consumer profiles. At this level, alerts are generated when deviations from the norm occur. Using machine learning, forensic comparison of account behaviors can be applied against peer groupings in an effort to discover abnormal activities, indicating money laundering schemes. Prior to the digitizing of money, financial institutions relied on personal interactions to identify unusual behavior that signaled possible money laundering activities, but in today's environment that is no longer the case. Today's environment requires the use of virtual machine learning agents, analogous to the human tellers and bank officers, that can provide knowledge regarding each customer and the transactions associated with different types of businesses.

The ability to monitor every single transaction for discovering all unusual behavior and looking for deviation from peer group behavior can be accomplished via machine learning forensics. The important aspect of this is defining what peer group behavior thresholds to develop and use. Peer group behavior might be defined by industry group, market segments, and individual profiles. These individual profiles might be based on such guidelines as average balances, total number of transactions over a given time frame, and other measurable activities. The point is that organizations need to be able to learn and adapt, comprehending new money laundering schemes as they arise.

Money launderers often know the basic thresholds to avoid and are continuously developing new ways to evade them. Rather than pushing a large amount of money through an account in a single transaction, criminals make multiple deposits that are less than the threshold limit, using different accounts, and then later aggregate the funds into a single account. This is known as *smurfing* and can involve hundreds of small transactions. Detecting such money laundering behaviors involves the technique of triangulation, where data points from diverse data sources are merged and used to detect suspicious behaviors.

There are several turnkey software packages for money laundering detection. One of them is GIFTS Software's Enhanced Due Diligence (EDD), which enables organizations to comply with the regulatory requirements of the PATRIOT Act. The software enables the user to monitor and identify fluctuations that may be inconsistent with the customer's normal business practice. Any account activity that exceeds the allowed variance, as defined by the organization, is brought to the attention of the appropriate staff through a selection of an online or offline report or e-mail alert. The user can then drill down to the transaction details for each of the results displayed and can sort the information by any of the field columns. Results are viewed directly through a browser for presentation to the inquiry regulatory agency or internal audit department.

Another vendor is Fiserve and its anti-theft and anti-money laundering software, which provides a user-friendly graphical investigation environment that make it fast; it provides easy-to-analyze alerts. As users click on each alert, they immediately have access to the transaction or series of transactions that triggered the alert.

Yet another firm is Actimize, formerly Searchspace, which is based on models of past criminal activity and peer profiles by industry type. Actimize performs adaptive profiling for discovering suspicious transactions by first comparing every transaction against its corresponding account history to determine if the behavior is unusual. Actimize allows an organization to insert its own business rules along with out-of-the-box detection models to cover cash and cash equivalent transactions, wires, ACH/IAT, securities orders and executions, insurance policies, and more. The software can improve detection of unusual

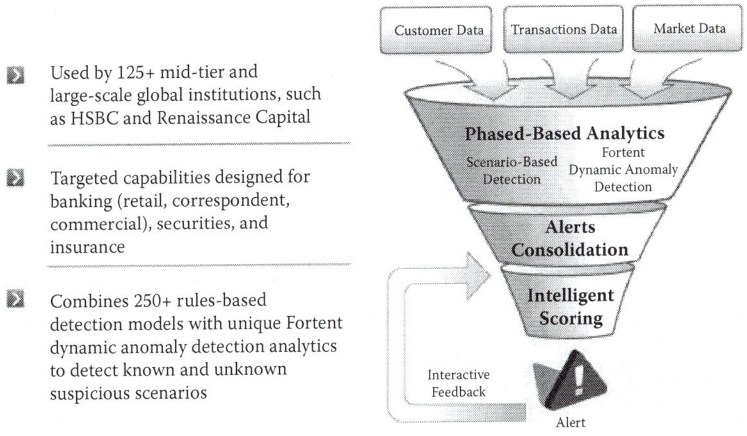
Used by 125+ mid-tier and large-scale global institutions, such as HSBC and Renaissance Capital
Targeted capabilities designed for banking (retail, correspondent, commercial), securities, and insurance
Combines 250+ rules-based detection models with unique Fortent dynamic anomaly detection analytics to detect known and unknown suspicious scenarios
Customer Data
Transactions Data
Market Data
Phased-Based Analytics
Scenario-Based Detection
Fortent Dynamic Anomaly Detection
Alerts Consolidation
Intelligent Scoring
Interactive Feedback
Alert

Figure 8.6 Actimize money laundering software solution.

tactics by comparing activity with peer group segments and historical behavior profiles (Figure 8.6).

For example, in one situation, this type of software discovered that a business account for a pizzeria was set up to launder money. The pizza restaurant seemed to have consistently high sales throughout the year with no lulls or especially busy periods. A review of its account history would not reveal suspicious activity, because the deposits were consistent. However, by comparing the pizzeria's transactions against an industry peer group, the account suddenly appeared very suspicious because similar restaurants tended to experience a dip in sales after the Christmas holiday season, and the profiled pizzeria did not. Similar types of industry-specific comparisons can draw out abnormal financial behavior indicating potential money laundering activity by organizations.

This approach automates the anti–money laundering operations by discovering unusual transactions considered to be risky. These are then communicated to the organization's compliance staff with an explanation as to why the transactions are considered suspicious, enabling the investigators to take action as necessary. As the Actimized graphic shows, the money laundering system relies on rule-based detection models and dynamic anomaly detection analytics, which the machine learning forensic investigator can discover. The top priority of the forensic investigator is to leverage information from diverse data sources to discover the detection of money laundering activity to look for any form of unusual behavior as opposed to looking for specific known forms of money laundering. This enables organizations to find even highly sophisticated schemes designed to elude detection via adaptive modeling using machine learning tools such as link analysis, text analytics, and clustering via neural network Self-Organizing Maps and decision tree software.

Index